U.S. Fish & Wildlife Service

Pearl Harbor
National Wildlife Refuge

*Draft Comprehensive Conservation Plan
and Environmental Assessment*

Pearl Harbor National Wildlife Refuge

Ka Nu'ukia

He lei momi. He pu'uhonua a kākou...

Ma ka lihikai o Pearl Harbor i nalo ai nā pālielie o Honouliuli a me Wahiawa i na ho'omohala kūkulu kaianoho no nā kanaka, a he pu'uhonua nui loa ho'i e like no ho'i me ka nui o ka nakilinaka o Alika. He waiwai nui ho'i kēia mau wahi elua no nā manu leleaoa a me na manu wai 'o Hawai'i nei. Nānā no ho'i nā i kanaka hoihoi loa i ke kilo manu in ā manu mai ka Wahi Kilo Manu o Betty Bliss mai, a e lilo pu ho'i lakou i ho'okahi me nā mea ola o ka aina. Ho'ohui ho'i nā ha'awina pilina nohona aina i nā haumana opio me nā aina pālielie wai/kai, nā holoholona on ka aina, a me na 'ike nohona ho'oilina.

He wahi lua'ole o Kalaeloa no kōna mau meakanu aina malo'o a me nā 'āpapa ako'ako'a i laha i ke kai malo'o, a he kumuwaiwai kulohelohe nui ho'i no ka lawelawe like 'ana no na oihana mālama i nā mea ola 'o ia 'āina. Moani ho'i ke 'ala o ka mai'apilo ma luna o na kumu wiliwili. Nui a lehulehu ho'i na 'Opea'ula ma nā puna wai loko pa'a. Ho'okipa aku ho'i nā huihuina kala o nā hinahina o 'Ewa i nā lima kōkua i ka ho'omohala ha'awina mālama 'āina, ke kōkua mālama mo'aukala, a me ka ho'okumu i nā polokalamu kōkua ho'opulapula 'āina no ka hō'ike 'ana aku i nā malihini i ka nani o na kula kahakai o 'Ewa nei e like no ho'i ka nānā 'ana o ia 'āina me ko ka wā ma mua loa.

Vision Statement

"...a string of pearls offering refuge to nature..."

Hidden along the shoreline of Pearl Harbor, surrounded by urban development, the Honouliuli and Waiawa wetlands offer oases for migratory birds from as far as the Arctic Tundra while providing all life requirements for Hawaiian waterbirds. Avid birdwatchers gaze into the Refuge from the Betty Bliss Observation Deck, reconnecting with nature. Environmental education links our youth to wetland ecology, native wildlife, and cultural heritage.

Kalaeloa, a unique coastal dryland plant and exposed coral reef community, serves as a model for a collaborative approach to natural resource management. Night blooming maiapilo perfume the air among beautiful wiliwili trees. 'Ōpae'ula flourish in the protective anchialine pools. A mosaic of silvery 'Ewa hinahina greets volunteers who sustain environmental education, historical preservation, and habitat restoration programs to allow visitors a glimpse of the coastal 'Ewa Plain as it was long ago.

Honouliuli wetland/©Laura Beauregard, USFWS

Pearl Harbor National Wildlife Refuge

Draft Comprehensive Conservation Plan and Environmental Assessment

Prepared by:

U.S. Fish and Wildlife Service
Oʻahu National Wildlife Refuge Complex
66-590 Kamehameha Highway, Room 2C
Haleʻiwa, Hawaiʻi 96712

U.S. Fish and Wildlife Service
Pacific Islands Planning Team
300 Ala Moana Boulevard, Room 5-231
Honolulu, Hawaiʻi 96850

August 2010

Comprehensive Conservation Plans provide long-term guidance for management decisions and set forth goals, objectives, and strategies needed to accomplish refuge purposes and identify the U.S. Fish and Wildlife Service's best estimates of future needs. These plans detail program planning levels that are sometimes substantially above current budget allocations and, as such, are primarily used for strategic planning and program prioritization purposes. The plans do not constitute a commitment for staffing increases, operational and maintenance increases, or funding for future land acquisition.

Table of Contents

Tables

Figures

Appendices

Note to Reviewers: Throughout the CCP document, all attempts have been made to use appropriate diacriticals related to the Native Hawaiian language (i.e., 'okina and kahakō). However, places where diacriticals may not appear occur in the maps and literature cited. Due to limitations of the Geospatial Information System (GIS) software used for the maps developed in the plan, diacriticals were unable to be used where place names or legend text appear. For references identified, if the title of the publication or original citation does not use diacriticals, references were left as is.

Readers' Guide

Native species discussed in this document are referred to by their Hawaiian names. Common English names and scientific nomenclature can also be found in the glossary in Appendix A. The U.S. Fish and Wildlife Service endeavors to be accurate in its use of the Hawaiian language and correctly spell Hawaiian words, including the diacritical marks that affect the meaning and aid in pronunciation. This guide is provided to simplify pronunciation for the reader.

When Captain Cook arrived in the Hawaiian Islands in 1778, the Hawaiians had a totally oral tradition. In 1820, western missionaries standardized a written version of the Hawaiian language that features 8 consonants and 5 vowels.

Consonants

H - as in English
K - as in English
L - as in English
M - as in English
N - as in English
P - as in English
W - after i and e pronounced v
   - after u and o pronounced like w
   - at the start of a word or after a,
      pronounced like w or v
(') - 'okina - a glottal stop

Vowels

A - pronounced like the a in far
E - pronounced like the e in bet
I - pronounced like the ee in beet
O - pronounced like the o in sole
U - pronounced like the oo in boot

Special Symbols

Two symbols appear frequently in Hawaiian words... the 'okina and the kahakō. These two symbols change how words are pronounced. The 'okina itself looks like an upside-down apostrophe and is a glottal stop - or a brief break in the word. An example of this in English is in the middle of the expression "uh-oh." The 'okina is an official consonant - just as any of the other consonants.

The kahakō is a stress mark (macron) that can appear over vowels only and serve to make the vowel sound slightly longer. The vowels ā, ē, ī, ō, and ū sound just like their non-stress Hawaiian vowels with the exception that the sound is held slightly longer. Missing the 'okina or kahakō can greatly change not only the how a word sounds, but also its basic meaning. A popular example of how an 'okina and a kahakō can change the meaning of a word is "pau":

• pau = finished, ended, all done
• pa'u = soot, smudge, ink powder
• pa'ū = moist, damp
• pā'ū = skirt

Unit Names

Honouliuli	*(hoh-noh oo-lee-OO-lee)*	meaning: dark bay
Waiawa	*(why-AH-vah)*	meaning: milkfish water
Kalaeloa	*(ka-lye-LOH-ah)*	meaning: the long point

Waterbirds

Ae'o (EYE oh)

Hawaiian Stilt *Himantopus mexicanus knudseni*

SPECIES STATUS:
Federally listed as Endangered
State listed as Endangered
State recognized as Indigenous

Laura Beauregard

'Alae ke'oke'o (ah-lye KAY oh KAY oh)

Hawaiian Coot *Fulica alai*

SPECIES STATUS:
Federally listed as Endangered
State listed as Endangered
State recognized as Endemic

Laura Beauregard

'Alae 'Ula (ah-lye OO-lah)

Hawaiian Moorhen *Gallinula chloropus sandvicensis*

SPECIES STATUS:
Federally listed as Endangered
State listed as Endangered
State recognized as Indigenous

USFWS

'Auku'u (ow-KOO oo)

Black-crowned Night Heron *Nycticorax nycticorax hoactli*

SPECIES STATUS:
State recognized as Indigenous

Laura Beauregard

Koloa Maoli (ko-LOWah MAOW-lee)

Hawaiian Duck *Anas wyvilliana*

SPECIES STATUS:
Federally listed as Endangered
State listed as Endangered
State recognized as Endemic

Brenda Zaun

Migrant Shorebirds

ʻAkekeke (ah-kay-Kay-kay)

Ruddy Turnstone *Arenaria interpres*

SPECIES STATUS:
State recognized as Indigenous
U.S. Shorebird Conservation Plan - High Concern

Michael Walther

Hunakai (hoo-nah-KYE)

Sanderling *Calidris alba*

SPECIES STATUS:
State recognized as Indigenous
Hunakai means "sea foam." Their habit of running along the receding waves on the shore in search of small sand crabs apparently reminded early Hawaiians of the sea foam or hunakai left behind by the waves. It shares the name with a coastal plant.

Michael Walther

Kioea (kee-oh-AYE-ah)

Bristle-thighed Curlew *Numenius tahitiensis*

SPECIES STATUS:
State recognized as Indigenous
IUCN Red List Ranking-Vulnerable

Laura Beauregard

Kōlea (KOHH-lay-ah)

Pacific Golden Plover *Pluvialis fulva*

SPECIES STATUS:
State recognized as Indigenous
U.S. Shorebird Conservation Plan - High Concern

Michael Walther

ʻŪlili (OOO-lee-lee)

Wandering Tattler *Heteroscelus incanus*

SPECIES STATUS:
State recognized as Indigenous
U.S. Shorebird Conservation Plan - Moderate Concern

Michael Walther

Native Plants - Herbs

'Ākulikuli (AAH-koo-lee-KOO-lee)

Sea Purslane *Sesuvium portulacastrum*

SPECIES STATUS:
State recognized as Indigenous

Laura Beauregard

'Aki'aki (AH-kee AH-kee)

Beach Dropseed *Sporobolus virginicus*

SPECIES STATUS:
State recognized as Endemic

Laura Beauregard

Hunakai (hoo-nah-KYE)

Beach Morning Glory *Ipomoea imperati*

SPECIES STATUS:
State recognized as Endemic
This plant shares its name with the shorebird Hunakai.

Forest & Kim Starr

'Ilima (ee-LEE-mah)

Yellow Ilima *Sida fallax*

SPECIES STATUS:
State recognized as Indigenous

Laura Beauregard

Pā'ūohi'iaka (PAAH OOO-oh-hee ee-AH-kah)

Oval-leaf Clustervine *Jacquemontia ovalifolia*

SPECIES STATUS:
State recognized as Endemic

Laura Beauregard

Native Plants - Shrubs

'Akoko (ah-KOH-koh)

Ewa Plains 'Akoko *Chamaesyce skottsbergii var. scottsbergii*

SPECIES STATUS:
Federally listed as Endangered
State listed as Endangered
State recognized as Endemic

Forest & Kim Starr

'Ewa hinahina (EH-vah HEE-nah-HEE-nah)

Round-leaved Chaff-flower *Achyranthes splendens var. rotundata*

SPECIES STATUS:
Federally listed as Endangered
State recognized as Endemic

Laura Beauregard

Ko'oloa'ula (koh oh-lowah OO-la)

Red Ilima *Abutilon menziesii*

SPECIES STATUS:
Federally listed as Endangered
State listed as Endangered
State recognized as Endemic

USBG

Maiapilo (mye-ah-PEE-low)

Pilo *Capparis sandwichiana*

SPECIES STATUS:
State recognized as Endemic

Mike Silbernagle

'Ōhelo kai (OHH-heh-loh KYE)

Hawai'i Desert-thorn *Lycium sandwicense*

SPECIES STATUS:
State recognized as Indigenous

Forest & Kim Starr

Native Plants - Trees

Naio (NYE-oh)

False Sandalwood *Myoporum sandwicense*

SPECIES STATUS:
State recognized as Indigenous

Forest & Kim Starr

'Iliahialo'e (ee-lee-AH-hee-ah-LOW ay)

Coastal Sandalwood *Santalum ellipticum*

SPECIES STATUS:
State recognized as Endemic

Forest & Kim Starr

Wiliwili (VEE-lee-VEE-lee)

Hawaiian Coral Tree *Erythrina sandwicensis*

SPECIES STATUS:
State recognized as Endemic

DOFAW

Native Fauna

'Ōpae'ula (OHH-pye OO-lah)

Hawaiian Red Shrimp *Halocaridina rubra*

SPECIES STATUS:
State recognized as Endemic

Mike Yamamoto

Pinapinao (pee-nah-PEE-now)

Orange-black Hawaiian Damselfly *Megalagrion xanthomelas*

SPECIES STATUS:
Federal Candidate species
State recognized as Endemic

D. J. Preston/Hawaii Biological Survey

Chapter 1. Introduction

Pearl Harbor was once an extensive, shallow embayment called Wai Momi (water of pearl) in the region of Puʻuloa (long hill) by the Hawaiians. The first people to arrive on the island of Oʻahu (around 100 to 300 BCE) would have seen verdant lands around the bay watered by streams running down from the Koʻolau Mountains, bordered by the arid ʻEwa Plain with its abundance of flightless land birds. Polynesian settlement, British arrival, sugarcane plantations, and U.S. military development have drastically changed the landscape and decimated the native bird population. Currently an active military base and the home of America's Pacific Fleet, Pearl Harbor was also the site of the infamous Imperial Japanese Navy attack of December 7, 1941, which launched the United States into World War II.

Amidst naval facilities and urban development, the Pearl Harbor National Wildlife Refuge (NWR or Refuge) was established in 1972 as mitigation for construction of the Honolulu International Airport's reef runway. The Honouliuli and Waiawa Units on the West and Middle Lochs of the harbor are managed under a cooperative agreement with the U.S. Navy to provide wetland habitat for four of Hawaiʻi's endangered waterbirds: aʻeo (Hawaiian stilt), ʻalae keʻokeʻo (Hawaiian coot), ʻalae ʻula (Hawaiian moorhen), and koloa maoli (Hawaiian duck). Located west of Honolulu on the ʻEwa Plain, the Kalaeloa Unit was established during Barber's Point Naval Air Station (NAS) base closure proceedings in 2001 to protect and enhance the habitat for the endangered coastal dryland plants ʻEwa hinahina and ʻakoko. Cooperative efforts between the Federal Aviation Administration, the State of Hawaiʻi, the U.S. Navy, and the U.S. Fish and Wildlife Service (Service) have made Pearl Harbor NWR a valued asset of the Oʻahu National Wildlife Refuge Complex (Complex) and a key Oʻahu wetland for recovery of endangered Hawaiian waterbirds.

1.1 Proposed Action

We, the U.S. Fish and Wildlife Service (Service), manage the Pearl Harbor National Wildlife Refuge as part of the National Wildlife Refuge System. We propose to adopt and implement a Comprehensive Conservation Plan (CCP) for the Refuge. This document is the Refuge's Draft Comprehensive Conservation Plan and Environmental Assessment (Draft CCP/EA). A CCP sets forth management guidance for a refuge for a period of 15 years, as required by the National Wildlife Refuge System Administration Act (16 U.S.C. 668dd et seq.) as amended by the National Wildlife Refuge System Improvement Act of 1997 (Pub. Law 105-57). The Administration Act requires CCPs to identify and describe:
- The purposes of the Refuge;
- The fish, wildlife and plant populations, their habitats, and the archaeological and cultural values found on the Refuge;
- Significant problems that may adversely affect wildlife populations and habitats and ways to correct or mitigate those problems;
- Areas suitable for administrative sites or visitor facilities; and
- Opportunities for fish and wildlife dependent recreation.

National Wildlife Refuge System (Refuge System) planning policy (Service Manual 602 FW 3, June 21, 2000) states that the purpose of CCPs is to: "describe the desired future conditions of a refuge and provide long-range guidance and management direction to achieve refuge purposes; help fulfill the National Wildlife Refuge System mission; maintain and, where appropriate, restore the ecological integrity of each refuge and the Refuge System; . . . and meet other mandates."

The Service has developed and examined alternatives for managing Pearl Harbor NWR through the CCP planning process. The various alternatives address the major issues and relevant mandates identified in the CCP process and are consistent with principles of sound fish and wildlife management. The Service has consolidated management options into two alternatives for Pearl Harbor NWR and has identified Alternative B as the preferred alternative. The draft preferred alternative appears to represent the best balanced approach for achieving the Refuge's purposes, vision, and goals; contributing to the National Wildlife Refuge System (Refuge System) mission; and addressing the relevant issues and mandates consistent with sound principles of fish and wildlife management. However, the preferred alternative may be modified between the draft and final document depending upon comments received from the public or other agencies and organizations. The Regional Director for the Service's Pacific Region will be the final decisionmaker regarding the alternative that will be adopted for implementation. For details on the specific components and actions comprising the range of alternatives, see Chapter 2.

1.2 Purpose and Need for the CCP

The purpose of the CCP is to provide the Refuge System, the Service, partners, and citizens with a management plan for improving fish and wildlife habitat conditions and infrastructure for wildlife, staff, and Refuge visitors for 15 years. An approved CCP will help ensure that the Service manages Pearl Harbor NWR to achieve its purposes, vision, goals, and objectives, and to help fulfill the Refuge System mission. Another purpose of the CCP is to provide reasonable, scientifically grounded guidance for improving the Refuge's subterranean, coastal, and wetland habitats for the long-term conservation of native plants, animals, and migratory birds. The CCP will identify appropriate actions for protecting and sustaining the cultural and biological features of coastal communities; endangered, threatened or rare species populations and habitats; and migratory shorebirds. The CCP will also evaluate priority wildlife-dependent recreation uses on the Refuge.

The CCP is needed for a variety of reasons. Primary among these is the need to improve degraded habitat conditions by removing pest plants and animals, such as kiawe shrubs, mongooses, and feral cats. There is also a need to address Pearl Harbor NWR's contributions to aid in the recovery of endangered species, and assess and possibly mitigate potential impacts of global climate change on the Refuge. The Service should continue to effectively work with current partners such as the Federal Aviation Administration, the State of Hawaiʻi, and the U.S. Navy, as well as seek new partnerships to restore habitats, improve environmental education and interpretive opportunities and volunteer programs, and recover endangered species populations.

1.3 Content and Scope of the CCP

This CCP provides guidance for managing Refuge habitats and wildlife, and administering public uses on Refuge lands. The Pearl Harbor CCP/EA is intended to comply with the requirements set forth in the Administration Act and the NEPA. Information included in the CCP includes:

- An overall vision for the Refuge, its establishment history and purposes, and its role in the local ecosystem (Chapter 1).
- Goals and objectives for specific conservation targets and visitor programs, as well as strategies for achieving the objectives (Chapter 2).
- A description of the Refuge's physical environment (Chapter 3).
- A description of conservation targets, condition, and trends on the Refuge and within the local ecosystem, a presentation of the key desired ecological conditions for sustaining the targets, and a short analysis of the threats to each conservation target (Chapter 4).
- An overview of the Refuge's visitor programs and facilities, a list of desired future conditions for each program, and other management considerations (Chapter 5).
- An analysis of the environmental effects associated with implementing the various management actions prescribed under the alternatives described in Chapter 2 (Chapter 6).
- A comprehensive list of species known or mentioned in the CCP/EA (Appendix A).
- Evaluations of existing and proposed appropriate public and economic uses for compatibility with the Refuge's purposes (Appendix B).
- An Implementation Plan needed to support the alternatives considered (Appendix C).
- Wilderness Review (Appendix D).
- Integrated Pest Management (Appendix E)

1.4 Planning and Management Guidance

The Service, an agency within the Department of the Interior, is the principal Federal agency responsible for conserving, protecting, and enhancing fish, wildlife, and plants and their habitats. Refuge management is guided by Federal laws, Executive orders, Service policies, and international treaties. Fundamental are the mission and goals of the Refuge System and the designated purposes of the Refuge as described in establishing legislation, Executive orders, or other documents establishing, authorizing, or expanding a refuge.

Key concepts and guidance of the Refuge System derive from the National Wildlife Refuge System Administration Act of 1966 as amended (16 U.S.C. 668dd et seq.), the Refuge Recreation Act of 1962 (16 U.S.C. 460k-460k-4), as amended, Title 50 of the Code of Federal Regulations (CFR), and the Fish and Wildlife Service Manual. The National Wildlife Refuge System Administration Act is implemented through regulations covering the National Wildlife Refuge System, published in Title 50, subchapter C of the Code of Federal Regulations. These regulations govern general administration of units of the Refuge System.

1.4.1 U.S. Fish and Wildlife Service Mission

The mission of the Service is "working with others, to conserve, protect, and enhance fish and wildlife and their habitats for the continuing benefit of the American people." National natural resources entrusted to the Service for conservation and protection include migratory birds, endangered and threatened species, interjurisdictional fish, wetlands, and certain marine mammals. The Service also manages national fish hatcheries, enforces Federal wildlife laws and international treaties on importing and exporting wildlife, assists with State and Territorial fish and wildlife programs, and helps other countries develop wildlife conservation programs.

1.4.2 National Wildlife Refuge System

The Refuge System is the world's largest network of public lands and waters set aside specifically for conserving wildlife and protecting ecosystems. From its inception in 1903, the Refuge System has grown to encompass 552 national wildlife refuges in all 50 States, and waterfowl production areas in 10 States, covering more than 150 million acres of public lands. More than 40 million visitors annually fish, hunt, observe and photograph wildlife, or participate in environmental education and interpretive activities on national wildlife refuges.

1.4.3 National Wildlife Refuge System Mission and Goals

The mission of the Refuge System is "to administer a national network of lands and waters for the conservation, management, and, where appropriate, restoration of the fish, wildlife, and plant resources and their habitats within the United States for the benefit of present and future generations of Americans" (Administration Act).

Wildlife conservation is the fundamental mission of the Refuge System. The goals of the Refuge System, as articulated in the Mission, Goals, and Refuge Purposes policy (601 FW1), follow:
- Conserve a diversity of fish, wildlife, and plants and their habitats, including species that are endangered or threatened with becoming endangered.
- Develop and maintain a network of habitats for migratory birds, anadromous and interjurisdictional fish, and marine mammal populations that is strategically distributed and carefully managed to meet important life history needs of these species across their ranges.
- Conserve those ecosystems, plant communities, wetlands of national or international significance, and landscapes and seascapes that are unique, rare, declining, or underrepresented in existing protection efforts.
- Provide and enhance opportunities to participate in compatible wildlife-dependent recreation (hunting, fishing, wildlife observation and photography, and environmental education and interpretation).
- Foster understanding and instill appreciation of the diversity and interconnectedness of fish, wildlife, and plants and their habitats.
- Provide and enhance opportunities to participate in compatible wildlife-dependent recreation (hunting, fishing, wildlife observation and photography, and environmental education and interpretation).

1.4.4 National Wildlife Refuge System Administration Act

Of all the laws governing activities on national wildlife refuges, the Administration Act exerts the greatest influence. The Administration Act was amended by the National Wildlife Refuge System Improvement Act of 1997 (Improvement Act). The Improvement Act included a unifying mission for all national wildlife refuges, a new process for determining compatible uses on refuges, and a requirement that each refuge will be managed under a CCP developed in an open public process. The Administration Act states that the Secretary shall provide for the conservation of fish, wildlife, plants, and their habitats within the Refuge System, and ensure that the biological integrity, diversity, and environmental health of the Refuge System are maintained. House Report 105–106 accompanying the Improvement Act states "...the fundamental mission of our System is wildlife conservation: wildlife and wildlife conservation must come first." Biological integrity, diversity, and environmental health are critical components of wildlife conservation. As later made clear in the Biological Integrity, Diversity, and Environmental Health Policy, "the highest measure of biological integrity, diversity, and environmental health is viewed as those intact and self-sustaining habitats and wildlife populations that existed during historic conditions."

Each refuge must be managed to fulfill the Refuge System mission as well as the specific purposes for which it was established. The Administration Act requires the Service to monitor the status and trends of fish, wildlife, and plants on every refuge. Additionally, six priority wildlife-dependent recreational uses are granted special consideration in the planning, management, establishment, and expansion of units of the Refuge System: hunting, fishing, wildlife observation and photography, and environmental education and interpretation. When determined compatible on a refuge-specific basis, these six uses assume priority status among all uses of the refuge in question. The overarching goal is to enhance wildlife-dependent recreation opportunities and access to quality visitor experiences on refuges, while managing refuges to conserve fish, wildlife, plants, and their habitats. The Service is directed to make extra efforts to facilitate wildlife dependent visitor opportunities.

When preparing a CCP, refuge managers must re-evaluate all general public, recreational, and economic uses (even those occurring to further refuge habitat management goals) proposed or occurring on a refuge for appropriateness and compatibility. No refuge use may be allowed or continued unless it is determined to be appropriate and compatible. Generally, an appropriate use is one that contributes to fulfilling refuge purposes, the Refuge System mission, or goals and objectives described in a refuge management plan. A compatible use is defined as a use that, in the sound professional judgment of the refuge manager, will not materially interfere with or detract from the fulfillment of the mission of the Refuge System or the purposes of the refuge. Updated Appropriateness Findings and Compatibility Determinations for existing and proposed uses for Pearl Harbor NWR are in Appendix B of this Draft CCP/EA.

The Administration Act also requires that, in addition to formally established guidance, the CCP must be developed with the participation of the public. Public comments play a role in identifying issues, guiding alternatives considered during development of the CCP, and selecting a preferred alternative. It is Service policy to develop CCPs in an open public process; the agency is committed to securing public input throughout the process.

1.5 Relationship to Previous and Future Refuge Plans

Planning has been a part of refuge operations since establishing refuges began. However, not all plans were completed in a comprehensive fashion, or with public participation considered adequate today.

1.5.1 Previous Plans

- Master Plan for the Hawaiian Wetlands National Wildlife Refuge Complex (USFWS 1985).
- Conceptual Management Plan for the Barbers Point Unit of the Pearl Harbor National Wildlife Refuge, Island of Oʻahu, Hawaiʻi (USFWS 1999).
- Draft Revised Recovery Plan for Hawaiian Waterbirds, Second Draft of Second Revision (USFWS 2005).

1.5.2 Future Planning

The CCP will be revised every 15 years or earlier if monitoring and evaluation determine that changes are needed to achieve refuge purposes, vision, goals, or objectives. The CCP provides guidance in the form of goals, objectives, and strategies for refuge program areas but may lack some of the specifics needed for implementation. Step-down management plans will therefore be developed for individual program areas, as needed, following completion of the CCP. Step-down plans require appropriate NEPA compliance. Several step-down plans (including the Habitat Management Plan, Visitor Services Plan, Inventory and Monitoring Plan, and Integrated Pest Management Plan) are appropriate to develop and/or update following CCP completion. All of the step-down plans should be based on the management goals, objectives, and strategies outlined in the CCP. The Integrated Pest Management Plan should address coordination with all other Federal, State, and regional agencies.

1.6 Refuge Establishment and Purposes

1.6.1 General

The Improvement Act directs the Service to manage each refuge to fulfill the mission of the Refuge System, as well as the specific purposes for which that refuge was established. Refuge purposes are the driving force in developing refuge vision statements, goals, objectives, and strategies in the CCP. Refuge purposes are also critical to determining the compatibility of all existing and proposed refuge uses.

Lands within the Refuge System are acquired and managed under a variety of legislative acts, administrative orders, and legal authorities. The official purpose or purposes for a refuge are specified in or derived from the law, Presidential proclamation, Executive order, agreement, public land order, donation document, or administrative memorandum establishing, authorizing, or expanding a refuge, refuge unit, or refuge subunit. The Service defines the purpose of a refuge when it is established or when new land is added to an existing refuge. When an addition to a refuge is acquired under an authority different from the authority used to establish the original refuge, the addition takes on the purposes of the original refuge, but the original refuge does not take on the purposes of the addition. Refuge managers must consider all of the purposes. However, purposes dealing with the conservation, management, and restoration of fish, wildlife, and plants and their habitats take precedence over other purposes in the management and administration of a refuge.

1.6.2 Pearl Harbor NWR Purposes Background

Pearl Harbor was first identified for protection by the Service in *Hawai'i's Endangered Waterbirds* (U.S. Bureau of Sport Fisheries and Wildlife 1970). This report recognized the ponds and tidal flats at Pearl Harbor Naval Base as one of four areas of major importance for waterbirds on O'ahu. The Cooperative Agreements that established the Honouliuli and Waiawa units of the Pearl Harbor NWR in 1972 (USBSFW 1972) identify the purpose of the units as being "...a wildlife refuge for rare and endangered species." The agreements further add, "The area shall be maintained and operated by the U.S. Bureau of Sport Fisheries and Wildlife, at its own expense, as part of the National Wildlife Refuge System." [Note: In 1974, the U.S. Bureau of Sport Fisheries and Wildlife became the

U.S. Fish and Wildlife Service. In 2010, the Pearl Harbor Naval Base and Hickam Air Force Base were realigned to become Joint Base Pearl Harbor-Hickam.]

The Service's purpose for acquiring the Kalaeloa Unit of the Refuge was first discussed in the *Preliminary Project Proposal (PPP) to Establish the Barbers Point Unit of the Pearl Harbor National Wildlife Refuge* (USFWS 1994). [Note: This original proposal included four distinct parcels of land, of which only one was eventually transferred to the Service. As such, only those purposes that directly relate to the one parcel will be discussed herewith. The name Barbers Point reverted to the original Hawaiian area designation, Kalaeloa, in 1999.] The PPP states that securing habitat for the endangered 'akoko and 'Ewa hinahina is the highest priority. Additionally, the cover memorandum for the PPP from the Deputy Director to the Regional Director, Region 1, U.S. Fish and Wildlife Service recognizes the 'ōpae 'ula, an endemic shrimp, as benefiting from the establishment of the Refuge.

The *Conceptual Management Plan for the Barbers Point Unit of the Pearl Harbor National Wildlife Refuge, Island of O'ahu, Hawai'i* (USFWS 1999a) described the Refuge purposes:
- Protect habitats of endangered plants, endangered birds, and other native plants, aquatic invertebrates, migratory birds and shorebirds, and other native animals;
- Restore and enhance in their natural ecosystems (when practicable) all species of animals and plants that are endangered or threatened with becoming endangered that occur on the Refuge Unit; and
- Conserve and enhance the natural diversity and abundance of native fauna and flora on the Refuge Unit for the benefit of current and future generations.

The Categorical Exclusion: Barbers Point Unit Addition of Parcel 2 (*Achyranthes* plant recovery area) to the Pearl Harbor National Wildlife Refuge, City and County of Honolulu, Hawai'i (USFWS 1999a) specifically states the purpose of Barbers Point Parcel 2 is, "… for the protection and recovery of endangered *Achyranthes splendens* var. *rotundata* plants and the conservation and enhancement of native coastal shrubland and dryland forest natural communities." Additionally, the document states that transfer of the property "… is recommended for the protection and recovery of endangered species, and other management to protect natural and historic resources in a portion of the 'Ewa coastal plain."

1.6.3 Refuge Purpose Summary

The following summary was developed by Refuge staff, based upon the purposes listed in the administrative documents which established the Refuge.

The purpose of the Pearl Harbor NWR is to protect, provide habitat, and aid in recovery efforts for four of Hawai'i's endangered waterbirds (a'eo, 'alae ke'oke'o, 'alae 'ula, and koloa maoli) in the Honouliuli and Waiawa Units; and the endangered plants 'Ewa hinahina and 'akoko in the Kalaeloa Unit.

1.7 Refuge Goals

Goals and objectives are the unifying elements of successful refuge management. They identify and focus management priorities, resolve issues, and link to refuge purposes, Service policy, and the Refuge System mission. A CCP describes management actions that help bring a refuge closer to its vision. A vision broadly reflects refuge purposes, Refuge System mission and goals, other statutory requirements, and larger-scale plans as appropriate. Visitor services and wildlife/habitat management goals then define general targets in support of the vision, followed by objectives that direct efforts into incremental and measurable steps toward achieving those goals. Finally, strategies identify specific tools and actions to accomplish objectives. The Pearl Harbor NWR vision statement is found on the inside front cover of this document. The following are our goals; their order does not imply any priority in this CCP.

Nā Pahuhopu o ka Puʻuhonua

- **Pahuhopu 1:** E kīaʻi a mālama hoʻi i nā pāleilei i loaʻa hoʻi kekahi wahi e mahuahua ai a e lilo hoʻi i wahi noho paʻa ʻole no nā manu ʻane make loa.

- **Goal 1:** Protect and manage seasonal wetland habitats to meet the life-history needs of endangered waterbirds to promote their recovery and also for the benefit of migratory birds.

- **Pahuhopu 2:** E kīaʻi a mālama hoʻi i nā ʻāpapa a hoʻomahuahua hou i nā lihikai ʻākoʻakoʻa ma nā kahakai i loʻa ai hoʻi nā wahi e ulu ai nā meakanu ʻane make loa a me ke kaiaola luaʻole.

- **Goal 2:** Restore and protect coastal coralline plain habitat at the Kalaeloa Unit.

- **Pahuhopu 3:** E ʻohiʻohi hoʻi in ā manaʻo ʻepekema e pili ana i ia wahi no ka hoʻomākaukau ʻana a e hoʻokupu hoʻi i haʻawina e holomua ai na manaʻo mālama ʻāina.

- **Goal 3:** Collect scientific information necessary to support adaptive management decisions.

- **Pahuhopu 4:** E hoʻomākaukau hoʻi kumuwaiwai no ka wehewehe ʻana a e hoʻoamopopo pu hoʻi i nā kanaka e pili ana i ka waiwai o ia ʻāina, nā pilina mālama ʻāina, a me nā moʻaukala e pili ana hoʻi no ia wahi o Pearl Harbor NWR.

- **Goal 4:** Provide interpretive and educational opportunities to enhance public understanding of and appreciation for the natural and cultural resources of Pearl Harbor NWR.

- **Pahuhopu 5:** E mālama hoʻi i nā moʻaukala a me nā moʻomeheu no ka pono o na kanaka mai kēia au a ia au aʻe e hiki mai ana.

- **Goal 5:** Protect historic and cultural resources for the benefit of present and future generations.

1.8 Relationship to Ecosystem Planning Efforts

When developing a CCP, the Service considers the goals and objectives of existing national, regional, and ecosystem plans; State/Territorial fish and wildlife conservation plans; and other landscape-scale plans developed for the same watershed or ecosystem in which the refuge is located. To the extent possible, the CCP is expected to be consistent with these existing plans and assist in meeting their conservation goals and objectives (Part 602 FW 3.3). This section summarizes some of the key plans that were reviewed by members of the planning team during CCP development.

Hawai'i's Comprehensive Wildlife Conservation Strategy, 2005. With passage of the Commerce, Justice, and State Appropriations Act of 2001, Congress mandated each State and Territory to develop its own comprehensive strategy. *Hawai'i's Comprehensive Wildlife Conservation Strategy* comprehensively reviews the status of the full range of the State's native terrestrial and aquatic species, over 10,000 of which are found nowhere else on Earth. Hawai'i's Species of Greatest Conservation Need include all native terrestrial animals, all endemic aquatic animals, additional indigenous aquatic animals identified as in need of conservation attention, a range of native plants identified as in need of conservation attention, and all identified endemic algae. This list includes: terrestrial mammal (1), birds (77), terrestrial invertebrates (~5,000), freshwater fishes (5), freshwater invertebrates (12), anchialine pond-associated fauna (20), marine mammals (26), marine reptiles (6), marine fishes (154), marine invertebrates (197), flora (over 600). Details on all the listed wildlife taxa are provided in fact sheets that contain information for taxa, closely related groups of species, and species facing similar threats.

U.S. Navy, *Naval Station Pearl Harbor (NAVSTA PH) Integrated Natural Resource Management Plan* (INRMP), December 2009. The purpose of the INRMP for Navy lands on O'ahu is to provide Navy planners and implementers of mission activities and natural resource managers sufficient biological background and management guidance to ensure NAVSTA PH's military mission goals are met without compromising natural resources present on Navy lands. In accordance with the Sikes Act of 1960, as amended, the Department of Defense (DOD) maintains a multipurpose, sustainable, natural resources management program. The Act also requires that all DOD conservation programs allow continued access to land, air, and water resources for realistic military training and testing, while ensuring that the natural and cultural resources are sustained in a healthy condition for future generations. This INRMP is a programmatic document intended to identify management objectives for natural resources. The INRMP emphasizes habitat protection for federally and State of Hawai'i listed threatened and endangered species and associated educational programs, preventive measures, and partnerships.

Draft Revised Recovery Plan for Hawaiian Waterbirds, Second Draft of Second Revision, May 2005. The ultimate goal of the recovery program is to restore and maintain multiple self-sustaining populations of Hawaiian waterbirds within their historical ranges. The recovery of the endangered waterbirds focuses on the following objectives:

- Increasing population numbers to statewide baseline levels (consistently stable or increasing with a minimum of 2,000 birds for each species);
- Establishing multiple, self-sustaining breeding populations throughout each species' historic range;

- Establishing and protecting a network of both core and supporting wetlands that are managed as habitat suitable for waterbirds, including the maintenance of appropriate hydrological conditions and control of invasive nonnative plants;
- For all four species, eliminating or controlling the threats posed by introduced predators, avian diseases, and contaminants; and
- For the koloa maoli, removing the threat of hybridization with feral mallards.

Draft Recovery Plan for Chamaesyce skottsbergii var. skottsbergii and Achvranthes splendens var. rotundata, 1994. On the 'Ewa Plain, both species occur on limestone substrate characterized by sinkholes and coralline rubble. Current threats are habitat loss due to development (including nearly complete loss of native habitat in the 'Ewa Plain), invasion of habitat by alien and parasitic native plant species, fire, infestation by damaging insects, destruction by cattle and feral animals, trampling by humans, over-utilization for commercial use (in the case of *Achyranthes*), and chemical spills and pollutants. In order to consider downlisting for either taxon, there must be at least three self-reproducing populations with a minimum of 1,000 reproductive plants per population in each of the two geographically distinct regions in which they occur. Populations should be growing beyond or stable at the minimum size and threats should be removed or controlled for at least 10 years prior to downlisting. [Note: *Chamaesyce skottsbergii* var. *skottsbergii* and *Achvranthes splendens* var. *rotundata* are referenced by their Hawaiian names, 'akoko and 'Ewa hinahina, respectively, in this CCP.]

U.S. Pacific Islands Regional Shorebird Conservation Plan, 2004. Conservation and restoration of shorebird habitats is essential for the protection of endangered and declining shorebird populations. Wetlands, beach strand, coastal forests, and mangrove habitats are particularly vulnerable on Pacific islands due to increasing development pressures and already limited acreage. Monitoring and research needs include assessment of population sizes and trends; assessment of the timing and abundance of birds at key wintering and migration stopover sites; assessment of habitat use and requirements at wintering and migration areas; exploration of the geographic linkages between wintering, stopover, and breeding areas; and evaluation of habitat restoration and management techniques to meet the needs of resident and migratory species. Education and public outreach are critical components of this plan. Resource management agencies of Federal, Territorial, Commonwealth, and State governments will need to work together with military agencies, nongovernmental organizations, and the scientific community. On a larger scale, coordination at the international level will be key to the conservation of vulnerable species, both migratory and resident.

1.9 Planning and Issue Identification

1.9.1 Issues to be Addressed in the CCP

The following issues are within the scope of the CCP/EA and are being addressed in the planning process.

Wildlife and Habitat Resources: Endangered waterbirds and plants are the primary management focus, but management also considers and includes migratory shorebirds, waterfowl, seabirds, and native plant species. Unique microhabitat (anchialine pools – tidally influenced pockets of coastal waters without direct physical connection to ocean that support unique flora and invertebrate fauna) is found throughout the Kalaeloa Unit and is in need of restoration activities. Several pest plant, animal, and insect species hinder staff from fulfilling the purposes for which the Refuge was established. Invasive plants such as California grass directly affect the habitat while invasive (and feral) animals such as mongooses and cats directly affect the species themselves. Endangered waterbirds are the primary management focus for the wetland units of the Refuge. As such, much of the existing Refuge acreage is excluded from visitor service opportunities to protect endangered species during their nesting and brood rearing period.

Facilities and Facilities Maintenance: The maintenance of current facilities includes vehicles and heavy equipment; boundary fencing; weather stations; ditches, dikes, and impoundments; water control structures; and wells and pumps. Due to the environmental conditions (e.g., constant wind containing salt spray, precipitation, warm temperatures, and high humidity) associated with this coastal marine environment, degradation of equipment and facilities is accelerated and often exceeds normally acceptable mainland standards for maintenance costs and schedules. The establishment of an onsite maintenance facility is needed. The current Refuge office is located in Hale'iwa at a General Services Administration rental location approximately 20 miles from the Refuge. The shared maintenance facility is on the James Campbell NWR, 40 miles from the Pearl Harbor NWR. The distance and logistics needed to transport supplies and equipment substantially adds to the cost of conducting refuge management activities.

Visitor Services Activities: Environmental education, interpretation, and wildlife observation are currently offered on a limited basis through special use permits and/or volunteer-docent lead tours. The presence of nesting endangered species throughout much of the calendar year, along with limited land base, restricts public access and refuge management activity. Maintaining access for shoreline fishing at the Kalaeloa Unit, which is State-controlled below mean high water, is important to the local community, and a condition of land acquisition.

Protection of Historical and Cultural Resources: Although there are no known cultural practice sites on the Refuge, an 'ulu maika (Hawaiian rolling stone) was found within an impoundment at the Honouliuli Unit indicating use of the area by Native Hawaiians. World War II pillboxes located at the Kalaeloa Unit have been vandalized. Protection of these sites from vandals and looters is a management concern. Appreciation for cultural and historical resources should become an interpretive and educational theme within the visitor services program.

1.9.2 Issues Outside the Scope of the CCP/EA

The Betty Bliss Memorial Overlook at the Honouliuli Unit is part of a larger, multiagency construction project that is outside the scope of this CCP. It is a component of the Pearl Harbor Historic Trail project, an 18.5-mile multiuse recreational trail that will highlight historic sites from the World War II Valor in the Pacific National Monument's USS Arizona Memorial to the west coast O'ahu town of Nānākuli. Under a previous agreement with the Hawai'i Department of Transportation (HDOT), NEPA compliance for the Betty Bliss Memorial Overlook will be included as part of the revised HDOT environmental assessment (EA) being prepared for Phase 1 of the Pearl Harbor Historic Recreation Trail improvement project. This EA is expected to be completed by early 2011. Construction of the overlook is anticipated to begin in late 2011 or 2012.

Chapter 2: Alternatives, Goals, Objectives, and Strategies

2.1 Introduction

The Service proposes to adopt and implement a CCP to guide the management and administration of the Refuge throughout the life of the CCP. This chapter presents and compares a range of reasonable alternatives for this proposed action, including a preferred alternative. It also includes information on the development of the alternatives, alternatives or components considered but dropped from further analysis, and elements or actions common to all alternatives. Table 1 summarizes, compares, and contrasts the alternatives.

2.2 Development of Alternatives

Initial alternatives were developed between fall 2009 and spring 2010 after initial scoping and public involvement. These alternatives were "Continue Current Management" (no action) and "Increase Native Habitat Restoration and Wetland Management" (preferred alternative). The two alternatives are described in detail in Section 2.5. Under both alternatives, the wetlands at the Honouliuli and Waiawa units are managed as core management areas as identified in the Recovery Plan for Hawaiian Waterbirds (USFWS 2005) and the Kalaeloa Unit is managed for endangered plant recovery. Also, under each alternative, the Betty Bliss Memorial Refuge Overlook will be constructed at the Honouliuli Unit as planned before initiation of the CCP process. This overlook, associated with the Pearl Harbor Historic Trail project, will provide new visitor opportunities for compatible wildlife observation, photography, and interpretation on the Honouliuli Unit of the Refuge.

2.3 Alternative Components Not Considered for Detailed Analysis

During scoping, public involvement, and the development of the objectives that make up each alternative, a variety of ideas and solutions were presented, explored, and debated. The following alternative components were considered but not selected for further analysis in this Draft CCP and EA for the reason(s) described.

2.3.1 Expansion of the Refuge

Pearl Harbor NWR was established in 1972 as mitigation for construction of the Honolulu International Airport Reef Runway. The Honouliuli and Waiawa units are managed under a cooperative agreement with the Navy. The Kalaeloa Unit was established in 2001 as a result of lands transferred from the Navy to the Service under the Department of Defense Base Realignment and Closure program. Adjacent urban land uses and planned development on the 'Ewa Plain precludes expansion of the unit. Additional Navy lands in the Pearl Harbor area were also considered for transfer to the Service, but due to legal liability concerns related to contaminant issues, these lands were not accepted. The only remaining wetland habitat in Pearl Harbor is the 70-acre Pouhala Marsh on the West Loch, which is managed by the Hawai'i Department of Land and Natural Resources'

Division of Forestry and Wildlife (DOFAW) as a wildlife sanctuary. Because no other wetlands exist in the area, none of the alternatives include an expansion of the Refuge.

2.3.2 Expansion of Visitor Opportunities within the Fenced Areas of the Refuge

This alternative component would open the Refuge for wildlife observation, wildlife photography, and/or interpretation. Overlooks are planned for construction outside the fenced areas only. Public access along the Kalaeloa Unit ocean coast for incidental fishing on adjacent State-owned shoreline will continue under both alternatives. It was determined unfeasible and undesirable to open the Refuge to any additional uses due to the need to limit disturbance to endangered species and the units' extremely small size. Logistical limitations such as the lack of safe, suitable, and legal access also factored into the decision to keep the Refuge closed.

2.3.3 No Mammalian Predator Removal

No mammalian predator (mongoose, rat, mouse, cat, and dog) control would be conducted on the Pearl Harbor Refuge. The lack of mammalian predator control would not protect adult and young endangered waterbirds, their nests, and habitat on the Refuge. Other resident and migratory waterbirds on the Refuge that are vulnerable to predation would also not be protected. Based upon available scientific information (Refuge studies, monitoring, and the Hawai'i Endangered Waterbird Recovery Plan), no predator control would not achieve Refuge goals necessary to promote recovery of Hawai'i's endangered waterbirds in the State.

2.3.4 Nonlethal Techniques to Remove Mammalian Predators

In accordance with 569 FW 1 (Integrated Pest Management), the Service chooses pest management methods by considering the following four factors (listed in their order of importance): human safety, environmental integrity, effectiveness, and cost. Live trapping and release of predators to other locations on O'ahu or the State is not a sound biological strategy. Transporting predators and releasing them has the potential to exacerbate resource management at other State, private, and Federal lands.

2.3.5 Public Trapping and Hunting to Remove Mammalian Predators

These actions are dismissed from consideration for this CCP for the following reasons: potential disturbance to endangered species (plants and animals), lower effectiveness for removal of mammals, safety of and potential conflicts with other Refuge users, potential conflicts with Refuge staff implementing on-the-ground management actions, and the mammalian predators present are not sought after species by the general hunting public.

2.4 Elements Common to All Alternatives

2.4.1 Implementation Subject to Funding Availability

Under each alternative, actions will be implemented over a period of 15 years as funding becomes available. Routine maintenance, repair, replacement, and improvement of existing facilities will continue, also dependent on funding.

2.4.2 Interagency Coordination and Collaboration

Ecosystem planning efforts discussed in Chapter 1, Section 1.8 involve collaboration among Federal and State agencies toward mutual goals.

2.4.3 Threatened and Endangered Species Protection and Recovery

The purpose of the Pearl Harbor NWR is to protect and provide habitat for four endangered waterbirds and two endangered plants ('Ewa hinahina and 'akoko). Protection of threatened and endangered species is common across all alternatives. The protection of federally listed species is mandated through the Endangered Species Act of 1973. It is also Service policy to give priority consideration to the protection, enhancement, and recovery of these species on national wildlife refuges. To ensure adequate protection, the Refuge is required to review all activities, programs, and projects occurring on lands and waters of the Refuge to determine if they may affect listed species. If the determination is that an action may adversely affect an endangered species then the Refuge conducts a formal review, known as a consultation, to identify those effects and means to mitigate those effects.

To benefit and protect endangered waterbirds, the wetlands on the Honouliuli and Waiawa Units will be managed as core wetland areas as designated in the Draft Revised Recovery Plan for Hawaiian Waterbirds (USFWS 2005) throughout the 15-year span of the CCP.

2.4.4 Archaeological and Cultural Resource Protection

Cultural resources on Refuge lands receive protection and consideration in accordance with Federal cultural resources laws, Executive orders, and regulations, as well as policies and procedures established by the Department of the Interior and the Service. Although the presence of cultural resources, including historic properties, does not preclude a Federal activity, the Refuge will seek to protect cultural resources whenever possible. Refuge management actions will support the State of Hawai'i's vision statement "to promote the use and conservation of historic and cultural resources for the education, inspiration, pleasure and enrichment of the public in a spirit of stewardship and trusteeship for future generations" (State Historic Preservation Plan 2010-2014).

During early planning of any projects, the Refuge will provide the Service Regional Historic Preservation Officer (RHPO) a description and location of all projects and activities that affect ground and structures, including project requests from third parties. Information will also include any alternatives being considered. The RHPO will analyze these undertakings for potential to affect historic properties and enter into consultation with the State Historic Preservation Division and other parties as appropriate. The Refuge will also ask the public and local government officials to identify any cultural resource impact concerns. This notification is generally done in conjunction with the review required by NEPA or Service regulations on compatibility of uses.

2.4.5 Fire Management

The suppression of wildfires and the use of prescribed or controlled fire are a long-standing part of resource protection, public safety, and habitat management on national wildlife refuges. In 2003, a Fire Management Plan which incorporated NEPA compliance was approved for the Refuge and provides detailed guidance for the suppression and use of prescribed fire. The plan outlines wildfire response and prescribed fire objectives, strategies, responsibilities, equipment and staffing; burn units; implementation; monitoring; and evaluation. The complete Fire Management Plan is available at the Oʻahu National Wildlife Refuge Complex Office.

2.4.6 Volunteer Groups

The Refuge currently has an active volunteer program involving about 200 individuals. These volunteers contribute over 600 hours annually, assisting with environmental education, biological monitoring, invasive species removal, native plant propagation, and anchialine pool restoration. The recruitment and use of volunteers will continue and is a vital component of many of the objectives outlined in the Draft CCP and EA.

2.4.7 Participation in Planning and Review of Regional Development Activities

The Service will actively participate in planning and studies for ongoing and future industrial and urban development, contamination, and other potential concerns that may affect the Refuge's wildlife resources and habitats. The Service will continue to cultivate working relationships with pertinent State and Federal agencies to stay abreast of current and potential developments and will utilize effective outreach tools and technologies and environmental education as needed to raise awareness of the Refuge's resources.

2.4.8 Adaptive Management

The small acreage and multiendangered species management for this Refuge results in complex wetland management strategies. Over time, wetlands naturally progress from open water to a more vegetated condition. During this progression, types, distribution, density, structure, and number of species change. These changes affect numbers, distribution, and use patterns of waterbirds. Specifically, waterbird species require slightly different nesting, chick rearing, and foraging habitats. As succession continues in a wetland, the vegetation response tends to favor one of more species life history requirements until dense monotypic vegetation covers so much of the wetland that it becomes less valuable to endangered waterbird species, which are present yearlong on the Refuge.

Water management strategies (pulsing, depth, duration of flooding, seasonality of flooding/drying) affect the rate of plant succession. Optimal water management provides the longest period of use for waterbirds before dewatering and vegetation management are needed to set back the successional stage to essentially an open water condition. After vegetation management (e.g., disking, mowing, herbicide application), the wetland succession cycle begins. Consequently, different parts of a wetland are used to meet the full range of life-history needs throughout the year. Areas of the wetland used at one time by one species for foraging might be used by another species during a different season or year for nesting or chick rearing. This management technique provides optimal habitat conditions and maximum use by a greater variety of waterbirds both seasonally and over time.

As a result of this seasonal rotational management strategy, acres of habitat presented for Objectives 1.1 – 1.4) in Chapter 2 may sum to more acres of wetlands than are available on the Refuge.

2.4.9 Integrated Pest Management

In accordance with 517 DM 1 and 569 FW 1, an integrated pest management (IPM) approach would be utilized, where practicable, to eradicate, control, or contain pest and invasive species (herein collectively referred to as pests) on Refuge lands. IPM would involve using methods based upon effectiveness, cost, and minimal ecological disruption, which considers minimum potential effects to nontarget species and the Refuge environment. Pesticides may be used where physical, cultural, and biological methods or combinations thereof, are impractical or incapable of providing adequate control, eradication, or containment. If a pesticide would be needed on Refuge lands, the most specific (selective) chemical available for the target species would be used unless considerations of persistence or other environmental and/or biotic hazards would preclude it. In accordance with 517 DM 1, pesticide usage would be further restricted because only pesticides registered with the U.S. Environmental Protection Agency (USEPA) in full compliance with the Federal Insecticide, Fungicide, and Rodenticide Act (FIFRA) and as provided in regulations, orders, or permits issued by USEPA may be applied on lands and waters under Refuge jurisdiction.

Environmental harm by pest species would refer to a biologically substantial decrease in environmental quality as indicated by a variety of potential factors, including declines in native species populations or communities, degraded habitat quality or long-term habitat loss, and/or altered ecological processes. Environmental harm may be a result of direct effects of pests on native species, including preying and feeding on them; causing or vectoring diseases; preventing them from reproducing or killing their young; outcompeting them for food, nutrients, light, nest sites or other vital resources; or hybridizing with them so frequently that within a few generations, few if any truly native individuals remain. Environmental harm also can be the result of an indirect effect of pest species. For example, decreased waterfowl use may result from invasive plant infestations reducing the availability and/or abundance of native wetland plants that provide forage during the winter.

Environmental harm may involve detrimental changes in ecological processes. For example, bufflegrass infestations can greatly alter fire return intervals, displacing native species and communities of bunch grasses, forbs, and shrubs. Environmental harm may also cause or be associated with economic losses and damage to human, plant, and animal health. For example, invasions by fire-promoting grasses that alter entire plant and animal communities, eliminating or sharply reducing populations of many native plant and animal species, can also greatly increase fire-fighting costs.

Throughout the life of the CCP, most proposed pesticide uses on Refuge lands would be evaluated for potential effects to Refuge biological resources and environmental quality. Pesticide uses with appropriate and practical best management practices (BMPs) for habitat management as well as cropland/facilities maintenance would be approved for use on Refuge lands where there likely would be only minor, temporary, and localized effects to species and environmental quality based upon nonexceedance of threshold values in chemical profiles. However, pesticides may be used on Refuge lands where substantial effects to species and the environment are possible (exceed threshold values) in order to protect human health and safety (e.g., mosquito-borne disease).

2.5 Alternative Descriptions

2.5.1 Alternative A: Continue Current Management

Honouliuli and Waiawa Units

Alternative A is the "no change" alternative required by NEPA. Management of threatened and endangered species would continue to focus on protection and production in the statewide effort to implement the Recovery Plan for Hawaiian waterbirds. Inventory and monitoring would continue to focus on waterbirds and aquatic invertebrate/vegetation, and water quality sampling. Waterbird surveys to determine species composition and numbers of individuals present on the Refuge would continue to be conducted once to twice monthly at each unit. Ground water quality (temperature, salinity, and dissolved oxygen) and quantity (gallons used for management) required for monthly State water use compliance will continue to be conducted and reported monthly. Water level monitoring and manipulation would continue at current scheduled intervals to meet the life history needs of endangered water birds. Water manipulation is used throughout the year to provide quality wetland/waterbird habitat. See section 2.6 for detailed discussion of water management. Control of invasive plant species would be modest, and intensive predator control would continue. Predator control is aimed at minimizing predator entry to the Refuge using fences, and eradicating or reducing and maintaining low numbers of mongooses, rats, mice, cats, and dogs that enter the Refuge. Live trapping and use of bait stations containing 0.005% dipahacinone rodenticides bait would continue to be used to control mongooses, rats, and mice. These species are euthanized when live-trapped. Live traps are used to capture cats and dogs on the Refuge. Predator control would be conducted by Refuge personnel or contracted control technicians. Prescribed fire, mechanical, and chemical methods would continue to be used to provide high quality wetland habitat to support all aspects of endangered waterbirds and seasonal habitat for migratory species on portions of the Refuge.

On the Honouliuli Unit, environmental education would continue in cooperation with the Hawai'i Nature Center on a seasonal basis, occurring from September into December. The Betty Bliss observation deck will be constructed at Honouliuli for interpretation, wildlife viewing, and photography.

Kalaeloa Unit

Management and protection would continue for the 14 existing anchialine pools. Cooperation with Bishop Museum on cataloging avian and other fossil remains from the pools would continue. Entry into the Refuge units would continue by special use permit (SUP) only. There would be no increase in facilities or programming for wildlife observation, photography, interpretation and environmental education, with a focus on maintaining the status quo. No new offices or maintenance facilities would be constructed. There will be no new programs and no new staff. The Refuge volunteer program will continue at the current level, benefiting a variety of Refuge programs.

2.5.2 Alternative B: Increase Native Habitat Restoration and Wetland Management

Under Alternative B, the Refuge staff would manage its resources to emphasize and increase native habitat restoration of the coralline plain at Kalaeloa Unit and wetland management at the Honouliuli and Waiawa units. This is the preferred alternative.

Kalaeloa Unit

At Kalaeloa, the existing restoration area of 25 acres would be expanded an additional 12 acres to incorporate the full 37 acres of the unit. The Refuge staff would emphasize control and reduction of invasive plants and propagation and planting of native plants, including two endangered species: the ʻakoko and ʻEwa hinahina. A trail system would be developed to reduce ground disturbance, protect plants, and improve visitor safety. An endangered plant restoration partnership with Leeward Community College would continue.

Protection and management would continue for the 14 existing anchialine pools. Up to 30 additional pool sites would be identified, evaluated, and restored. Viable anchialine pools would be surveyed to determine if translocation of pinapinao listed as candidates for endangered status is feasible. The Refuge staff would coordinate efforts with Service Ecological Services staff to facilitate experimental translocation of these species.

Restoration of endangered and native plants and additional anchialine pools would increase, with Kalaeloa functioning as a living classroom for both Hawaiʻi's residents and visitors. Onsite work activities for volunteers that include such jobs as invasive plant removal, path clearing, and replanting of native species would be developed. University of Hawaiʻi students (undergraduate and graduate levels) would design and conduct onsite research projects that correspond with Refuge management goals and objectives while mentoring a Kapolei High School student during the entire process. A University of Hawaiʻi student would help local high school students develop learning stations and an interpretive guided tour of Kalaeloa, thus creating a source of trained, local interpreters available to provide guided tours to groups visiting Kalaeloa. Up to 1,500 students a year could participate in the guided tour and learning stations.

Cooperation with Bishop Museum cataloging avian fossils would continue. Refuge staff, working with Bishop Museum and the Smithsonian Institution, would pursue an indepth paleontological study of the Kalaeloa Unit to confirm genetic identification of prehistoric bird remains.

Honouliuli and Waiawa Units

Under Alternative B, the Refuge would manage its resources to increase the level of effort on wetland habitat management to potentially augment capacity for endangered waterbirds. Management of threatened and endangered species would focus on protection and production in the statewide effort to implement the Recovery Plan for Hawaiian Waterbirds. Pond level manipulation would continue at current scheduled intervals to meet the life-history needs of endangered waterbirds. The Refuge would conduct mangrove removal on 5 acres at Honouliuli Unit with associated dike protection and maintain previously cleared intertidal flat at Waiawa Unit.

Wildlife inventory and monitoring frequency would increase with continued focus on waterbirds and aquatic invertebrate/vegetation response to habitat management. Current levels of control of invasive plant species and intensive predator control would increase slightly. Installation and use of a predator-proof fence at Honouliuli may be pursued if determined feasible. The Refuge would work with partners and adjacent landowners to determine feasibility of developing a Refuge overlook at Waiawa (along the Pearl Harbor Historic Trail).

All Units

These alternatives represent broad, thematic approaches to management and administration of the Refuge, recognizing the latitude managers have in focusing human and fiscal resources within the framework of Refuge System laws and policy (Table 1). The alternatives reflect direction in the Administration Act, Service policy for administration and management of refuges, and a host of ongoing conservation initiatives affecting the Hawaiian Islands. The alternatives were also developed to address a suite of issues, and indeed are structured to track the issues, challenges, and opportunities presented in Chapter 1. As an integrated EA and CCP, the details of the alternatives are described in terms of the main components of a CCP, namely measurable objectives and strategies to achieve those objectives. Most importantly, these alternatives are designed to help Pearl Harbor NWR contribute to the mission of the Refuge System; meet the purposes for which the Refuge was established in 1972 and expanded in 2001, and help achieve the Refuge vision, goals, and objectives.

A step-down plan to inventory and monitor climate change-related variables and trends on all units would be developed. A maintenance shed would be constructed on one of the Units. All Refuge units would continue to be closed to general public entry, except for year-round access at the Betty Bliss Memorial Overlook. Entry into the Refuge would continue to be by SUP only.

2.6 Goals, Objectives, Strategies, and Rationale

Goals and objectives are the unifying elements for successful, adaptive refuge management. They identify and focus management priorities, resolve issues, and link to refuge purposes, Service policy, and the Refuge System mission.

A CCP describes management actions that help bring a refuge closer to its vision. A vision broadly reflects the refuge purposes, Refuge System mission and goals, other statutory requirements, and larger-scale plans as appropriate. Goals then define general targets in support of the vision, followed by objectives that direct effort into incremental and measurable steps toward achieving those goals. Finally, strategies identify specific tools and actions to accomplish objectives. Unless specifically stated, all objectives are applicable throughout the life of this plan.

In the development of this CCP, the Service has prepared an EA. The EA evaluates alternative sets of management actions derived from a variety of management goals, objectives, and implementation strategies. The goals for the Pearl Harbor NWR throughout the life of the CCP are presented on the following pages. Each goal is followed by one or more objectives that pertain to it. The goal order does not imply any priority in this CCP. Some objectives pertain to multiple goals and have simply been placed in the most reasonable spot. Similarly, some strategies pertain to multiple objectives and for clarity these strategies are listed under each relevant objective. Following the goals, objectives, and strategies, a brief rationale is provided. This rationale generally describes how management strategies will be implemented to achieve the intended objectives. The rationale may also, where necessary, discuss means to minimize potential impacts to nontarget species and habitats. It also provides further background information pertaining to the importance of an objective relative to legal mandates for managing units of the Refuge System, including refuge purpose, trust resource responsibilities (federally listed threatened and endangered species and migratory birds), and maintaining/restoring biological integrity, diversity, and environmental health.

Table 2.1: Management Alternatives Summary

Pearl Harbor NWR Management Alternatives Summary			
Key Themes	**Objectives**	**Alt A** **Continue Current Management**	**Alt B** **Increased Native Habitat Restoration**
Threatened, Endangered and Sensitive Species			
Waiawa and Honouliuli Units Seasonal wetland habitats	**1.1. Provide seasonal wetland habitat for ae'o loafing/foraging**	17 acres	22-35 acres
	1.2. Manage seasonal wetland habitat for ae'o breeding	5-8 acres	9-13 acres
	1.3. Provide seasonal wetland habitat for 'alae ke'oke'o and 'alae 'ula loafing and foraging	5-8 acres	10-15 acres
	1.4. Provide seasonal wetland habitat for 'alae ke'oke'o and 'alae 'ula breeding	3-5 acres	5-8 acres
Kalaeloa Unit Coastal coralline plain habitats	**2.1. Restore and maintain dry coastal shrubland**	25 acres	37 acres
	2.2. Protect and restore anchialine pools	14 anchialine pools	14-44 anchialine pools
Inventory, Monitoring, and Research			
Inventory	**3.1. Conduct inventory and monitoring to document progress and evaluate management strategies**	Continue existing inventory and monitoring.	Increase inventory and monitoring frequency.
Monitoring		Work with Pacific Islands Climate Change Cooperative to develop monitoring protocol to understand effects of climate change on the Refuge.	

Key Themes	Objectives	Alt A Continue Current Management	Alt B Increased Native Habitat Restoration
Research	3.2. Facilitate research and scientific assessments at the Refuge to guide management decisions	Partner with Bishop Museum to catalog fossil bones.	Same as A plus pursue an indepth avian paleontological survey at Kalaeloa Unit.
Public Use and Services			
Outreach	4.1. Provide a quality environmental education program at the Honouliuli and Kalaeloa Units.	<2,500 students	<5,500 students
Public Uses	4.2. Promote understanding and appreciation of natural and cultural resources.	Overlook constructed at Honouliuli Unit.	Same as A plus conduct feasibility study for overlook at Waiawa Unit.
Historic and Cultural Resources			
Historic Remnants	5.1. Protect World War II structures at the Kalaeloa Unit.	Existing fence and screening maintained. Public entry limited by Special Use Permit.	

2.6.1 Goal 1: Protect and manage seasonal wetland habitats to meet the life-history needs of endangered waterbirds to promote their recovery and also for the benefit of migratory birds.

Objective 1.1: Provide seasonal wetland habitat for aeʻo loafing and foraging.		
Provide seasonal wetland habitat for loafing and foraging aeʻo year-round on 15 -20 acres of the Honouliuli Unit and 10-20 acres of the Waiawa Unit. Habitat for aeʻo loafing and foraging has the following characteristics: • Open water (1-6") and mudflat (saturated and dry) interspersed with 30-60% cover of emergent vegetation (e.g., cattail), grasses (e.g., sprangletop, knot-grass, millet), and sedges (e.g., saltmarsh bulrush, California bulrush, *Fimbrystlis* sp.) providing a mosaic; • <25% cover of pest plants including marsh fleabane, *Batis*, California bulrush, and California grass; • Documented predation (e.g., by mongooses, cats, and dogs below 10 individual aeʻo per year; • Using water manipulation strategies throughout the year create soil and water condition enhancing and perpetuating invertebrate production and diversity.		
Strategies Applied to Achieve Objective	Alt A	Alt B
Total acreage meeting objective characteristics	18-25	25-40
• Flooding after vegetation treatment (mowing, tilling, herbicide) to promote foraging	✓	✓

	Alt A	Alt B
• Drawdown approximately April-June (control fish and promote invertebrates/algal growth, plant response)	✓	✓
• Pulse water to promote abundance and availability of invertebrates	Monthly	Twice monthly
• Standard chain link fencing, live-trapping, and bait stations to reduce predation (e.g., by mongooses, cats, dogs, rats, cattle egrets)	✓	✓
• Construct predator-proof fence using new fence design and materials generally along existing fence alignment		✓
• Control pest plants using IPM techniques including water level control, herbicide application, mowing, and rototilling (See attached regional IPM Appendix E)	✓	✓

Rationale:

Ae'o require different loafing and foraging habitats during the breeding (late February through July) and nonbreeding seasons. Recently hatched ae'o (<14 days old) require shallow water of less than 2 in to forage. During the remainder of the year, fledgling and adult ae'o can forage in water as deep as 6 in.

Seasonally regulating water depth (pulsing) stimulates germination of desirable and beneficial plant species, controls undesirable plants, and encourages the production of a variety of macro-invertebrates that serve as an important food source for young and adult ae'o. In addition to providing forage, seasonally regulated water depths provide a mosaic of open water and vegetation as microhabitat for stilt thermoregulation and cover during inclement weather.

Mowing, herbicide application, and rototilling are all techniques suitable for creating the mosaic of desired vegetation, open water, and mudflats by controlling dense contiguous patches of *Batis*, California grass, marsh fleabane, California bulrush, water hyssop, or cattail. These management techniques also benefit a variety of other wetland-dependent species including koloa maoli, 'alae 'ula, 'alae ke'oke'o, wintering waterfowl, and shorebirds, primarily by providing valuable feeding and loafing habitat.

Vegetation control is accomplished to some degree all year. This yearlong control consists mainly of mechanical treatment, such as mowing dikes to reduce and minimize predator concealment cover and control invasive plants. To minimize potential predation by cattle egrets that follow mowing equipment feeding on invertebrate prey, this type of control is terminated just prior to the time stilt nests begin hatching and does not resume until hatching is over in critical areas of the Refuge. This period is generally from April into June, depending on the nesting chronology that year. Seasonally, mainly during the period of August through mid October, more intense habitat enhancement occurs. The exact timing is dependent on endangered waterbird nesting cycles and arrival of winter migrants from their breeding grounds on other continents. When young waterbirds are capable of flight and can move among wetland impoundments or to other wetlands work is initiated.

Objective 1.2. Manage seasonal wetland habitat for ae'o breeding.

Manage seasonal wetland habitat for breeding ae'o from February through July on 3-5 acres of the Waiawa Unit and 6-8 acres of the Honouliuli Unit with the following characteristics:
- Open water (<3 in) and mudflat (saturated and unsaturated) with <25% cover of cattail, grasses, and sedges providing a mosaic;

- Undulating, irregular bottom topography creating unsaturated mudflats with gradual slopes during drawdown for nesting adjacent to foraging habitat;
- Units remain closed to general public use to prevent disturbance, except for the new Betty Bliss Memorial Overlook at Honouliuli which is located to minimize potential disturbance
- Management activities by refuge staff are timed and conducted to minimize disturbance;
- Predation by dogs, cats or mongooses limited to no more than 5 documented events per year, a hatching rate of at least 3 eggs per nest, and at least 2 chicks fledged per nest;
- <25% cover of pest plants including marsh fleabane, *Batis*, water hyssop, California bulrush, and California grass;
- Abundant macro-invertebrates for foraging with densities of 480-720 invertebrates/yd^2.

Strategies Applied to Achieve Objective	Alt A	Alt B
Total acreage meeting objective characteristics	5-8	9-13
• Flooding for prebreeding (as a follow-up to mowing/rototilling to create nesting habitat)	✓	✓
• Slow drawdown rate (control fish and promote invertebrates/algal growth, plant response)	✓	✓
• Pulsing water to promote invertebrates for broods	annually	twice monthly
• Fencing, live-trapping, and bait stations to reduce predation by mongooses, rats, cats, dogs and mice	✓	✓
• Control invasive plants and create openings in rank vegetation using IPM techniques including water level control, herbicide applications, mowing, and rototilling	✓	✓
• Public use closures	✓	✓

Rationale:

Breeding ae'o require unsaturated mudflat habitat for building nests. Initial (prebreeding) water-level drawdowns help establish unsaturated mudflats for nesting. Initiation of the drawdown is timed to coincide with minimal or no 'alae ke'oke'o nesting or chick rearing. This drawdown timing method is part of an overall cycle of wetting and drying of habitat, making it suitable for a greater number of individuals throughout the year and increasing species diversity. Thus, ae'o nesting habitat temporally follows where 'alae ke'oke'o nesting habitat existed previously.

Declining water levels increase areas of suitable nesting habitat. The target distance between nest site to vegetation and water is approximately 0-20 ft. These slow breeding season drawdown rates also stimulate ample numbers and diversity of invertebrates throughout the brood rearing period, allowing adult ae'o with broods to establish feeding territories and reduce interbrood conflicts that can result in injury or death to young chicks.

Ae'o are very easily disturbed during the nesting season. Since they nest in the open on exposed mudflats they evolved behaviors to help protect nests and young. One behavior of the adult is to depart the nest when perceived danger is detected, leaving the nest, eggs, or young exposed to ground or avian predators and the weather. Eggs can also be destroyed by prolonged exposure to high temperature, wind chill, and rain, all of which occur frequently in Hawai'i. Human disturbance must be minimized during the nesting period to reduce the risk of nest abandonment. Thus, public access is closed during nesting season.

Ae'o nests, eggs, and young are also vulnerable to a variety of predators including rats, mice, mongooses, bullfrogs, dogs, cats, cattle egrets, and 'auku'u. It is critical to control predators during the nesting season, thereby increasing nesting and fledging success.

Objective 1.3. Provide seasonal wetland habitat for 'alaeke'oke'o and 'alae 'ula loafing and foraging.

Manage seasonal wetland habitat for loafing/foraging 'alae 'ula and 'alaeke'oke'o throughout the year on 5-7 acres of seasonal wetlands at Waiawa Unit, 7-10 acres of seasonal wetlands at Honouliuli Unit, and associated dikes with the following characteristics:

- Mudflat (dry and saturated) and open water (<1-18 in) interspersed with 30-60% cover of tall (3-8 ft) emergent vegetation, grasses, and sedges that provide seed and green browse and a mosaic of concealment cover, open water, and thermal cover;
- <25% cover of invasive plants including marsh fleabane, *Batis*, water hyssop, California bulrush, and California grass;
- Adjacent short (<4 in), grassy uplands (especially dikes) for foraging;
- Interspersed vegetation with sufficient edge providing visual barriers to maximize territories available for breeding;
- Predation levels by dogs, cats or mongooses of no more than 5 individual 'alae ke'oke'o and 1 'alae 'ula per year;
- Tilapia numbers maintained at a low level promoting algal growth and other desirable plants such as widgeon grass (*Ruppia maritime*) as forage;
- Abundant epiphytic invertebrates (e.g., dragonflies), crayfish, and aquatic benthic/nektonic macroinvertebrates to provide an important source of forage.

Strategies Applied to Achieve Objective	Alt A	Alt B
Total acreage meeting objective characteristics	7-11	12-17
• Extended hydro period November-March to promote epiphytic invertebrates		✓
• Flood-up after vegetation treatment (mowing, tilling, etc) to promote foraging	✓	✓
• Slow drawdown rate (control fish and promote invertebrates/algal growth, plant response)	✓	✓
• Fencing, live-trapping, and bait stations to reduce vertebrate pest predation	✓	✓
• Control invasive plants and create openings in rank vegetation using IPM techniques including: water level control, herbicide application, mowing, brush cutting, excavation, and rototilling	✓	✓
• Pulsing water to promote young food plant growth for foraging		✓
• Mangrove removal on 5 acres at Honouliuli with associated dike protection		✓
• Implement use of a predator proof fence at Honouliuli		✓

Rationale:
While 'alaeke'oke'o and 'alae 'ula occupy similar loafing and foraging habitat, there are differences between the two species. 'Alae ke'oke'o use earlier succession stages of wetland habitat with greater open water to vegetation ratio. They also typically occupy deeper water than 'alae 'ula, which prefer late successional stages comprised of dense, robust vegetation. 'Alae ke'oke'o spend more time loafing in a

flock on open water and dikes; whereas, 'alae 'ula are more solitary and use open water primarily as a corridor between areas of suitable habitat.

Mowing, herbicide application, and rototilling are all techniques suitable to open dense contiguous patches of *Batis*, California grass, marsh fleabane, California bulrush, water hyssop, or cattail dominated areas in order to create a mosaic of vegetation, open water, and mudflats. These techniques also return nutrients to the wetland ecosystem and benefit a variety of other waterbirds including koloa maoli, wintering waterfowl, and shorebirds.

Mangrove is not native to the Hawaiian archipelago and was introduced to reduce sedimentation resulting from agricultural practices, mainly sugarcane growing. Since introduction, it has spread along shorelines of the main islands and into the lochs of Pearl Harbor on O'ahu. The outward growth from the shoreline reduces endangered and migratory waterbird foraging habitat and potential native fish species habitat. Removal will increase intertidal mudflat foraging area for endangered, other resident, and migratory waterbirds and increase food availability. Expanding foraging areas for these species will help meet recovery goals. Native fish species might also benefit from the more open accessible shoreline for various life-history needs during the year.

Installation of a predator-proof, boundary fence is planned for the Honouliuli Unit of the Refuge. Vertebrate pests (dogs, cats, mongooses, rats, and mice) kill birds and destroy nests, not only on the Refuge but throughout the State of Hawai'i. Site-specific ongoing and intensive predator control programs are necessary and common throughout the State where efforts are being made to manage and protect populations of ground nesting birds. These programs are an essential component for the recovery of the populations of many endangered species, including the a'eo, 'alaeke'oke'o, 'alae 'ula, and potentially the koloa maoli.

Predator-proof fences are now being used successfully and on very large scales (tens and hundreds of thousands of acres) in New Zealand and other countries, but they have not yet been used in Hawai'i. The current standard chain-link fence that surrounds most of the Honouliuli Unit is not effective at keeping dogs (and people) outside of the Refuge. Cats are known to climb over the fence and smaller mammals easily pass through the fence; therefore, the need exists for the current year-round predator control program within the fence line. Some predators such as feral and trespass dogs and cats and exotic mongooses are known to kill adult birds as well as destroy nests and kill young birds. The terrain and current alignment of a fence around the Honouliuli Unit make it the most practical and feasible unit to initially install a predator-proof fence. Although the initial installation costs would be high, a predator-proof fence, properly installed and maintained, would greatly reduce the need for and cost of the current ongoing intensive predator control program. This could result in a long-term savings of cost and effort, and most importantly, the further reduction of predators within the Refuge would increase the success of nesting endangered waterbirds and the survival of both adult and young birds.

Ongoing monitoring would be needed to determine the full extent of the effect of the fence on both predator and endangered waterbird populations. Lessons learned and experience gained from the installation and use of this fence will benefit future management decisions on this and other wetland refuges. Note: predator-proof fence refers to the ability of the fence to restrict movement of terrestrial predators (in this case, mammals) and does not include avian predators.

Objective 1.4. Provide seasonal wetland habitat for ʻalae ʻula and ʻalae keʻokeʻo breeding.

Provide and intensively manage seasonal wetland habitat for breeding ʻalae ʻula and ʻalae keʻokeʻo throughout the year on 1-3 acres on Waiawa Unit and 3-5 acres on Honouliuli Unit on a rotational basis to meet the following characteristics:

- Mudflat (dry and saturated) and open water (<1-18 in) interspersed with 30-60% cover of tall (3-8 ft) emergent vegetation, grasses, and sedges that provide seed and green browse and a mosaic of concealment cover, open water, and thermal cover;
- <25% cover of invasive plants including marsh fleabane, *Batis*, water hyssop, California bulrush, and California grass;
- Predation levels by dogs, cats or mongooses of no more than 5 individual ʻalae keʻokeʻo and 1 ʻalae ʻula per year;
- Interspersed vegetation with sufficient edge providing visual barriers to maximize territories available for breeding;
- Brood rearing habitat in close proximity to nesting habitat; and stable water levels during nesting period

Strategies Applied to Achieve Objective	Alt A	Alt B
Total acreage meeting objective characteristics	3-6	4-8
• Extended hydroperiod to promote epiphytic invertebrates		✓
• Flooding to sufficiently inundate emergent vegetation	✓	✓
• Slow drawdown rate (control *Tilapia* and promote invertebrates and plant response)	✓	✓
• Fencing, live-trapping, and bait stations to reduce predation by vertebrate pests	✓	✓
• Control pest plants using IPM techniques including herbicide application, mowing, and rototilling	✓	✓
• Mowing, rototilling, and brush cutting to create openings in *Batis*, California grass, marsh fleabane, and California bulrush-dominated areas and promote a mosaic of vegetation/open water to maximize territories for ʻalae keʻokeʻo	✓	✓
• Maintain stable water levels during laying and incubation	✓	✓
• Partial to complete public closure to minimize human disturbance	✓	✓

Rationale:

ʻAlae ʻula and ʻalaekeʻokeʻo prefer stable water levels for nest building and nesting. When preparing an impoundment for ʻalae ʻula and ʻalae keʻokeʻo nesting, water levels are raised to a depth of 8-15 in and maintained at a constant level to provide adequate nest sites that are secure from mammalian predation. Fluctuating water levels are not desirable, requiring nesting adults to continually build the nest up or have it isolated on dry ground vulnerable to mammalian predation.

During brood-rearing periods, water levels are pulsed infrequently to provide physical barriers between brood territories and provide greater availability of macroinvertebrates that are eaten by adults in breeding condition and also fed to developing chicks. These invertebrates are an important protein source necessary for survival and proper development.

Part of the Statewide recovery effort for endangered waterbirds involves producing adequate numbers of offspring to increase populations to a sustainable level and then maintaining that level. Providing a mosaic of open water and desirable plant species promotes the greatest number of nesting and brood rearing territories, while minimizing strife between family units.

The amount of vegetative cover in a managed wetland varies with the duration between habitat management actions. The succession from open water to a more vegetation-dominated wetland favors different species. 'Alae ke'oke'o are adept at nesting in a more open setting, where there is approximately 30% cover of emergent vegetation. 'Alae 'ula prefer more vegetated cover for nest concealment with around 60% cover. Because of rapid and yearlong plant growth in Hawai'i, habitat manipulation generally requires removal of all or nearly all vegetation (generally every 2-3 years) from a managed wetland to increase the time before follow-up actions. In the habitat preparation phase, dewatering followed by mowing, tilling, and herbicide application are used to setback emergent succession, control invasive plants, and achieve the open water-emergent cover mosaic. During the managing phase when water is in the impoundment, water level manipulation (raising, lowering, or maintaining a constant level) is used to create the desired percentage of short and tall emergent plants and open-water interspersion. Each impoundment can be managed independently in this manner varying the habitat to meet life-history needs of waterbirds and other native wildlife.

Ample food supply is important to build and maintain a healthy breeding population at a given site. Exotic fish, particularly tilapia, are known to compete for food eaten by 'alae 'ula and 'alae ke'oke'o. They also degrade water quality, which can affect invertebrate densities and plant growth. During habitat manipulation, slow draw-downs of water levels are used to concentrate undesirable fish and ultimately remove them from the environment. Following their death during dewatering, the remains are allowed to dry and decompose naturally or are tilled into the soil increasing soil nutrients that aid in promoting invertebrate and plant response. Botulism is a concern and evidence of botulism poisoning is closely monitored during periods when decomposition is occurring.

'Alae 'ula and 'alae ke'oke'o are less susceptible to disturbance during nesting compared with ae'o, and this relates to their nest location, nesting habitat, and response to disturbance. Since 'alae 'ula and 'alae ke'oke'o nest in open water or dense vegetation with concealment, their response to disturbance is to remain motionless on the nest. As a result, limited and controlled public use occurs during the nesting season. It is difficult to see a nest even at a relatively close distance.

Rotational management, including water manipulation, is needed to accommodate the multiendangered species management on a yearlong basis. This technique of having different habitat conditions on that same area of land but in a different season enhances the ability to recover endangered waterbird production and maintenance habitat.

Recognizing public tours and educational programs are important, access for such activities is restricted in areas where nesting and brood rearing is concentrated. The locations of nests are monitored and visitors either directed away from the areas or led quickly through the area to minimize human disturbance.

2.6.2 Goal 2: Restore and protect coastal coralline plain habitat at the Kalaeloa Unit.

Objective 2.1: Restore and manage dry coastal shrubland habitat.

Manage 25 - 37 acres of dry coastal shrubland habitat characterized by the following:
- Coral limestone substrate with pockets containing sandy organic humus soil;

- < 20 stems per acre of woody invasive species including marsh fleabane, kiawe, and koa haole; no mature kiawe
- <25% cover of herbaceous invasive plants (e.g., bufflegrass, khaki weed);
- Patchy distribution of low growing (2-8 in), native woody species (e.g., kou, 'ilima, beach naupaka, pilo, wiliwili, naio) as a mosaic;
- Endangered plants ('Ewa hinahina, 'akoko) distributed in appropriate microhabitat (e.g., suitable moisture-retentive soils with wind/sun protection).

Strategies Applied to Achieve Objective	Alt A	Alt B
Total acreage meeting objective characteristics	25	37
• Unit is closed to general public access to minimize human disturbance	✓	✓
• Fence boundary to prevent trampling of endangered plants		✓
• Develop formal trail system for guided tours to reduce ground disturbance, protect plants, and improve visitor safety		✓
• Control pest plants and animals using IPM techniques including herbicide application, mowing, rototilling, trapping, and rodenticides bait stations.	✓	✓
• Harvest seed with subsequent propagation and outplanting of endangered and native plant species	✓	✓

Rationale: The rare coastal coralline environment that occurs on the Kalaeloa Unit is a small remnant of this unique habitat that once occurred across much of the 'Ewa Plain along the south shore of O'ahu. This natural plant community has almost been lost due to urban, industrial, and agricultural development and severe invasion by many pest species of plants and animals. The remaining and partially restored habitat on the Refuge is home to small and isolated populations of endangered and rare native plant species. Dominant pest plants (e.g., kiawe, koa haole and others) have been greatly reduced on much of the area but where they still occur their presence can result in poor or inadequate germination and survival conditions for many sensitive or endangered native plants. Continual control of these pest plants will be required to prevent them from once again expanding their presence on the Refuge and outcompeting the remaining native plants. This Refuge unit provides a small area where this rare, unique habitat can be protected. Restoring and protecting this habitat is vital to maintaining the biological integrity of the Refuge. The Refuge also provides a critical site where the genetic integrity of endangered plants can be maintained and where seed reserves can be harvested for future propagation and restoration.

Presently mammals have not been considered a serious limiting factor to recovery and perpetuation of endangered plants at the Kalaeloa Unit. While rodents known to eat seeds and seedling plants are known to occur, they have not been documented inhibiting natural germination and expansion of native plants. This is not to say that could not change in the future and control of these species become necessary.

Currently approximately 25 acres on the Unit are under active management, with no management occurring on the remaining 7 acres of the Unit. Under Alternative A, management would continue to reduce/remove invasive species, restore native plants (including endangered species) and protect the existing anchialine pools on the current 25 acres of managed lands. Under Alternative B, management would be undertaken on the remaining 7 acres to include removal of mature kiawe trees, removal and control of other invasive species, and initiate restoration through natural regeneration and outplanting of native plants. Also, under Alternative B identification and restoration of additional anchialine pools would take place across the entire Unit.

A foot trail system on the Kalaeloa Unit will protect the ground surface from disturbance, protect native and endangered plants, and provide for public safety by controlling and designating route(s) for human foot traffic. Safety issues that are a concern on this Unit and would be mitigated by a trail system include an uneven ground surface that is strewn with loose rocks, many natural and partially hidden holes resulting from the ancient coralline nature of this site and persistent large thorns from kiawe trees. The trail system will provide additional opportunities for viewing and maintenance of endangered plants and restored anchialine pools, education opportunities in viewing of a restored Hawaiian coastal plant community, restored functioning anchialine pools, and historic World War II military artifacts.

Harvest of seeds and outplanting of endangered and other native plants may be accomplished by Refuge staff, volunteers or contractors. Propagation of seeds is accomplished by local contractors who have the both the necessary facilities and expertise to accomplish this task.

While prescribed fire is a valuable and viable tool, its use at Kalaeloa would require close coordination and careful preparation because of the proximity of the Refuge to an airport approach path and runway.

Objective 2.2: Protect and restore anchialine pools.

Protect and maintain 14 existing and restore an additional 15-30 anchialine pools on the Kalaeloa Unit inhabited by native shrimps: the 'ōpae 'ula, a species of special concern, and the predatory shrimp *Metabetaeus lohena*, which is a candidate for endangered species listing. Anchialine pools are characterized by the following:
- Limited to fossil coral reef;
- Tidally influenced land-locked bodies of water (nearly fresh to ocean strength) without a surface connection to the ocean;
- Algal growth provides forage for a native invertebrate community.

Strategies Applied to Achieve Objective	Alt A	Alt B
Number of Pools Protected/Restored	14	29-44
• Remove pest plants (e.g., kiawe, marsh fleabane, koa haole) in close proximity to pools by hand pulling and mechanical removal	✓	✓
• Unit remains closed to general public access to reduce human disturbance	✓	✓
• Develop trail system for use by authorized environmental education programs and limited guided public tours to reduce disturbance to ground surface adjacent to pools and improve safety	✓	✓
• Establish an experimental population of candidate listed pinapinao		✓

Rationale:
Anchialine pools are a rare and distinctive habitat. Plants and animals found here are uniquely adapted to life in these isolated coastal sinkholes. Please refer to Chapter 4 for a more complete description of anchialine pool habitat.

A foot trail system on the Kalaeloa Unit will aid in protecting the anchialine pools by controlling and designating route(s) for human foot traffic which will reduce disturbance to soil and plants near the pools which affect the conditions of the pools.

Threats to the pinapinao include loss of suitable water habitats and predation by introduced fish species that feed on the naiads. Predation by crustaceans and nonnative birds, such as bulbuls, cardinals, and mynas, may also pose a threat to all life phases of the pinapinao. Pinapinao currently do not occur on the Refuge, but based on data collected from anchialine pools on the Refuge, there is a high potential for successful translocation of eggs and/or larval forms of this species to the Kalaeloa Unit. A translocation would involve movement of the available life stage from the existing site on Oʻahu to the Refuge. A successful translocation to the Refuge would create another population, adding to the security of the overall population, allowing its potential expansion into other anchialine pools, allowing radiation and colonization to other suitable habitat on the ʻEwa Plain, and aiding in sustaining a more stable and geographically dispersed population to reduce the need to list the species as threatened or endangered.

2.6.3 Goal 3. Collect scientific information necessary to support adaptive management decisions.

Objective 3.1. Conduct inventory and monitoring to document progress and evaluate management strategies.

Throughout the life of the CCP, conduct high-priority inventory and monitoring (survey) activities that evaluate resource management and public-use activities to facilitate adaptive management. These surveys contribute to the enhancement, protection, use, preservation, and management of wildlife populations and their habitats on- and off-refuge lands. Specifically, they can be used to evaluate achievement of resource management objectives identified in this CCP. These surveys have the following attributes:

- Data collection techniques would likely have minimal animal mortality or disturbance and minimal habitat destruction;
- Minimum number of samples (e.g., water, soils, vegetative litter, plants, macro-invertebrates, vertebrates) to meet statistical analysis requirements would be collected for identification and/or experimentation in order to minimize long-term or cumulative impacts;
- Proper cleaning of investigator equipment and clothing as well as quarantine methods, where necessary, would minimize the potential spread or introduction of invasive species;
- Projects will adhere to scientifically defensible protocols for data collection, where available and applicable.

Objective as written above applies to alternatives. *The following is a list of survey activities needed to support management decisions on the Refuge.*	Alt A	Alt B
• Inventory and monitor native habitat and endangered plant species (vegetation survey)		✓
• Inventory and map invasive plants		✓
• Annually inventory and monitor invasive plant species to determine effectiveness of control measures and need for future management actions		✓
• Monitor and report on water quality at wetland units on a monthly basis	✓	✓
• Monitor and report on water quality in anchialine pools on a quarterly basis	✓	✓
• Survey entire Kalaeloa Unit for presence of additional anchialine pools for potential restoration		✓
• Monitor and report on water use of all units on a monthly basis	✓	✓

	Alt A	Alt B
• Monitor water levels of wetland units	weekly	3 times/week
• Assess vegetation on an annual basis, prior to habitat management work (August)		✓
• Monitor wildlife populations, especially endangered waterbirds	monthly	Twice monthly
• Monitor nesting and fledgling success of endangered waterbirds	monthly	weekly
• Annually assess vertebrate pest and predator species		✓
• Participate in joint wildlife surveys with State of Hawai'I such as bi-annual state-wide waterbird surveys	✓	✓
• Monitor data for climate change protocol on all units	✓	✓

Rationale:

The National Wildlife Refuge System Administration Act of 1966, as amended (16 U.S.C. 668dd-ee) requires that we"… monitor the status and trends of fish, wildlife, and plants in each refuge." Surveys would be used primarily to evaluate resource response to assess progress toward achieving Refuge management objectives derived from the Refuge System mission, Refuge purpose(s), and maintenance of biological integrity, diversity, and environmental health (601 FW 3). Determining resource status and evaluating progress toward achieving objectives is essential to implementing adaptive management on Department of the Interior lands as required by policy (522 DM 1). Specifically, results of surveys would be used to refine management strategies, where necessary, over time in order to achieve resource objectives. Surveys would provide the best available scientific information to promote transparent decisionmaking processes for resource management over time on Refuge lands.

Climate change is expected to place enormous pressure on coastal refuges particularly vulnerable to sea-level rise resulting from melting glaciers and thermal expansion of oceans. Estimates by the Intergovernmental Panel on Climate Change project that global sea level will rise 0.6-2 ft by the end of the century. Sea-level rise threatens to erode shorelines, inundate low-lying areas, and contaminate freshwater resources through saltwater intrusion. Other impacts of climate change include species' range shifts, phenological changes, decoupling of species assemblages, hydrological changes, and changes in disturbance regimes. Such impacts could result in dramatically different ecosystem compositions than currently exist on the Refuge, and planning decisions should be considered in light of this issue.

Objective 3.2. Facilitate research and scientific assessments at the Refuge to guide management decisions.

Throughout the life of the CCP, conduct high-priority research projects that provide the best science for habitat and wildlife management on and off refuges. Scientific findings gained through these projects would expand knowledge regarding life-history needs of species and species groups as well as identify or refine habitat and wildlife management actions. Research also will reduce uncertainty regarding wildlife and habitat responses to refuge management actions in order to achieve desired outcomes reflected in resource management objectives and to facilitate adaptive management. These research projects have the following attributes:
- Adhere to scientifically defensible protocols for data collection, where available and applicable, in order to develop the best science for resource management
- Data collection techniques would likely have minimal animal mortality or disturbance and minimal habitat destruction
- Collect the minimum number of samples (e.g., water, soils, vegetative litter, plants, macroinvertebrates, vertebrates) to meet statistical analysis requirements for identification and/or

experimentation in order to minimize long-term or cumulative impacts

- Utilize proper cleaning of investigator equipment and clothing as well as quarantine methods, where necessary, to minimize the potential spread or introduction of invasive species
- Often result in peer reviewed articles in scientific journals and publications and/or symposiums

Objective as written above applies to alternatives. *The following is a list of research and scientific assessments needed for the Refuge:*	**Alt A**	**Alt B**
Develop a vegetation cover map of Pearl Harbor NWR	✓	✓
Investigate and monitor the impacts of pest plants and animals on Refuge landscapes	✓	✓
Develop a new soils survey map	✓	✓
Investigate movements of endangered waterbirds (e.g. inter- and intra-island movement)	✓	✓
Determine survival and predation rates of endangered waterbirds	✓	✓
Pursue an in-depth avian paleontological study of Kalaeloa to confirm genetic identification of bones		✓

Rationale:

The Refuge System encourages compatible research activities on refuge lands. Research and monitoring projects on refuge islands enhance scientific understanding of the ecosystems and lead to better management. Fossilized bird bones were found while Service scientists were restoring several small tidal pools, known as anchialine pools. Over the past century, the pools had been filled in with rubble, rocks, and debris by agricultural, military, residential, and commercial activities. The discovery of the fossils provides a more complete picture of the natural bird diversity of a coastal dryland forest on Oʻahu. The fossilized bones discovered so far are those of an extinct hawk, long-legged owl, Hawaiian sea eagle, petrel, two species of crow, Hawaiian finches, Hawaiian honeyeaters, and the moa nalo (a turkey-sized, flightless gooselike duck that was the largest of the native Hawaiian birds). Further work is needed to confirm the identification of each species.

The ages of the fossilized bones are unknown at this time and require further testing using radiocarbon analysis. Avian bones found at similar sites on the ʻEwa Plain date back from 1,000-8,000 years ago. The discovery of these ancient bird bones, including several species now extinct and maybe even new species not known before, is a great reminder of the truly unique history and wonderful diversity of Hawaiʻi's birds and the need to protect what is still left. The Service is working with the Smithsonian Institution and Bishop Museum to properly clean, store, and preserve the bones. The Smithsonian is also providing technical assistance to Bishop Museum and the Service to properly identify and catalog the recently discovered fossils. Interest is high amongst all involved to continue with a more in-depth paleontological study of the area, but further work is dependent upon the availability of funding.

2.6.4 Goal 4: Provide interpretive and educational opportunities to enhance public understanding of and appreciation for the natural and cultural resources of Pearl Harbor NWR.

Objective 4.1. Provide a quality environmental education program at the Honouliuli and Kalaeloa Units.

Environmental education programs will have specific learning objectives and diverse opportunities with the following attributes:

- Meet State standards for learning;
- Based on Refuge and endangered species recovery management programs;
- Support the mission of the Service;
- 90% of programs are teacher-led;
- Support the Service's "Connecting Children with Nature" program
- Seasonal program (October–December) at Honouliuli Unit provides educational visits for up to 60 third grade students per day, 5 days a week, 3,500 students per year;
- A seasonal program that provides educational visits for up to 1,500 high school and college students per year at Kalaeloa Unit

Strategies Applied to Achieve Objective	Alt A	Alt B
• Maintain partnership for providing environmental education opportunities primarily by Leeward Community College staff at Kalaeloa on native and endangered plant restoration	✓	✓
• Maintain partnerships for providing environmental education opportunities to third grade students at Honouliuli	<2,500 students	<3,500 students
• Provide seasonal program for high school and college students at Kalaeloa	100 students	1,500 students

Rationale:

With its variety of natural resources, facilities, and proximity to major population centers, Pearl Harbor NWR is in a position to offer local education agencies, teachers, and students an opportunity to study endangered species and natural resource management and conservation issues in an outdoor setting. However, a small land base (leading to concerns regarding disturbance to endangered species) and staff availability limit the level of environmental education that can be provided. Since Refuge establishment, educators such as Hawai‘i Nature Center have been using the Refuge units as an outdoor classroom to enhance course curricula. The demand for environmental education is high and expected to grow.

Waiawa Unit is closed to the public because of its small size, access issues, and close proximity to U.S. Naval facilities in Middle Loch, Pearl Harbor. Private property must be crossed to get to the Refuge and then access via a bike path to reach the area near the Refuge fence line. The bike path is not designed for vehicular traffic and general motorized vehicular access is prohibited.

Objective 4.2. Promote understanding and appreciation of natural and cultural resources.		
Interpretive programs promote understanding and appreciation of natural and cultural resources and their management on all lands and waters in the Refuge System.		
Strategies Applied to Achieve Objective	**Alt A**	**Alt B**
• Work with Hawai'i Department of Transportation to construct an overlook at Honouliuli	✓	✓
• Research feasibility of developing an overlook for Waiawa		✓
• Maintain existing signs and interpretive materials	✓	✓

Rationale: Interpretive programs promote understanding and appreciation of natural and cultural resources and their management on all lands and waters in the Refuge System. An inadequate land base and staff availability limit onsite interpretive opportunities to the previously approved Betty Bliss Memorial Overlook at Honouliuli. This overlook, associated with the Pearl Harbor Historic Trail, will provide new visitor use opportunities for wildlife observation, photography, and interpretation.

There is a potential for developing an overlook at the Waiawa Unit. No planning for this overlook has been undertaken. If deemed desirable and feasible, the overlook would be placed along the fence line of the Unit and provide for more public viewing and wildlife photography opportunities, and allow the Refuge opportunities to interpret the natural resources, management techniques and strategies, and military history of this area.

2.6.5 Goal 5: Protect historic and cultural resources for the benefit of present and future generations.

Objective 5.1. Protect World War II structures at Kalaeloa Unit.		
Strategies Applied to Achieve Objective	**Alt A**	**Alt B**
Maintain fence and closure to the public	✓	✓
Maintain screening with native plants	✓	✓

Rationale: The transfer of the Kalaeloa property to the Service included the need "…to protect natural and historic resources in a portion of the 'Ewa coastal plain." Physical historic remnants within the unit include World War II-era gunnery bunkers. Association with historical events, although intangible in nature, is an important aspect of cultural resources. Although no Hawaiian cultural resource sites have been identified within the Refuge units, the Refuge recognizes the value of conserving oral and written histories of the Pearl Harbor and Kalaeloa region. In trusteeship for future generations, the Service will conduct activities, plans, and programs in a manner consistent with the preservation and enhancement of historic and cultural property.

Chapter 2: Alternatives, Goals, Objectives, and Strategies

Figure 2.1 Honouliuli Unit, Alternative B

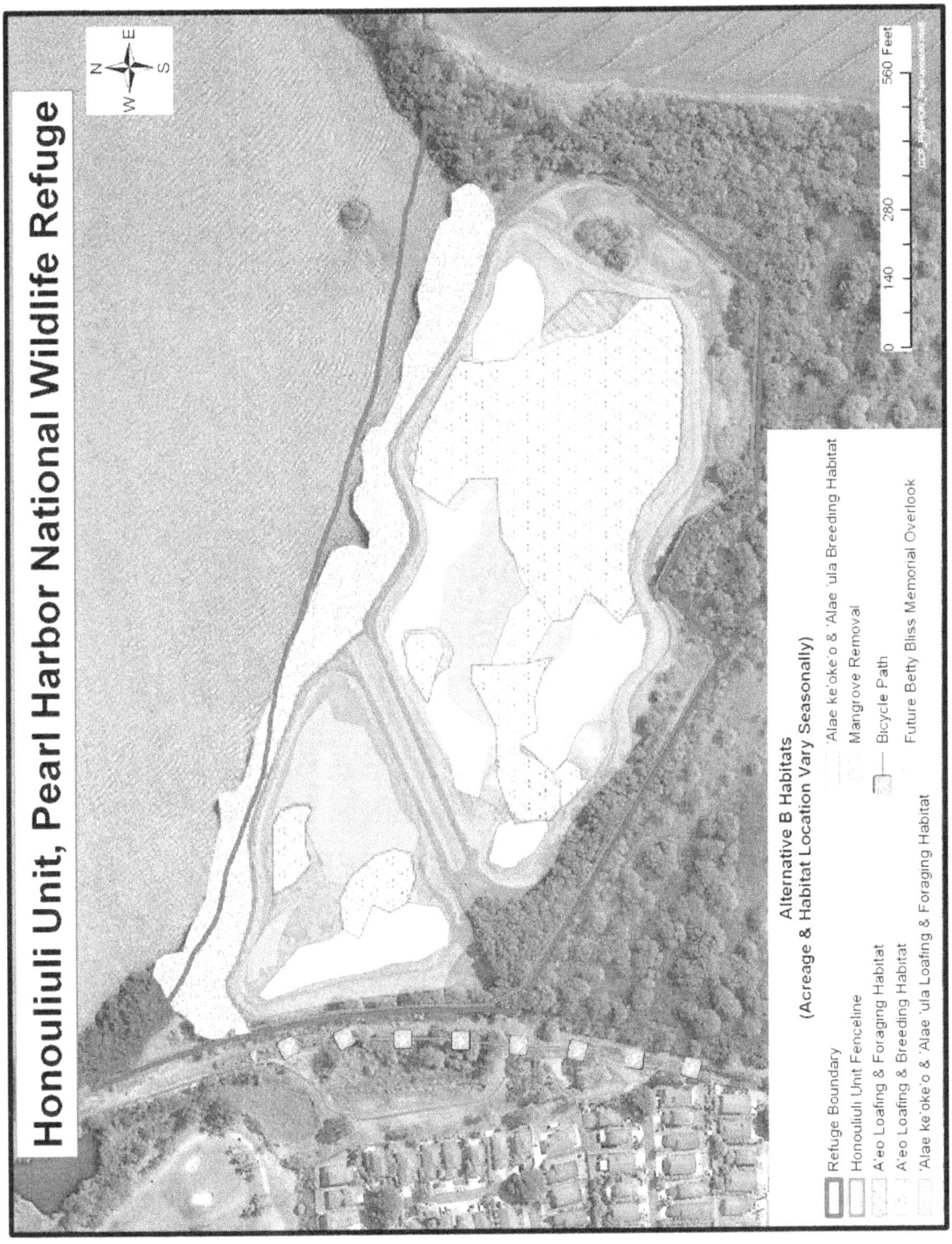

Honouliuli Unit, Pearl Harbor National Wildlife Refuge

Alternative B Habitats
(Acreage & Habitat Location Vary Seasonally)

Refuge Boundary
Honouliuli Unit Fenceline
A'eo Loafing & Foraging Habitat
A'eo Loafing & Breeding Habitat
'Alae ke'oke'o & 'Alae 'ula Loafing & Foraging Habitat
'Alae ke'oke'o & 'Alae 'ula Breeding Habitat
Mangrove Removal
Bicycle Path
Future Betty Bliss Memorial Overlook

0   140   280   560 Feet

To preserve the quality of our map, this side was left blank intentionally.

Figure 2.2 Waiawa Unit, Alternative B

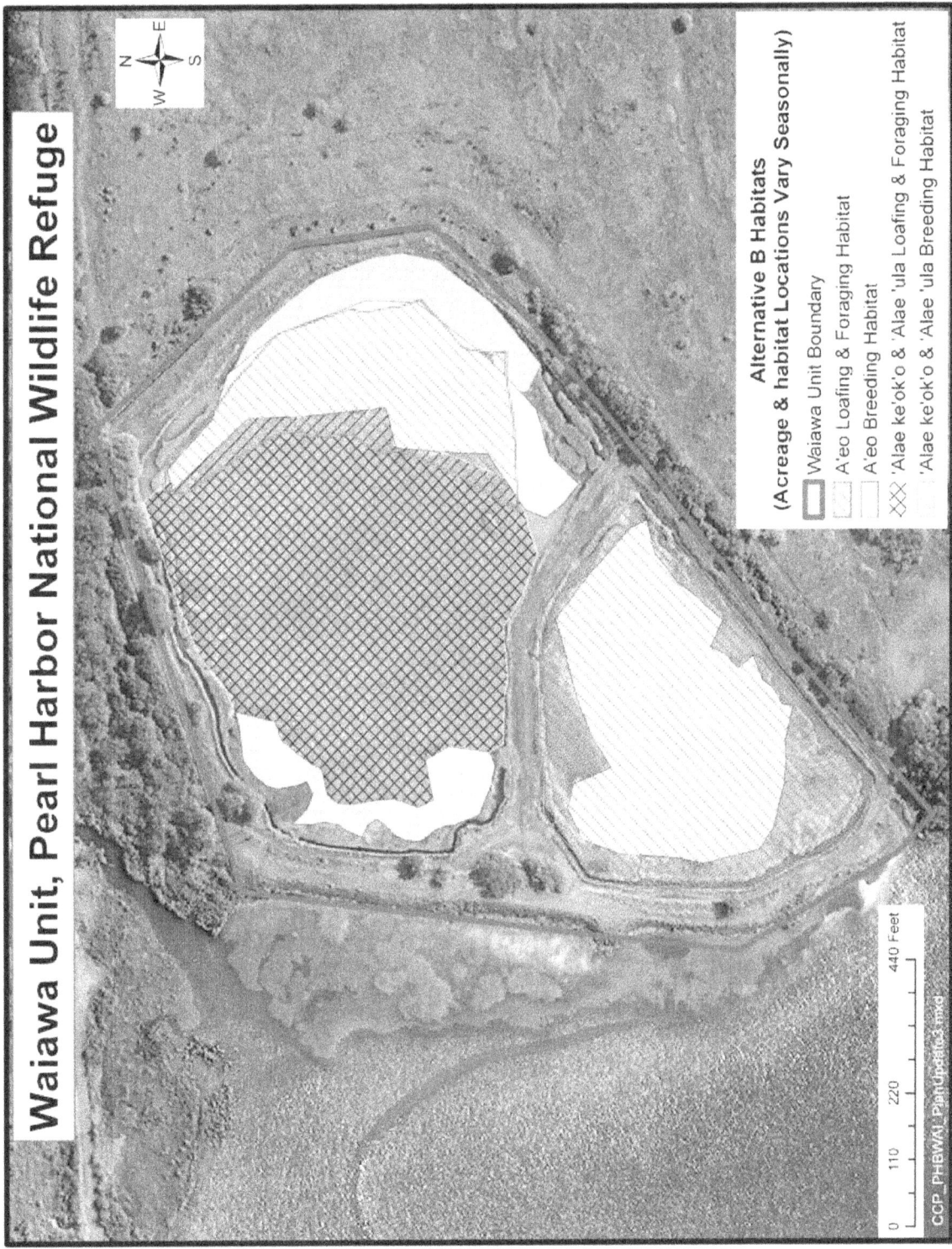

To preserve the quality of our map, this side was left blank intentionally.

Figure 2.3 Kalaeloa Unit, Alternative B

To preserve the quality of our map, this side was left blank intentionally.

Chapter 3. Physical Environment

3.1 Refuge Introduction

The O'ahu National Wildlife Refuge (NWR) Complex is located on the Island of O'ahu, within the State of Hawai'i. The Complex consists of James Campbell NWR, Pearl Harbor NWR, and O'ahu Forest NWR. Management of the Complex is conducted from the Service office located in Hale'iwa on the north shore of O'ahu (Figure 3.1).

Pearl Harbor NWR is comprised of three units on the southern portion of O'ahu: the Waiawa Unit, the Honouliuli Unit, and the Kalaeloa Unit (Figure 3.2). The Waiawa Unit (Figure 3.3) is 24.5 acres and is located on the west side of the Pearl City Peninsula, which divides the Middle Loch from the East Loch within Pearl Harbor. The Honouliuli Unit (Figure 3.4), covering 36.5 acres, is located on the west shore of the West Loch of Pearl Harbor. The newest unit, Kalaeloa (Figure 3.5), is located on the flat coastal Ewa Plain approximately 7 miles southwest of Pearl Harbor. This unit, which was formerly part of the Barbers Point Naval Air Station, is 37.4 acres.

3.2 Climate

Located 2,400 miles southwest of the nearest continental landmass, the Hawaiian Islands are the most isolated archipelago in the world. The climate of Hawai'i is generally constant throughout the year, with only minor periods of diurnal and seasonal variability. During the summer season (May-September), temperatures are slightly warmer, conditions are drier, and trade winds originate from the northeast direction. The winter season (October- April) is characterized by cooler temperatures, higher precipitation, and less equable winds. The trade winds also produce differences within the two physiographic provinces. On the windward or northeastern side of O'ahu, climatic conditions are relatively wet and strongly influenced by patterns of orographic rainfall. The leeward areas in the southern and western portion of the island experience decreased winds, less rain, and are subject to southerly Kona storms (Juvik and Juvik 1998).

O'ahu climate is influenced by three interacting climatic factors: (1) the Hadley cell, (2) the oceanic position of the major Hawaiian Islands, and (3) topography. The Hadley cell is a system of atmospheric circulation that is propelled by warm air rising near the equator and cool sinking air in the subtropics. In the Northern Hemisphere, air flowing within this system is reflected by the Earth's rotation to create northeasterly winds referred to as trade winds (Juvik and Juvik 1998, Lau and Mink 2006). Wind patterns, rainfall distribution, and other climatic conditions are also affected by the geographic location of Hawai'i.

Trade winds in Hawai'i originate from a high- pressure system located northeast of the archipelago called the North Pacific anticyclone. During the summer season, this system is stable and trade winds occur 80-95 percent of the time (Oki 2005). This high-pressure cell further regulates Hawai'i's climate because it shifts seasonally, causing trade wind and precipitation differences. During the winter and spring season, the North Pacific anticyclone moves further south and weakens, causing less persistent trade winds (50-80 percent of the time) and a greater chance of storms (Lau and Mink 2006).

Furthermore, the varied topography of the island affects the climate. The alignment, shape, and height of the mountains moderate wind patterns and cause moist air to rise near the mountain ranges. Excess clouds accumulate near mountain peaks and enhance precipitation amounts, referred to as orographic rainfall (Juvik and Juvik 1998, Lau and Mink 2006). The coastal, leeward sides of the mountains receive less precipitation because the air loses moisture as it ascends the windward side (Oki 2005).

Hurricanes can also result in intense rain and wind. Hurricane Iwa (1892) and Iniki (1992) brought damaging winds of 117 and 143 mph, respectively. These climate differences determine vegetation patterns, which in turn can affect local hydrological movements of surface and especially ground water (DBEDT 2007, Sack and Frole 2006).

Prevailing ocean currents surrounding the island influence weather patterns by moderating the surrounding surface air temperatures as a result of differential heat adsorption and advection of heat. Ocean currents around the Hawaiian Islands are moderated by the North Pacific anticyclone, a clockwise gyre that extends from the tropics to the North Pacific. The east to west flowing North Equatorial Current splits at the island of Hawai'i, creating a northern branch current that is 65 miles wide called the North Hawaiian Ridge Current. Ocean surface water temperatures surrounding O'ahu range from a mean of 75°F from February to April, to about 81°F between August and October (Juvik and Juvik 1998, Lau and Mink 2006).

The units of the Pearl Harbor NWR are located on the leeward physiographic zone of O'ahu. This geographic location results in lower rainfall, larger drainage basins, and more intermittent streams than regions more exposed to trade winds. During the dry season, day temperatures in Pearl Harbor are between 87-89°F and night temperatures range between 72-76°F. Wet season temperatures are slightly lower, with day temps ranging between 76-78°F. The difference between day and and night temperatures varies by 15-20°F. Average relative humidity in the region varies between 58-60 percent. Between 2002 and 2008, average annual rainfalls at the Waiawa and Honouliuli Units were recorded as 18.40 in and 24.60 in, respectively. Due to its location in the lee of the Ko'olau Range, Pearl Harbor is somewhat protected from the normal trade winds resulting in mean annual wind speeds of 12 mph (Department of Navy 2001, HECO 2004).

The semi-enclosed coastal waters offshore of the Waiawa and Honouliuli Units are referred to as the Pearl Harbor estuary. Water temperature in the harbor ranges between 73-84°F. This estuary receives freshwater inputs from streams, groundwater springs, urban runoff, and rainfall. Thus, salinity level measurements in the harbor fluctuate from 10- 37 percent (Englund et al 2000, Department of Navy 2001).

The climate near the Kalaeloa Unit is slightly warmer and drier than conditions in the Pearl Harbor Units. Data collected by NOAA at Barbers Point between 1970 and 2000 reported a minimum monthly average of 64.7°F in February and a maximum of 88.8°F in August (NOAA 2002). The mean annual precipitation in the area is approximately 25 in, with winter months receiving the most

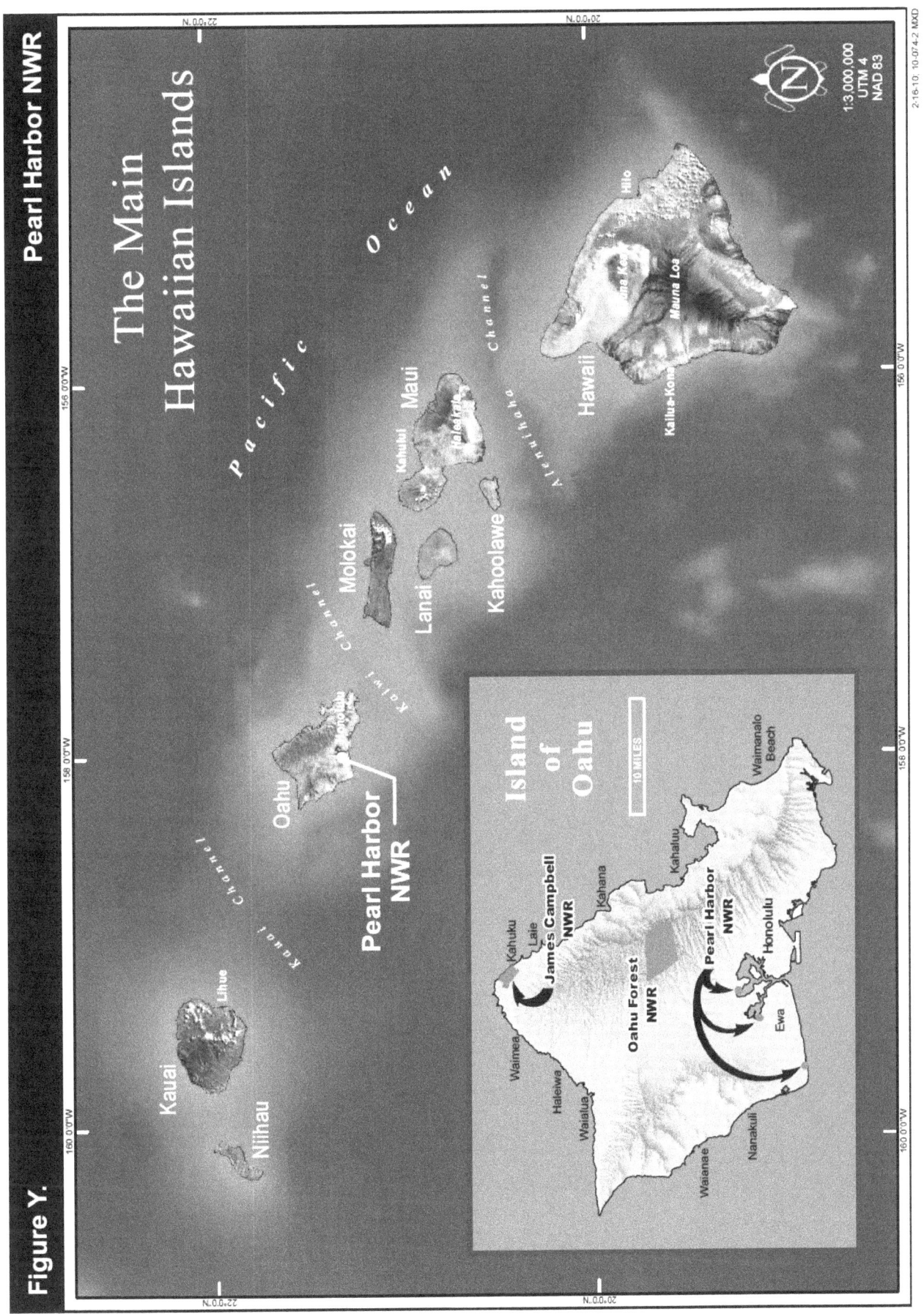

Figure Y.

Pearl Harbor NWR

The Main
Hawaiian Islands

To preserve the quality of our map, this side was left blank intentionally.

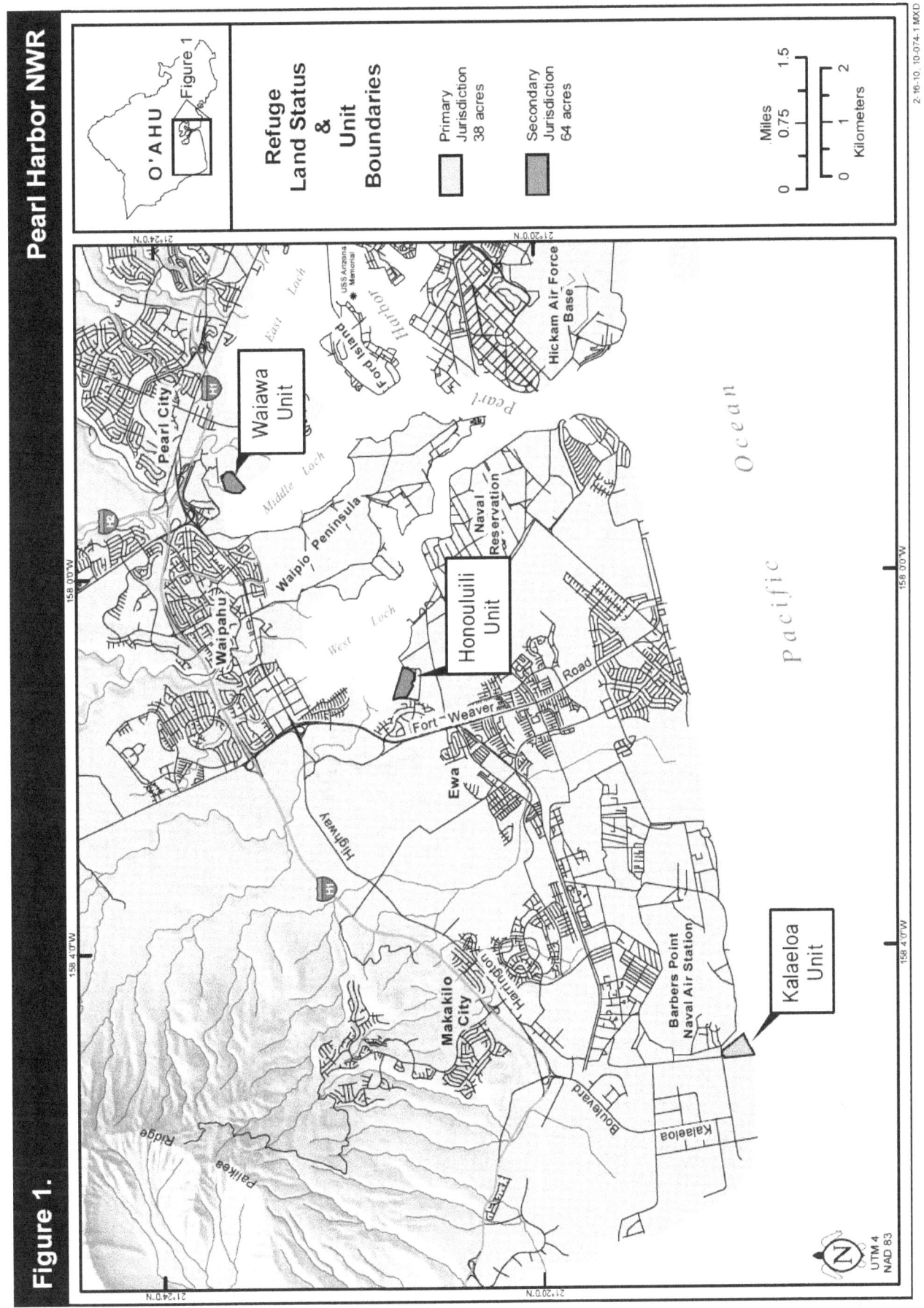

Figure 1.

Pearl Harbor NWR

Refuge Land Status & Unit Boundaries

Primary Jurisdiction 38 acres

Secondary Jurisdiction 64 acres

To preserve the quality of our map, this side was left blank intentionally.

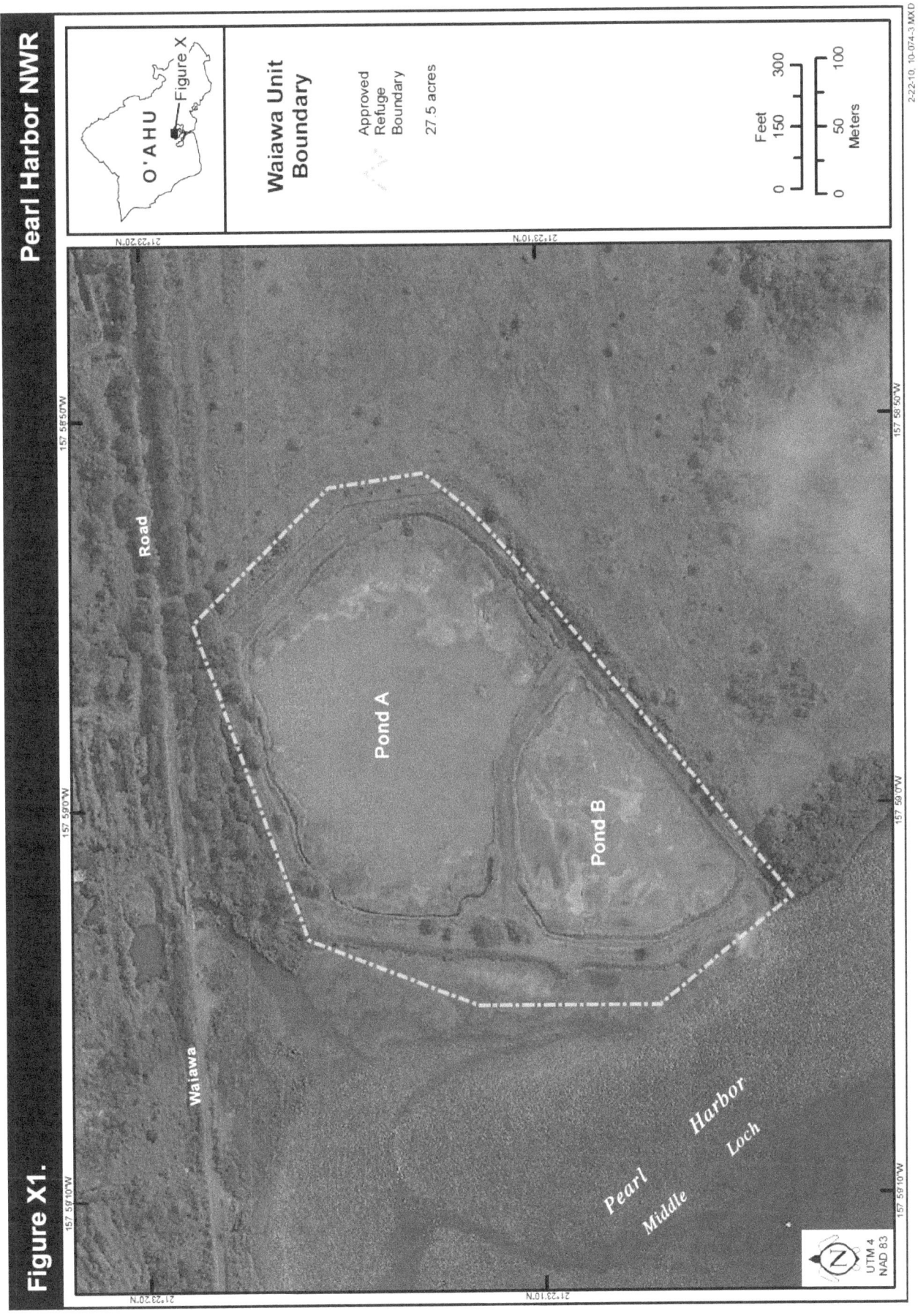

Figure X1.

Pearl Harbor NWR

O'AHU

Figure X

Waiawa Unit Boundary

Approved Refuge Boundary

27.5 acres

Feet
Meters

Pond A

Pond B

Road

Waiawa

Pearl Harbor
Middle Loch

To preserve the quality of our map, this side was left blank intentionally.

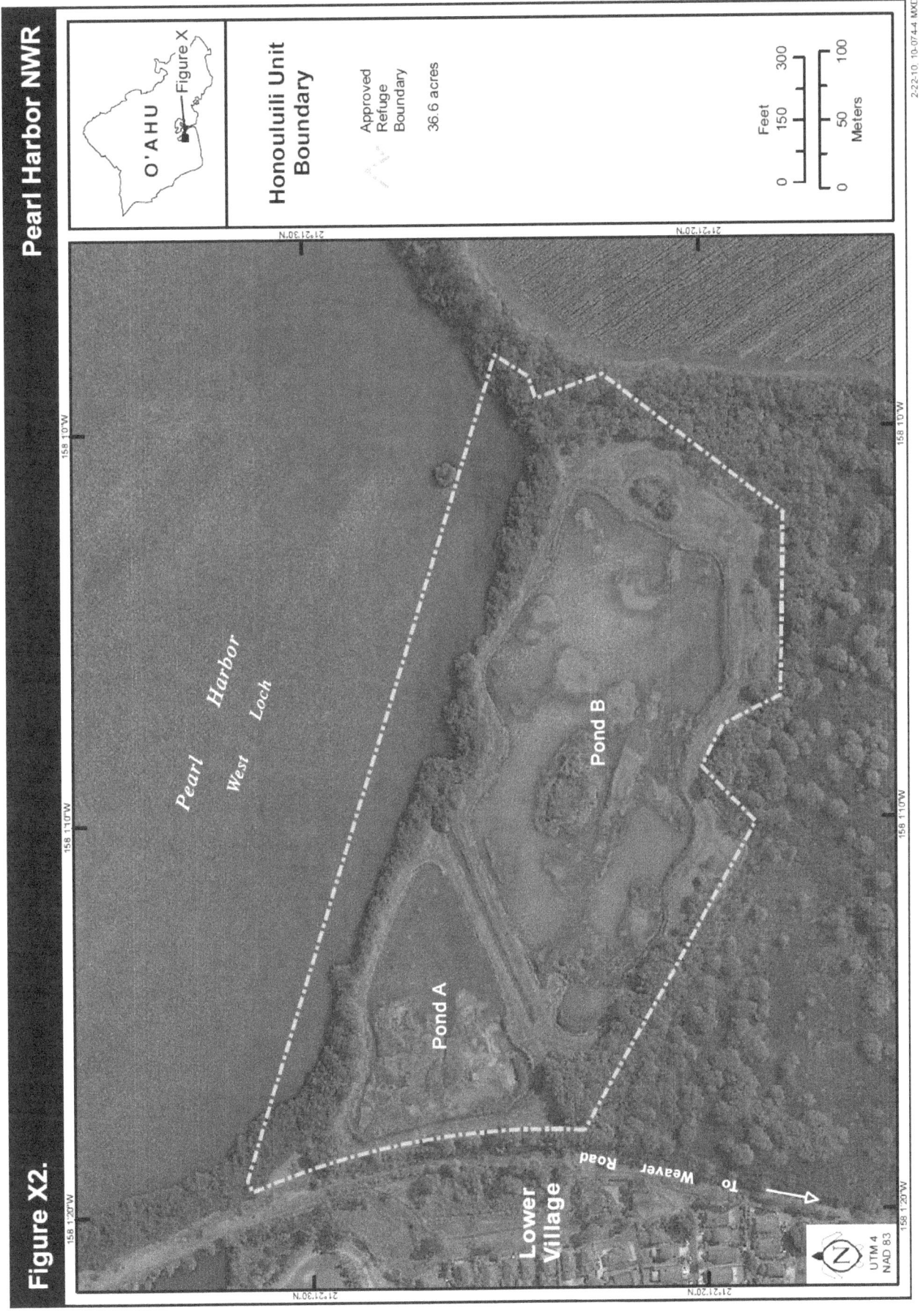

Figure X2.

Pearl Harbor NWR

Honouluili Unit Boundary

Approved Refuge Boundary

36.6 acres

To preserve the quality of our map, this side was left blank intentionally.

Figure X3.

Pearl Harbor NWR

Kalaeloa Unit Boundary

Approved Refuge Boundary

37.9 acres

To preserve the quality of our map, this side was left blank intentionally.

rainfall (Tsuru and Cline 2004, PBR Hawaii 2007). NOAA reported that the annual rainfall for Kalaeloa in 2006 and 2007 was 20.41 in and 12.40 in. Mean annual wind speeds recorded at Kalaeloa are about 13 mph (HECO 2004). Because of its location on the open coast, the Kalaeloa Unit is more exposed to Kona storms than the units within Pearl Harbor.

3.3 Geology and Soils

The Hawaiian Islands were formed by a series of volcanic eruptions that occurred at hotspots beneath the Earth's crust. As the tectonic plate slowly drifted, magma welled up from fixed spots creating a linear chain of islands. O'ahu is the third largest island in the chain and encompasses a total land area of 597.1 square miles. The island is mostly composed of the heavily eroded remnants of two large Pliocene shield volcanoes that broke the surface of the Pacific Ocean at different times and continued building to eventually form a single island. The western Wai'anae volcano is approximately 2.7-3.4 million years old. It consists of shield lavas overlain by a thick sequence of post-shield alkalic basalt. The Ko'olau Volcano on the east formed about 2.2-2.5 million years ago and is comprised of shield lavas, referred to as Ko'olau Basalt, as well as rejuvenated stages, termed the Honolulu Volcanics. The sea level around O'ahu has repeatedly fluctuated during various glacial epochs. During a period of higher sea level, a coral reef platform developed around the perimeter of the island. This platform currently makes up the island's shoreline (Juvik and Juvik 1998).

Soils on the island of O'ahu were classified by the U.S. Department of Agriculture (USDA) Soil Conservation Service. Soils and sediments on low-lying areas of O'ahu have been influenced primarily by periods of changing sea levels and human modifications (Juvik and Juvik 1998).

The Pearl Harbor soils developed from deposition of terrestrial and marine sediments (Macdonald and Abbott 1970). The southern shoreline is composed of raised coralline limestone that was partially caused by upward seafloor warping or tilting in response to the weight of the larger islands of Maui and Hawai'i (Juvik and Juvik 1998). The original Ko'olau volcano land surface near the harbor is covered by a layer of alternating beds of limestone, tuff, alluvium, and marine clays that is 1,069 ft thick. Wetlands within the harbor are lined with eroded materials from the upper elevations of the mountain ranges such as oyster beds, reef, gravel, and mud deposits. Long periods of deposition of calcareous and noncalcareous sediments to the lower regions of Pearl Harbor formed a hard layer known as caprock (Englund et al 2000).

The Kalaeloa Unit lies on the coastal 'Ewa Plain, which encompasses the southwestern portion of the island west of Pearl Harbor. The 'Ewa Plain was produced by sea level changes during the Pleistocene epoch, roughly 2-3 million years ago. This area is underlain by a broad platform of elevated limestone reef material and partially covered by accumulated alluvium from the mountains. Along the coast, the hard calcareous materials are highly permeable, and the caprock ranges from 750-1,000 ft thick (Char and Balakrishnan 1979, NAVFACENGCOM 1998, PBR 2007).

All of the Pearl Harbor Units are of the Lualualei-Fill land- 'Ewa Association and primarily belong to the Pearl Harbor Series. This series occurs on level coastal plains between 0 to 5 ft in elevation and is associated with Kaloko and Kea'au soils. The soils formed in alluvium washed from material weathered from basic igneous rocks and deposited within peat or muck. In addition to various deposits from the Koʻolau and Waiʻanae mountain ranges, large areas of Pearl Harbor were intentionally filled with materials during the early 1900s (Department of Navy 2001).

3.3.1 Waiawa Unit

The USDA has identified the following soil type within the Waiawa Unit:

Pearl Harbor clay (Ph): Pearl Harbor clay is classified within the Pearl Harbor Series. It is composed of very poorly drained soils found on low, nearly level coastal plains. The surface layer is very dark gray, mottled clay and the subsoil is very dark gray/grayish-brown mottled clay that has angular and subangular blocky structure. The surface layer is neutral (pH 6.6-7.3) and characteristically 12in thick, while the subsoil is mildly to moderately alkaline (pH 7.4-8.4) and about 19 in thick. The substratum is muck or peat. Permeability is identified as slow and runoff is very slow. This type of soil was typically used for taro, sugarcane, and pasture (Foote et al. 1972).

3.3.2 Honouliuli Unit

The following four soil types have been identified within the Honouliuli Unit:

Fill land, mixed (FL): This land type commonly occurs near the ocean and includes areas that have been filled with material from other sources, such as material dredged from the ocean or hauled from garbage sites (Foote et al. 1972).

Helemano silty clay, 30- 90 percent slopes (HLMG): The surface layer of this soil, which is approximately 10 in thick, is neutral dark reddish-brown silty clay. The subsoil is dark reddish-brown and dark-red silty clay that has subangular blocky structure. The subsoil is about 50 in thick and neutral to slightly acid (pH 7.3-6.5). The substratum is soft, highly weathered basic igneous rock. Small areas of rock outcrop, steep stony land, and eroded spots may also occur with this soil. Because this soil occurs on the slopes of V-shaped gulches, runoff is medium to very rapid and the erosion hazard is severe to very severe. Permeability is defined as moderate (Foote et al. 1972).

Kaloko clay, noncalcareous variant (Kfb): The noncalcareous variant of the Kaloko series occurs in slight depressions on the coastal plains of Oʻahu. More acidic and grayer than the other soils in the Kaloko series, this soil is underlain by noncalcareous material. The surface layer is very dark gray clay, while the subsoil is gray or grayish-brown prismatic clay. The substratum is massive clay and silty clay. Small areas of very deep, well-drained alluvial soils were also identified in drainageways. The permeability of this soil is ranked as slow, runoff is very slow, and the erosion hazard is none to slight (Foote et al. 1972).

Waipahu silty clay, 0-2 percent slopes (WzA): This soil occurs on level, dissected marine terraces. Approximately 12 in thick, the surface layer is dark grayish-brown silty clay. The subsoil is dark-brown silty clay that has prismatic structure (vertical axis of aggregates longer than horizontal). It is about 58 in thick and the lower portion of the subsoil is excessively sticky and plastic (Foote et al. 1972). Both the surface and subsoil are slightly acidic (pH 6.1-6.5). Below the subsoil, the substratum is clayey alluvium. Also included in this soil classification were small areas of Hanalei, Honouliuli, and Waialua soils. Foote et al. (1972) classified the permeability of this soil as moderately slow, the runoff as slow or very slow, and the erosion hazard as none to slight.

3.3.3 Kalaeloa Unit

The Kalaeloa Unit features only a thin layer of soil classified as the following two types:

Coral outcrop (CR): Coral outcrop, which is comprised of coral or cemented calcareous sand, can be found on Oʻahu between 0-100 ft in elevation. It is geographically associated with Jaucas, Keaʻau, and Mokulēʻia soils. Within the cracks, crevices, and depressions of the coral outcrop, a thin layer of friable, red soil material can be found. Sparse nonnative vegetation typically grows in coral outcrop (Foote et al. 1972).

Beaches (BS): This land type consists of light-colored sands derived from coral and seashells; however, some beaches are darker in color due to basalt and andesite (Foote et al. 1972).

3.4 Hydrology

The hydrologic processes that occur in the Hawaiian Islands are unique compared to continental landmasses or temperate zones. Drainage basins are typically small and streams are characterized by steep longitudinal profiles and numerous waterfalls. The island of Oʻahu has 57 perennial streams. Streamflow depends on the climatic and geological features of the area. For example, some streams on Oʻahu have lengthy dry reaches under natural conditions due to permeable underlying rock. Oʻahu also has a vast amount of groundwater, which supplies most of the domestic water supply (Lau and Mink 2006).

The combination of intense storms, steep terrain, and urban land uses causes flooding in certain areas of Oʻahu. The Flood Insurance Rate Maps (FIRM) prepared by the Federal Emergency Management Agency's National Flood Insurance Program depict flood hazard areas throughout the State. The maps classify land into four zones depending on the expectation of flood inundation.

Pearl Harbor estuary was formed when a signification sea level rise at the end of the last glacial period (about 15,000 years ago) flooded the alluvial valley floor. Sedimentation from upland areas formed small deltas that divide Pearl Harbor into three main bays or lochs (West Loch, Middle Loch, and East Loch) that join to form a single channel to the ocean. The initial configuration of these lochs has been altered by decades of sea level changes, siltation, and erosion. The estuary continues to receive runoff from central Oʻahu. Sediment input is estimated to be greater than 96,000 tons per year, while freshwater input is estimated between 50-100 million gallons per day (mgd) (Department of Navy 2001).

The Pearl Harbor watershed is bounded by Wahiawā Town to the north, the Koʻolau Mountains to the east, and the Waiʻanae Mountains to the west. The Pearl Harbor watershed drains 134 square miles or 22 percent of the island. Historically, seven perennial streams entered Pearl Harbor: Halawa, ʻAiea, Kalauao, and Waimalu Stream fed into the East Loch; Waiawa Stream entered into the Middle Loch; and Waikele and Honouliuli Streams supplied freshwater to the West Loch. Today, several of these streams are considered intermittent or nonfunctional; however, all carry storm drainage into Pearl Harbor. The total stream input into Pearl Harbor is estimated between 8-56 mgd. A series of five large freshwater springs (Kalauao, Waiau, Waimano, Waiawa, and Waikele) also add water to the estuary along the shoreline. The combined discharge of these springs ranges from 61.4-127.7 mgd (Oceanit et al. 2007, Stearns and Vaksvic 1931).

Groundwater in the Pearl Harbor area is primarily comprised of a freshwater lens floating on a brackish-water transition zone and saltwater. This basal aquifer is confined due to the low-permeability coastal caprock that impedes the discharge of fresh ground water from the lens. Beneath the freshwater lens, in the dike-free volcanic rocks, freshwater mixes with underlying saltwater to create a brackish-water transition zone. The Pearl Harbor aquifer encompasses approximately 120.92 square miles, extending from Red Hill to the crest of the Wai'anae Mountains; thus, it underlies all three units of the Pearl Harbor NWR. The freshwater lens in the Pearl Harbor area is considered to be the most important source of freshwater for the island of O'ahu and the most heavily exploited aquifer in the State of Hawai'i. Withdrawals from the aquifer ranged from 200 mgd in the 1970s to 100 mgd in 2000. Current modeling indicates that the sustainable yield for the aquifer is 178 mgd. Groundwater levels in southern O'ahu range from about 25-30 ft above sea level inland to about 15-20 ft above sea level near the shore, where the water is confined by caprock (Miller et al. 1999, Oki 2005, Liu 2006).

The Pearl Harbor area also supports a variety of natural and manmade wetlands. A 1999 U.S. Army Corps of Engineers (USACE) wetland study estimated that wetlands constitute a total of 456.41 acres in the Pearl Harbor area. The hydrology of each wetland is determined by inflows and outflows of water, soil contours, and subsurface connection. In turn, these hydrologic conditions greatly influence the structure and function of wetlands by affecting species composition and richness, salinity, primary productivity, organic accumulation, and nutrient cycling (Mitsch and Gosselink 1993). A more detailed discussion of wetlands is provided in Section 4.9.2.

3.4.1 Waiawa Unit

The Waiawa Unit consists of two diked ponds, referred to as Mauka Pond and Makai Pond, located on the northeastern banks of the Middle Loch. The manmade ponds have silty bottoms with varying depths and are separated by a narrow soil berm. Artificial nesting islands are scattered throughout the ponds. Water levels within the ponds are manipulated for management purposes; however, levels also fluctuate due to natural conditions such as rainfall and evaporation. Water control structures using flashboards are used to maintain suitable water levels for management purposes. The Makai Pond is maintained 3-10 in deep. This shallow level creates a mudflat habitat that is preferred by nesting a'eo. Mauka Pond is generally maintained at a deeper level to provide habitat for waterfowl, 'alae'ula, and 'alae'oke'oke.

Until 2003, the wetland area was supplied by the Waiawa Springs complex located outside the unit boundaries. Water from this natural spring was pumped from a cistern into the ponds. This system was abandoned due to a substantial decline in water quantity. The current water supply for the ponds is a 350 gallon/min artesian well that was drilled into the brackish water lens. Water is discharged from the well into each wetland management unit. Pond water then drains to the ocean through a short outlet at the southern end of the unit.

Water quality parameters are recorded from the outflow that supplies the wetlands. The average temperature of the water being pumped into the pond is 76.3 °F and the average salinity is 6.7 parts per thousand (ppt). Salinity levels within the ponds fluctuate tremendously depending on the season and water levels, with higher salinities during the summer. No surface waters drain directly into the wetland area. Waiawa Stream enters the Middle Loch of the Pearl Harbor estuary below the unit at the midsection of the peninsula. Estuary depth adjacent to the Waiawa Unit ranges 22-35 ft and increases toward to channel opening (Department of Navy 2001).

Approximately 70 percent of the Waiawa Unit of the Pearl Harbor NWR is defined as Zone A by the FIRM. Zone A is defined as an area that has a 1 percent annual chance of flooding, or a 100 Year Floodplain. The remaining portion of the Waiawa Unit is identified as Zone D, which encompasses areas in which hazards have not been determined.

3.4.2 Honouliuli Unit

The two freshwater impoundments within the Honouliuli Unit lie on the edge of the West Loch. The unit is comprised of a 4-acre pond (Pond 1) and a 13.5-acre pond (Pond 2) that are separated by a central drainage channel connected to the harbor. Similar to the Waiawa Unit, water levels and salinities in these ponds are manipulated to accommodate waterbird habitat. In general, water levels are maintained between 2- 24 in deep. However, water levels are frequently pulsed to encourage invertebrate species population as forage for the birds. The Service alternates dewatering every 2 years to eliminate unwanted vegetation and fish and then refilled at moderate rates to increase invertebrate populations. Water is fed to the ponds from a cistern type well located on the unit that was used during the sugar cane era. Water enters each of the ponds by separate pipes at the inland side of the ponds and is discharged by pumping water from each pond into the central drainage channel. This drainage channel is tidal and empties to the harbor; however, back flow often causes blockage due to the accumulation of mangrove, silt, and other debris. Riprap and dikes line the harbor side of the wetland areas to prevent seawater from entering the ponds. Both ponds have a hard substrate bottom.

Water measurements taken in Pond 1 between 2001-2004 showed an average water temperature of 78.3°F with an average salinity of 2.86 ppt. Measurements taken in Pond 2 during the same time interval revealed an average water temperature of 77.9°F with an average salinity of 3.94 ppt. Water measured directly from the outfall between 2002-2007 had an average water temperature of 76.6°F and an average salinity of 1.58 ppt. The ponds have gradually freshened since the Service has reduced harbor water from leaking into the ponds.

The FIRM shows that almost 80 percent of the Honouliuli Unit is classified as Zone D. Approximately 4 percent of the Refuge is identified as Zone A and a smaller portion is Zone X500, defined as a 500 Year Floodplain, which has a 0.2 percent annual chance of flood inundation. The remainder of the unit (roughly 8 percent) is outside of the 1 and 0 percent annual chance floodplains.

3.4.3 Kalaeloa Unit

Groundwater in the vicinity of the Kalaeloa Unit is the result of the hard but slightly permeable limestone caprock that is characteristic of the 'Ewa coastal zone. The caprock functions as a barrier restricting the seaward flow of freshwater and increasing the freshwater lens. Near the shoreline, the water table is roughly at sea level and the basal groundwater is brackish due to the hydraulic connection to the ocean (NAVFACENGCOM 1998, Oceanit et al. 2007). In addition the to caprock aquifer, groundwater exists in a deep confined aquifer in the basalt. The chloride content of this aquifer ranges from 250 mg/l to 1,000 mg/l (Department of Navy 1999). Neither of the aquifers are recognized as acceptable for potable use by the State of Hawai'i.

There are no perennial streams, drainages, or significant surface water features near the Kalaeloa Unit. However, karst features have developed throughout the intact limestone from dissolution by standing groundwater. The level of development of subterranean openings in the 'Ewa limestone is unknown, but numerous sinkholes across the 'Ewa Plain and the anchialine ponds in the Refuge and adjoining areas suggest that there may be substantial connectivity. A further discussion of sinkholes and anchialine ponds is found in Section 4.9.3.

The FIRM indicates that the shoreline portion of the Kalaeloa Unit (approximately 18.5 percent of the unit) is defined as Flood Zone A. This Zone has flood elevations ranging from 6-8' and is subject to coastal flooding and tsunami inundation (Park 1999). The larger, more inland portion of the Unit is defined as Flood Hazard Zone D.

3.5 Topography/Bathymetry

The interior portions of O'ahu gradually slope inward to a broad central valley. In contrast, the outer seaward slopes are tall and steep as a result of erosion from wind, rain and sea. Bathymetric mapping reveals that giant landslides and the associated slope failures are a significant component to the erosional history of the island (Polhemus 2007).

Since the submergence of ancient river valleys, the Pearl Harbor region has developed into a nearly level coastal plain (Stearns 1966, Elliot and Hall 1977). The central plain slopes to low-lying and flat wetlands along the shore. Elevations increase from the Pearl Harbor channel toward the inland Kamehameha Highway. The maximum elevation in the area is 20 ft above mean sea level at Makalapa Crater on the eastern portion of the harbor (Department of Navy 2001).

The topographic conditions of the Waiawa and Honouliuli Units are similar. The wetland areas are at sea level and have essentially no slope. Embankments on the Waiawa Unit rise 6-8' above mean sea level (Shaw Environmental 2004). Topography near the Kalaeloa Unit is also comparable. The southern 'Ewa Plain slopes gently southward to the coastal edge. Elevations range from 65 ft above mean sea level along the northern boundary to sea level at the southern boundary near the Kalaeloa Unit (Earth Tech 2001a). This area is defined as having karst topography, with sinkholes interspersed between coralline rock masses (Char and Balakrishnan 1979).

The sea floor in Pearl Harbor is largely comprised of a soft substrate, such as terrigenous mud and calcareous sand. This soft material covers the limestone platform that encircles the harbor's shoreline. The limestone platform slopes to the channel floor, which is covered by a thicker layer of sand and mud (Department of Navy 2001). The Waiawa and Honouliuli Units that are confined within this protective harbor are slightly more protected than the coastal Kalaeloa Unit. Offshore, fringing reefs parallel the coastline, except at the mouth of Pearl Harbor. These reefs help to dissipate wave energy from ocean swells and southerly storms; however, signs of erosion along the coastline are still evident (Fletcher et al 2002).

3.6 Environmental Contaminants

The Agency for Toxic Substances and Disease Registry defines a contaminant as "a substance that is either present in an environment where it does not belong or is present at levels that might cause harmful (adverse) health effects." Contaminants commonly include pesticides and pesticide residues, industrial chemicals, fertilizers, metals, and other toxic substances. By altering biological or physical processes, contaminants may produce adverse effects to an ecosystem.

During the last century, a wide variety of human activities have contributed to contamination of the Pearl Harbor area including industrial and military activities, private industrial operations, extensive sugarcane and pineapple agricultural uses, golf courses, and residential development. Joint Base Pearl Harbor-Hickam (JBPHH) is in the process of combining two historic bases into a single joint installation to support both Air Force and Navy missions. The former Pearl Harbor Naval Complex included six major military facilities encompassing approximately 12,600 acres of land and water. During an Initial Assessment Study in 1983, 30 potential hazardous waste sites were identified (NOAA 1992). The Pearl Harbor Naval Complex was placed on the National Priorities List (NPL) of the Nation's most contaminated hazardous waste sites on October 14, 1992 (Pearl Harbor Natural Resource Trustees 1999). This designation was due to metals, organic compounds, and petroleum hydrocarbons found in the soil, groundwater, and sediment. Subsequent to clean-up processes and follow-up investigations, no immediate threats currently exist at JBPHH (EPA 2008).

Because the two wetland units are located on this large and active military base, there is potential for contamination associated with shipping, infrastructure, and personnel support activities. For example, during the 1996 Chevron Pipeline Oil Spill, a pipeline ruptured and began discharging bunker fuel oil into Waiau Stream and the East Loch of Pearl Harbor (Pearl Harbor Natural Resource Trustees 1999).

In addition, three sewage outfalls are in the vicinity of Pearl Harbor, Sand Island, Fort Kamehameha, and Honouliuli. Until 2005, the U.S. Navy Wastewater Treatment Facility at Fort Kamehameha discharged effluent near the Pearl Harbor channel entrance. A new high-density polyethylene ocean outfall pipe currently discharges effluent at a water depth of approximately 150 ft. This system allows for greater diffusion in deeper waters, thus decreasing contamination levels and improving water quality in the harbor.

3.6.1 Waiawa Unit

The Waiawa Unit of Pearl Harbor NWR is located adjacent to an old Navy Pearl City Landfill, which has been established as a Superfund clean-up site under the Comprehensive Environmental Response, Compensation, and Liability Act (CERCLA). The landfill covers roughly 67 acres to the south of the Waiawa Unit on the northwestern portion of the Pearl City Peninsula. The landfill operated as an official sanitary landfill 1965-1976. Construction debris, ground maintenance material, pesticides, scrap metal, petroleum products, demolition debris, biodegradable wastes, and digested sewage sludge were deposed of at the landfill. Hazardous wastes may also have been disposed of at the site (Shaw Environmental, Inc. 2004).

Research on the biological and human health risks associated with possible contaminants entering the Refuge has been occurring since 1991. A Draft Final Baseline Risk Assessment of the area determined that potential contaminants from the landfill are not expected to impact the Waiawa Unit because groundwater flows in a southeastern direction and any contaminants currently emptying into the ponds will decrease in concentration over time. Contamination concentrations in the unit are low due to low flow rates, mixing, and tidal influence from the shallow water table (Shaw Environmental, Inc. 2004). Some surface water runoff may collect in low portions of the unit; however, this water is not directed toward the ponds.

Interim removal action activities were performed at the Pearl City Peninsula Landfill, which consisted of capping soil in certain areas and repairing cracks on existing landfill cover. These activities were conducted south and east of the Waiawa Unit at the following locations: Burn Disposal Area, Black Sands Area, Black Sand Patches, and the Asbestos Areas. A figure of these sites is shown in the Remediation Verification Report (The IT Group 2000). A Long-Term Monitoring Program of the landfill is in progress to ensure that harmful levels of contaminants are not leaching into the groundwater from the landfill. This program conducts field activities such as monitoring groundwater and landfill gas, inspecting sites, and carrying out maintenance activities (Shaw Environmental, Inc. 2004).

Additional environmental contamination has been identified on military properties in areas surrounding the unit. Polychlorinated biphenyl (PCB) contamination was reported at five sites on Ford Island and four on the eastern shore of the estuary. This contamination has been attributed to the operation and maintenance of electrical PCB-containing transformers (Earth Tech 2000).

3.6.2 Honouliuli Unit

Building 49 Auxiliary Power Plant, located on Arizona Road at the edge of the West Loch of Pearl Harbor, was designated as a Superfund site. Built in 1943, Building 49 is a 672-square foot concrete block structure that once contained an emergency generator and transformer containing PCBs. An underground storage tank was used to store fuel for the generator; a drain system stretches from the building to an underground injection well. The primary risks to human health and the environment at Building 49 were due to the presence of PCBs in soil and interior concrete and hydrocarbon fuels present in subsurface soil. Removal actions were conducted 1999-2002 and no further action is required within or beneath the building. Due to the distance from the site, it was determined that there was no impact to the endangered species located at the Honouliuli Unit (Earth Tech 2006).

3.6.3 Kalaeloa Unit

The Kalaeloa Unit is located adjacent to an active airfield, former Naval Air Station (NAS), and adjoins two large petroleum refineries and other heavy industrial activities at the neighboring Campbell Industrial Park. Basewide contaminants surveys conducted by the Navy and level 1 preacquisition surveys by the Service did not detect any evidence of contaminants within the Kalaeloa Unit. However, contaminants have been identified in the vicinity of the unit throughout the former NAS. Potential sources of environmental contamination that were identified on the base included the following: underground and aboveground storage tanks, asbestos, hazardous materials, Installation Restoration Program sites, lead, medical/biohazardous waste, ordnance, pesticides, PCBs, radon, radioactive materials, wastewater discharge, and dry wells. Based on preliminary information, 47 potentially contaminated Points of Interest were recognized on the base (USFWS 1999b).

The Barbers Point (Honouliuli) ocean sewer outfall discharges treated effluent through the Honouliuli Ocean Outfall located approximately 1.5 miles east of the unit. The plant discharges 37ft^3/s at a distance of 10,500' from the shore. Continuous studies have found that this outfall does not have a quantifiable impact on nearby coral and benthic communities (Lau and Mink 2006). The Honouliuli Wastewater Treatment Plant is regulated by the National Pollution Discharge Elimination System program and local permit (Park 1999).

Potential hazardous pollutants and materials may be produced during the process of converting raw materials to finished products at nearby Campbell Industrial Park. Due to the concern about the large concentration of industrial and commercial activities, a CLEAN Emergency Management Plan (1997) was developed to identify and address issuess. Pollutants identified that could affect the former NAS are anhydrous ammonia, chlorine, and sulfur dioxide (NAVFACENGCOM 1998).

3.7 Land Use

This section presents an overview of land uses within and adjacent to the units of Pearl Harbor NWR that have the potential to influence Refuge conditions. Relevant local and regional land use designations and policies affecting land use are also discussed.

Under the State Land Use Law (Act 187), Hawai'i Revised Statute Chapter 205, all lands and waters in the State are classified into four districts: Agriculture, Rural, Conservation, and Urban. Conservation Districts, under the jurisdiction of DLNR, are further divided into five subzones: Protective, Limited, Resource, General, and Special (Hawaii Administration Rules, Title 13, Chapter 5). Land use is also dictated by zoning ordinances from the City and County of Honolulu, the 13th largest municipality in the United States.

The Pearl Harbor watershed today/
Photo: JBPHH Navy

The O'ahu General Plan is a comprehensive document with objectives and policies to address the physical, social, economic, and environmental concerns affecting the City and County of Honolulu. Island planning is further divided into eight regional areas that are guided by Development Plans or Sustainable Communities Plans (DPP 2006). The Waiawa and Honouliuli Units are located in the Central O'ahu Sustainable Community Plan area, and the Kalaeloa Unit is located in the 'Ewa Development Plan area.

The Administration Act identifies six priority wildlife dependent visitor uses on refuges: recreational hunting, recreational fishing, wildlife observation and photography, environmental education, and interpretation. According to the Refuge Recreation Act of 1962, all recreational activities must be compatible with the primary purpose of the Refuge.

Other laws or policies that may affect land use include: the Endangered Species Act of 1973; the Clean Water Act (CWA) or Federal Water Pollution and Control Act; the Migratory Bird Treaty Act of 1918; Executive Order 11988 (Floodplain Management); Executive Order 11990 (Protection of Wetlands), the Hawai'i Coastal Zone Management Act of 1977 (Hawai'i Revised Statutes, Chapter 205A); JBPHH safety and security policies; and the Master Plan for the Hawaiian Wetland NWR Complex (1983).

The Pearl Harbor watershed has significantly changed over the years due to agricultural, military, and commercial activities. Prior to European contact, the Pearl Harbor watershed was utilized by Hawaiians for fishing, food gathering, and fish cultivation in fishponds. Historically, the peninsula was also used for rice and watercress cultivation prior to military occupation (Elliot and Hall 1977). The completion of the harbor entrance channel in 1911 was accompanied by the increased opportunity for species introductions from military ships (Coles et al 1997) and sedimentation from upland areas. In addition, the conversion of shorelines to accommodate docking of U. S. Navy ships and disposal of wastes into the harbor greatly altered conditions.

The construction of the Honolulu International Airport Reef Runway further altered the existing land uses of the area. The Pearl Harbor NWR was established in 1972 as mitigation for reducing shorebird habitat by runway construction.

3.7.1 Waiawa Unit

The Waiawa Unit is surrounded by the City and County of Honolulu Pearl Harbor Historic Trail to the north, former agricultural land to the east, and the waters of Pearl Harbor to the west and south. The Pearl Harbor Historic Trail extends from Waipi'o Point Access Road to the Wai'anae Coast. In addition, the 49-acre Leeward Community College, which is part of the University of Hawai'i system, is located 0.3 miles inland of the unit and the H-1 Highway is found further north. The Waiawa Unit is surrounded by an 8 ft chain-link fence, except the portion adjacent to the harbor water. Waiawa Stream runs through the center of the Pearl City Peninsula, delivering urban runoff from upland communities. Scattered commercial, residential, and industrial uses occur inland of the peninsula in the communities of Pearl City and Waipahu. (Denslow 2005).

In addition to wetland management by the Service, volunteer activities occasionally occur on the Unit. The Service, with the assistance of NOAA, initiated the Waiawa Unit Mangrove Removal Project to create shallow, intertidal habitat by removing a dense stand of introduced red mangroves. The exotic red mangrove alters habitat essential for native estuarine species and displaces foraging habitat for waterbirds and shorebirds. In addition, mangrove encroachment alters shoreline hydrodynamics and sedimentation.

The Waiawa Unit, and the majority of the land in the vicinity, is classified as Urban by the 2005 State of Hawaii Land Use District Boundaries Map (Figure 1-5). A portion of land north of the Waiawa Unit is designated as Agricultural. According to the ordinances from the City and County, the Waiawa Unit is zoned as a Restricted Preservation District (P-1).

3.7.2 Honouliuli Unit

The Honouliuli Unit area has been used as a car dump and salt evaporation ponds, and cultivated for sugarcane production. Currently, the wetland unit is surrounded by a variety of uses. A City and County of Honolulu Pearl Harbor Historic Trail borders the eastern portion of the unit. The West Loch Village subdivision and the 18-hole municipal West Loch Golf Course are located immediately east of the trail. Along the southern border of the unit, the Pearl Harbor West Loch Naval Magazine stretches southeast along the shoreline to Iroquois Point. Various agricultural lessees also use this land. Several additional residential developments (West Loch Estates, 'Ewa Gentry, and 'Ewa Villages) exist within close proximity to the unit. Waikele Stream opens into the northern portion of the West Loch. The 70-acre Pouhala Marsh, the largest remaining wetland habitat in Pearl Harbor, which is managed by the State as a wildlife sanctuary, is also located on the West Loch.

The Honouliuli Unit is included within an area designated as Agricultural by the 2005 State of Hawai'i Land Use District Boundaries Map, with adjacent portions of Urban land. Agricultural land adjacent to the Refuge units is mostly composed on sugar cane fields. According to the ordinances from the City and County, the Honouliuli Unit is zoned as a Federal and Military Preservation District.

3.7.3 Kalaeloa Unit

The Kalaeloa Unit is bordered by the Point Cruz Road to the north, the Kalaeloa (John Rodgers) Airport runway to the east, and the Pacific Ocean to the south. Kalaeloa Airport is a general aviation facility with three operational runways, a control tower, and support facilities. The U.S. Coast Guard Air Station Barbers Point shares Kalaeloa Airport and the airfield functions as a "reliever airport" for the nearby Honolulu International Airport. To the west of the unit, a concrete storm water drainage canal and Saratoga Avenue separate the unit from Campbell Industrial Park. This job center is the largest industrial park in Hawai'i, housing nearly 250 businesses and employing roughly 4,000 people. The Kalaeloa Unit is accessed by West Perimeter Road, a small, gravel service road that transverses the western and southern portion of the unit (USFWS 1999a).

Also in close proximity to the Kalaeloa Unit, the following land uses can be found: University of Hawai'i West O'ahu campus, Department of Hawaiian Home Lands residential developments, Ocean Pointe residential area, Kapolei Business Park, State and County government facilities, and commercial shopping centers. Further north is the City of Kapolei, and 'Ewa residential communities lie to east.

The unit is located at the former Barbers Point Naval Air Station, which was once considered the largest naval air station in the Pacific. The station was closed on July 1, 1999, and the majority of the original 4,603 acres was transferred to the State of Hawai'i (Kakesako 2005). This land, which encompasses roughly 3,695 acres, is referred to as the Kalaeloa Community Development District. Currently, 25 percent (929 acres) of the base is owned by the U.S. Navy, 44 percent (1,621 acres) has been transferred or conveyed to other government and private parties, and the remaining 31 percent (1,146 acres) is designated as unallocated (HCDA 2006). Of the land currently under State control, the State Department of Transportation is the largest landowner, managing 750 acres for the Kalaeloa Airport and 91 acres of roads. Unallocated land is either pending conveyance to a government agency or the agency has withdrawn their interest in receiving lands.

Several planning documents have been developed to support development at Kalaeloa. In 1996, the NAS Barbers Point Reuse Commission adopted a Community Redevelopment Plan to guide the conveyance of surplus lands in the area. Redevelopment responsibility was transfered to the Hawai'i Community Development Authority (HCDA) in 2002. The Kalaeloa Unit and its surrounding area are also defined as an Urban district by the 2005 State of Hawai'i Land Use District Boundaries Map. The Kalaeloa Unit is zoned as a Federal and Military Preservation District, per City and County ordinances.

3.7.4. Land Use and the Refuge Today

In the highly developed and degraded landscape along the south shore of O'ahu, the three units of the Pearl Harbor National Wildlife Refuge provide critical, permanently protected areas of wildlife habitat. At the time the Honouliuli and Waiawa wetland units of the Refuge were established in the 1970s, they had very little actual value to native wildlife; only significant potential value. Years of intensive management effort have forced back the ravages of invasive species and repaired other land abuses resulting in two very small but high quality and high value managed wetland areas. This ongoing effort has created two of the most critically important and permanently protected wetland sites for endangered waterbirds in the State of Hawai'i.

Endangered species are a trust responsibility for the Service, as is also the management of National Wildlife Refuges. The 2009 State of the Birds Report prepared by the National Audubon Society noted that "… more than one-third of all U.S. listed (endangered) bird species occur in Hawai'i…." Located in a highly urbanized area, residential and commercial development in the Pearl Harbor area will continue for decades to come, increasing the need and critical wildlife value of these Refuge units. Within this landscape and in the face of continuing development pressures, the ability to restore and protect additional wetland areas needed for the recovery of the four endangered Hawaiian waterbirds will be increasingly difficult. The Hawaiian Waterbird Recovery Plan designates both the Honouliuli and Waiawa Units as core management areas for these endangered species. This designation recognizes that these areas are vital and must continue to be intensively managed as critical habitat components for these species.

Also within this landscape, the Kalaeloa Unit is truly a unique example of the dry coastal shrubland habitat that once extended along most of the 'Ewa plain. The small remnant populations of endangered plants as well as other rare native flora, including an endemic subspecies of naio found only at this site, are clear indicators of the critical importance of this managed and protected Refuge unit to these endangered species.

In this highly altered and degraded landscape, vigilant management of these units of the Pearl Harbor NWR will be needed to ensure their continued critical contribution to endangered waterbird and plant species of Hawai'i.

Chapter 4: Refuge Biology and Habitat

The following section provides a summary of conservation targets (species or habitats) that are important to the biological integrity and management of Pearl Harbor NWR. This discussion includes the location of the conservation target within the Refuge, regional or national trends, habitat or ecosystem requirements, and limiting factors or threats to the existence of the target.

4.1 Endangered Hawaiian Waterbirds

Pearl Harbor NWR was established to provide protected habitat for four of Hawai'i's endangered waterbirds. According to the Draft Revised Recovery Plan for Hawaiian Waterbirds, Second Draft of Second Revision, the Refuge is designated as a core wetland, which is an area essential to the recovery and delisting of all four waterbird species. This Refuge is one of the five core wetland complexes located on O'ahu that are continually managed for endangered waterbirds. Pearl Harbor NWR includes two managed manmade wetlands used mainly as breeding and foraging habitat for ae'o, 'alae ke'oke'o, and 'alae 'ula. In addition to the five core wetlands, 12 supporting wetlands on O'ahu provide additional seasonal habitat or support smaller populations of Hawaiian waterbirds (USFWS 2005a).

Statewide, the primary causes of population decline for these four endangered waterbirds includes loss of wetland habitat, predation by introduced animals, altered hydrology, habitat alteration by invasive nonnative plants, and disease. In addition, environmental contaminants may also potentially threaten populations in certain areas. No critical habitat has been designated for any of Hawai'i's endangered waterbirds. The general recovery objectives for the endangered waterbirds, as described in the Draft Revised Recovery Plan for Hawaiian Waterbirds, are the following: stabilize or increase species populations to greater than 2,000 individuals; establish multiple self-sustaining breeding populations throughout their historic ranges; protect and manage core and supporting wetlands Statewide; eliminate or control the threat of introduced predators, diseases, and contaminants; and remove the Statewide threat of the koloa maoli hybridizing with mallards.

4.1.1 Ae'o (*Himantopus mexicanus knudseni*) or Hawaiian Stilt

The ae'o is an endemic subspecies in the Hawaiian Islands, which is part of a superspecies complex of stilts found in various parts of the world (Robinson et al. 1999). The U.S. Pacific Islands Regional Shorebird Conservation Plan considers the ae'o as highly imperiled because of its low population level (Engilis and Naughton 2004). Over the past 25 years, the ae'o population has shown a general upward trend Statewide. Annual summer and winter counts have shown variability from year to year. This fluctuation can be attributed to winter rainfall and successful reproduction. The State population size of this resident nonmigratory shorebird fluctuates between 1,200-1,500 individuals with a 5-year average of 1,350 birds (USFWS 2005a). Adult and juvenile dispersal has been observed both intra- and inter-island within the State.

O'ahu has the largest number of ae'o in the State, with an estimated 35-50 percent of the population residing on the island. Furthermore, some of the largest concentrations can be found at James Campbell NWR and the Honouliuli and Waiawa Units of Pearl Harbor NWR. The Ki'i Unit of James

Campbell NWR and the Waiawa Unit and Honouliuli Unit of the Pearl Harbor NWR are the most productive, with birds numbering near 100 or above during survey counts (Figure 4-1).

Ae'o favor open wetland habitats with minimal vegetative cover with water depths less than 9.4 in, as well as tidal mudflats. Ae'o nest from mid-February to late August. Nesting sites consist of simple scrapes on low relief islands within and/or adjacent to ponds. Ae'o tend to be opportunistic users of ephemeral wetlands to exploit seasonal abundance of food, feeding on small fish, crabs, polychaete worms, terrestrial and aquatic insects, and tadpoles (Robinson et al. 1999, Rauzon and Drigot 2002).

Although the ae'o is considered imperiled, it is believed to have high recovery potential with a moderate degree of threat. Barn owls and pueo (the endemic Hawaiian short-eared owl) are known predators of adult ae'o. Known predators of eggs, nestlings, and young consist of small Indian mongooses, cats, rats, dogs, 'auku'u, cattle egrets, common mynas, 'akekeke, laughing gulls, American bullfrogs, and large fish. Current and continued threats to foraging and breeding birds on Refuge lands include predation by introduced vertebrates, invasive plants, disease, and environmental contaminants. In 1988 and 1996, fuel and oil spills impacted ae'o causing direct harm or mortality in the Waiawa Unit. The Waiawa and Honouliuli have ongoing costly control programs for mongooses, cats, and rats (Robinson et al. 1999, USFWS 2005a).

Figure 4.1 Monthly waterbird survey data for ae'o March 1989 - July 2008.

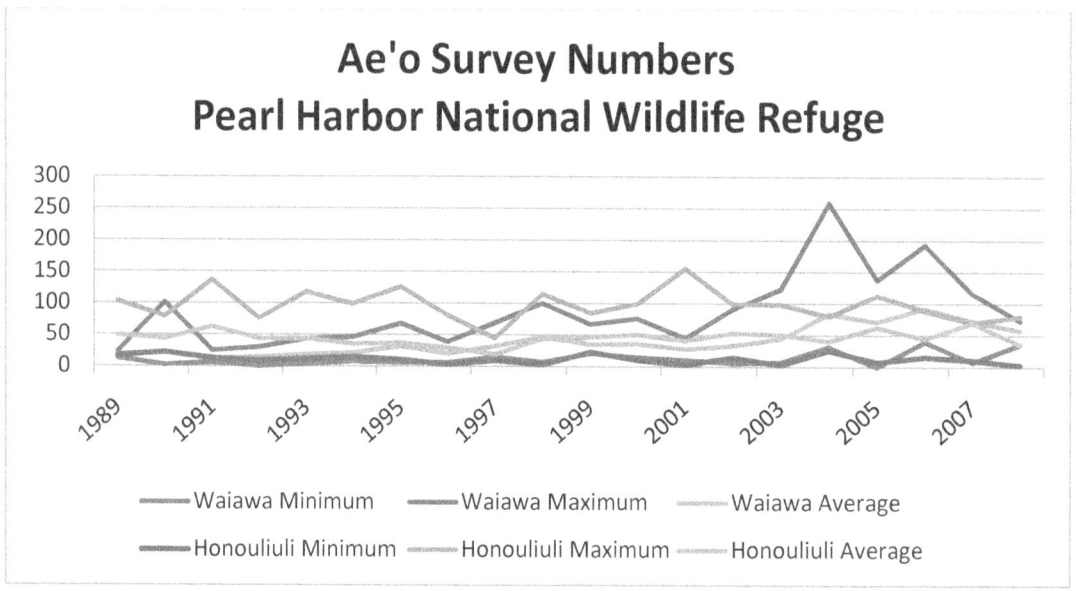

4.1.2 'Alae ke'oke'o (*Fulica alai*) or Hawaiian Coot

The 'alae ke'oke'o is an endangered species endemic to the main Hawaiian Islands, except Kaho'olawe, and has occurred sporadically as a vagrant to the Northwestern Hawaiian Islands, as far west as Kure Atoll. The Draft Revised Recovery Plan for Hawaiian Waterbirds lists the 'alae ke'oke'o as having high potential for recovery and a low degree of threats. The North American Waterbird Conservation Plan considers the 'alae ke'oke'o as a species of high concern. The State population of 'alae ke'oke'o has fluctuated between 2,000-4,000 birds with the O'ahu population fluctuating between 500-1,000 birds. Similar to the ae'o, this fluctuation is attributed to seasonal rainfall and successful reproduction. Large numbers of 'alae ke'oke'o occur in the Honouliuli Unit, with peak counts in 2005-2006 reaching nearly 350 'alae ke'oke'o (Figure 4-2). Interisland dispersal is most likely influenced by seasonal rainfall patterns and food abundance (Brisbin et al 2002, USFWS 2005a).

Figure 4.2 Monthly survey data for 'alae ke'oke'o March 1989 - July 2008.

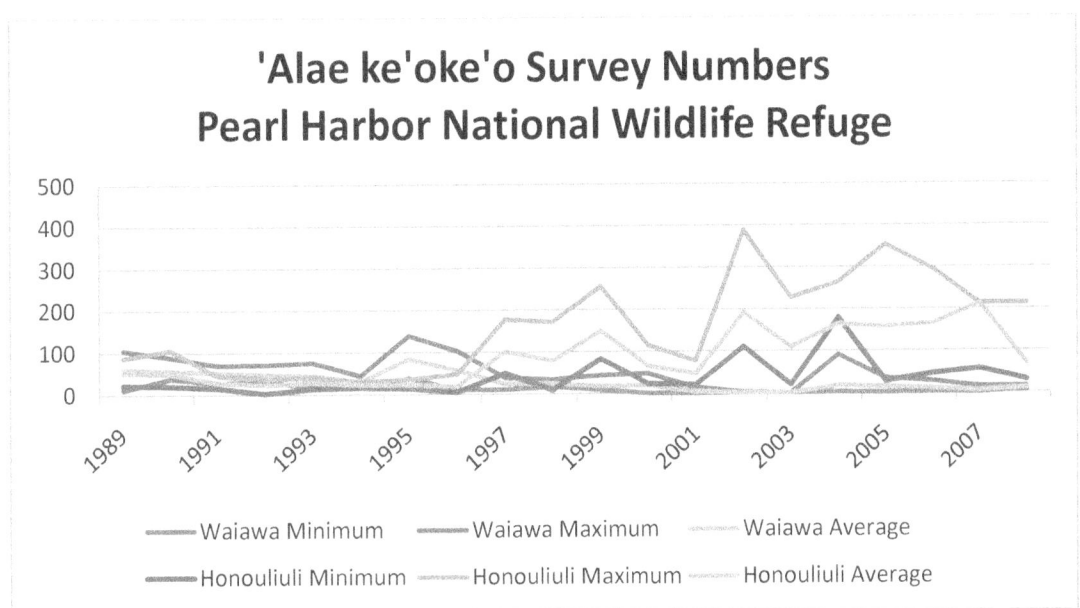

'Alae ke'oke'o are usually found on island coastal plains and prefer freshwater ponds or wetlands, brackish wetlands, and manmade impoundments. They prefer open water that is less than 11.8 in deep for foraging and nesting habitat that has open water with emergent aquatic vegetation or heavy stands of grass. Nesting occurs mostly March-September, with opportunistic nesting occurring year round depending on rainfall. 'Alae ke'oke'o will construct floating nests of aquatic vegetation, semifloating nests attached to emergent vegetation, or in clumps of wetland vegetation. False nests are also sometimes constructed and used for loafing or brooding platforms. Highly productive nesting has consistently occurred at Pond 2 of the Honouliuli Unit. 'Alae ke'oke'o feed on seeds and leaves of aquatic and terrestrial plants, freshwater snails, crustaceans, tadpoles of marine toads, small fish, and aquatic and terrestrial insects (Schwartz and Schwartz 1949, Brisbin et al. 2002).

Introduced cats, dogs, and mongooses are the main predators of adult and young 'alae ke'oke'o. Other predators include the 'auku'u, cattle egret, and large fish. 'Alae ke'oke'o are susceptible to avian botulism outbreaks in the Hawaiian Islands (Brisbin et al. 2002).

4.1.3 'Alae'ula (*Gallinula chloropus sandvicensis*) or Hawaiian Moorhen

The 'alae'ula is an endemic, nonmigratory subspecies of the common moorhen (*Gallinula chloropus*). It is believed the subspecies originated from stray migrants from North America that colonized Hawai'i. Although the 'alae'ula previously occurred on all the main Hawaiian Islands except Lana'i and Kaho'olawe, this species is currently only found on the islands of Kaua'i and O'ahu. A population was reintroduced to Moloka'i in 1983, but no individuals remain on the island today. The 'alae'ula is considered to have a high potential for recovery with a moderate degree of threats. The North American Waterbird Conservation Plan considers the common moorhen as a species of moderate concern because of its many subspecies (Hawaii Audubon Society 2005, Kushlan et al. 2002, USFWS 2005a).

'Alae'ula are very secretive; thus, population estimates and long term population trends are difficult to approximate. The Statewide population appears to be stable, with an average annual total of 314 birds between 1977 and 2002. Approximately half of this population occurs on O'ahu. Seasonal trends in population estimates occur because more 'alae'ula are observed in the winter than the summer months due to greater visibility in fields (Engilis and Pratt 1993, Hawaii Audubon Society 2005, USFWS 2005a).

The key features for 'alae'ula habitats are: (1) dense stands of emergent vegetation near open water; (2) slightly emergent vegetation mats; and (3) shallow freshwater areas. 'Alae'ula will nest on open ground and wet meadows, as well as on banks of waterways and in emergent vegetation over water. The habitats in which they can be found are generally below 410 ft elevation. Typically, nesting areas have standing water less than 24 in deep. Nesting occurs year round, with the majority of nesting activity occurring from March through August. Nesting is dependent on water levels and growth of suitable emergent vegetation (Bannor and Kiviat 2002, Engilis and Pratt 1993, USFWS 2005a).

Although the specific diet of 'alae'ula is not known, it is presumed the species is an opportunistic feeder. Cats, dogs, mongooses, and bullfrogs are known predators with 'auku'u and rats as possible predators. The 'alae'ula is highly susceptible to human and introduced predator disturbance (Byrd and Zeillemaker 1981, Bannor and Kiviat 2002, USFWS 2005a).

Figure 4.3 Monthly survey data for 'alae'ula March 1989 - July 2008.

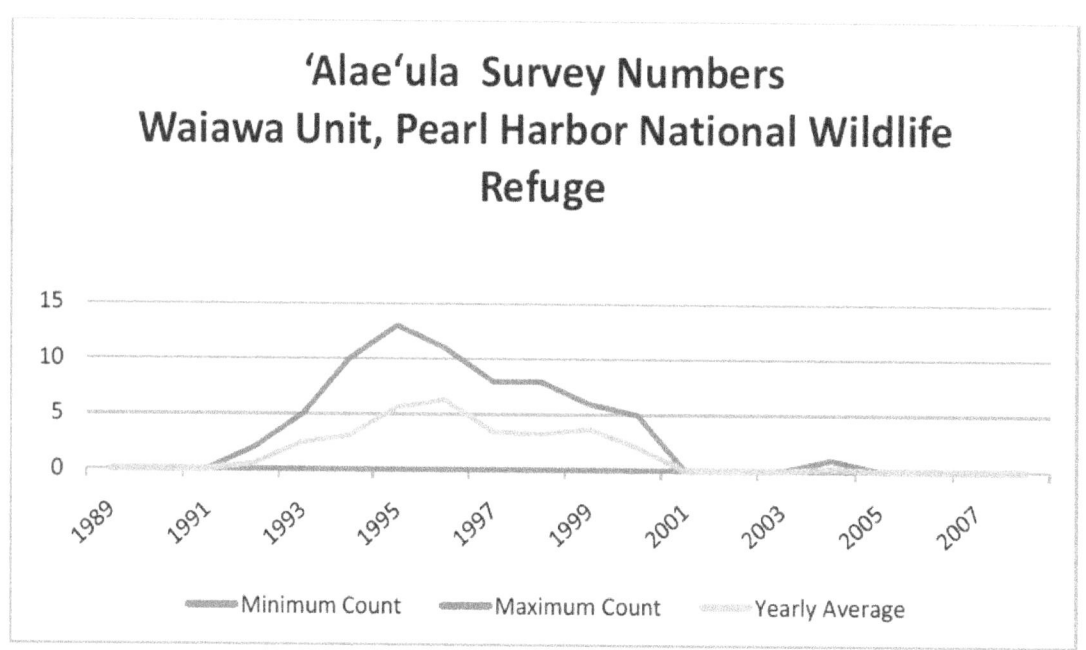

4.1.4 Koloa maoli (*Anas wyvilliana*) or Hawaiian Duck

The koloa maoli is an endangered waterfowl endemic to the Hawaiian Islands. The former range of the koloa includes all the main Hawaiian Islands except Lana'i and Kaho'olawe. Currently, the only naturally occurring population of koloa maoli exists on Kaua'i with repatriated populations on O'ahu, Hawai'i, and Maui. The Draft Revised Recovery Plan for Hawaiian Waterbirds lists the koloa maoli as having a high potential for recovery and a high degree of threat due to hybridization with mallard ducks, the greatest threat to this species' continued existence. The current Statewide population of pure koloa is estimated at 2,200 birds; approximately 2,000 individuals occur on Kaua'i and the remainder reside on the island of Hawai'i. Birds on O'ahu and Maui are thought to be koloa-mallard hybrids, with estimated counts of 300 and 50 birds, respectively. Although hybridization is still a threat on the islands of Kaua'i and Hawai'i, the koloa maoli population on these two islands appear to be stable. Because koloa are capable of interisland dispersal, it is possible that pure koloa maoli still occur on O'ahu (USFWS 2005a, Engilis et al. 2002, Hawaii Audubon Society 2005, Uyehara et al. 2007).

The koloa maoli uses a varied array of habitat types that include natural and manmade lowland wetlands, flooded grasslands, river valleys, mountain streams, montane pools, forest swamplands, aquaculture ponds, and agricultural areas. The Pearl Harbor NWR units provide suitable habitat for foraging, loafing, pair formation, and breeding. The majority of nesting occurs from March through June with broods observed year-round. Nests are placed in dense shoreline vegetation of small ponds, streams, ditches, and reservoirs. Types of vegetation associated with the nesting sites of koloa include fetched and bunch-type grasses, rhizominous ferns, and shrubs. The diet consists of aquatic invertebrates, aquatic plants, seeds, grains, green algae, aquatic mollusks, crustaceans, and tadpoles (Engilis et al. 2002, USFWS 2005a).

Figure 4.4 Monthly survey data for mallard-koloa hybrids March 1989 - July 2008.

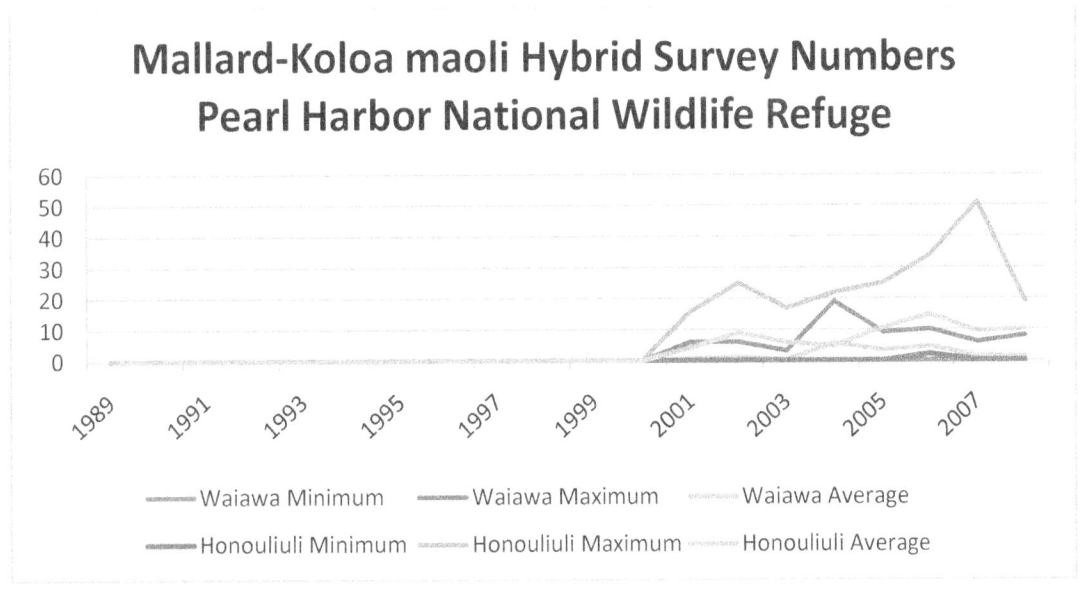

In addition to hydridization concerns, other hazards exist for koloa maoli. Known predators of eggs and chicks include mongooses, cats, dogs, and possibly rats. 'Auku'u, largemouth bass, and bullfrogs have been observed to take ducklings. Avian diseases are another threat to koloa maoli with outbreaks of avian botulism occurring annually throughout the State. In 1983, cases of adult and duckling mortality on O'ahu were attributed to aspergillosis and salmonella. In order for pure koloa maoli to exist on O'ahu, the removal of all hybrids and the elimination of all sources of mallard ducks will need to occur (Engilis et al. 2002).

4.2 Other Hawaiian Waterbirds

4.2.1 'Auku'u (*Nycticorax nycticorax hoactli*) or Black-crowned Night-heron

The indigenous 'auku'u is a cosmopolitan species resident to the main Hawaiian Islands. The black-crowned night-heron is a species of moderate concern in North America; however, 'auku'u in Hawai'i are not given this designation.

'Auku'u use a wide range of aquatic habitat types including mountain streams, lowland ponds and estuaries, aquaculture farms, and suburban/urban waterways. The 'auku'u is diurnal in Hawai'i and is known to forage on crustaceans, insects, fish, frogs, and mice. They have been observed eating the eggs and young of the endangered ae'o, koloa, and 'alae ke'oke'o. This species may also be a predator of 'alae'ula eggs and young. Nesting occurs in colonies in December through February in Hawai'i. 'Auku'u are susceptible to human disturbance during nesting (Davis 1993, Hawaii Audubon Society 2005, Mitchell et al. 2005, USFWS 2005a).

Figure 4.5 Monthly waterbird survey data for 'auku'u from March 1989 to July 2008.

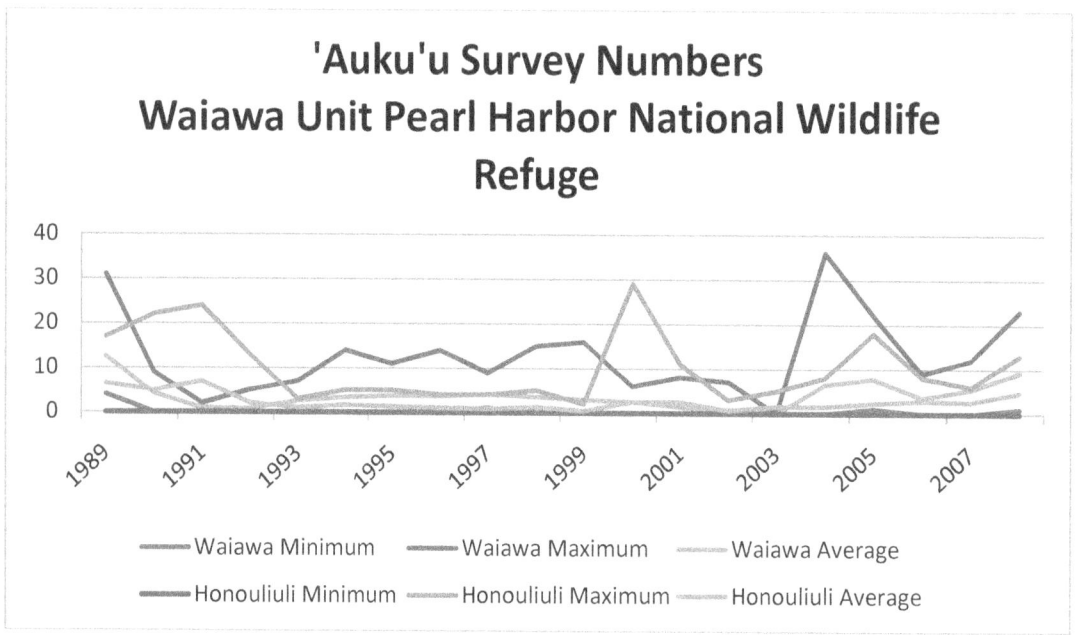

4.3 Migratory Waterfowl

For centuries, migratory ducks, geese, and other waterfowl have wintered on the Hawaiian Islands September-May. The most common winter migrants observed include koloa moha or northern shoveler, koloa mapu (northern pintail), mallard, lesser scaup, green-winged teal, and American wigeon.

Koloa mapu / Photo J.M.Garg

4.4 Migratory Shorebirds

The Pacific Island Region functions as an essential migratory habitat for maintaining global shorebird populations. Pearl Harbor NWR is an important piece of the wintering grounds for shorebirds in the Hawaiian Islands. 35 species of shorebirds have been recorded on the Refuge. The most common migratory shorebirds by order of abundance on Oʻahu wetland refuges are the kolea (Pacific golden-plovers), ʻakekeke (ruddy turnstones), hunakai (sanderling), and ʻulili (wandering tattler). The only resident shorebird is the aeʻo. The majority of the migratory shorebirds utilize the Refuge August-April (Engilis and Naughton 2004).

Shorebirds primarily utilize wetlands and tidal flats; however, estuaries, grasslands, and uplands are also important habitats. Although large portions have been altered for urban development, Oʻahu offers the most diverse shorebird habitat of all the Hawaiian Islands. Grasslands and beaches are important habitats for the kolea and the kioea (bristle-thighed curlew). Oʻahu golf courses support an estimated 1,900 kolea during the winter, and this species has even been observed roosting on urban rooftops (Engilis and Naughton 2004).

The Service developed the U.S. Pacific Islands Regional Shorebird Conservation Plan over concerns of declining shorebird populations and loss of habitat. Threats to shorebirds in the Pacific region include habitat loss, invasive nonnative plants, nonnative animals (predation, disease, competition), human disturbance, and environmental contaminants. Population estimates and conservation status for shorebirds are provided in Table 4-1. The kolea is the most common shorebird in the Pacific Region, with Hawaiʻi supporting a substantial portion of the Alaskan breeding population during winter. The kioea is the only migratory species that exclusively winters in the Pacific. Thus, the Pacific Region is considered to be a critical area for supporting hemispheric populations of both these species (Engilis and Naughton 2004).

Table 4.1. Shorebirds of Primary Conservation Importance in the Pacific Region.

Species	Hawai'i Winter Population	Regional Trend	Conservation Category
Kolea	15,000 – 20,000	Unknown	High Concern
Ae'o	1,200 – 1,600	Unknown	Highly Imperiled
Kioea	800	Unknown	High Concern
'Ulili	1,000	Unknown	Moderate Concern
'Akekeke	5,000 – 7,000	Unknown	Low Concern

Source: Engilis and Naughton (2004)

4.5 Native Invertebrates

The Kalaeloa Unit's anchialine pools provide habitat for two species of native shrimps and potentially suitable habitat for a native damselfly. One of the native shrimps and the damselfly are currently candidate species for listing under the Endangered Species Act.

4.5.1 'Ōpae 'ula (*Halocaridina rubra*) or Hawaiian Red Shrimp

The ōpae'ula is a tiny (less than 0.5") reddish shrimp of the family Atyidae found only in Hawai'i's brackish water anchialine pools. It is the most common species of anchialine shrimp in Hawai'i and can reach 10 to 15 years of age, an unusually long time for a tiny crustacean. This species is known to occur on the islands of Hawai'i, Maui, and O'ahu. They graze on the film of algae and diatoms growing on rocks and other hard surfaces. This endemic species is threatened by loss of habitat due to coastal development, the introduction of nonnative predatory fishes, and perhaps by collection for the pet trade. Its Hawaiian name literally means "red shrimp."

The shrimp are most abundant on the Island of Hawai'i but are also found in Pearl Harbor NWR's Kalaeloa Unit, where they were first found in 2004 in a recently restored anchialine pool. This species occurs in a range of colors from red, pink, white, light yellow/clear, and banded (red/clear). Eight different genetic lineages of 'ōpae 'ula exist in Hawai'i. Data show that a lineage was confined to a particular region of a single Hawaiian Island, with each island harboring at least two lineages. Kalaeloa is the unique exception because it is the only location in Hawai'i where two distinct lineages are found to coexist.

Kalaeloa 'ōpae 'ula / Photo FWS

4.5.2 *Metabetaeus lohena*

Metabetaeus lohena (no common name) is a species of native shrimp historically reported from at least 61 anchialine pools on the islands of Maui, Hawai'i, and O'ahu. It is slightly larger than the ōpae 'ula, growing up to 0.7 in in length. Its body coloration ranges from pale pink to brilliant red, and it is primarily a predator, feeding largely on the more common 'ōpae 'ula.

The species is threatened by habitat degradation and loss, predation by nonnative fish, and potentially overcollection by the aquarium hobby market. In 2005, the Service determined that the species warrants listing under the Endangered Species Act, and it was added to the candidate list.

In 2010, *Metabetaeus lohena* was documented in restored anchialine pools at the Kalaeloa Unit. Population estimates are not easily made since the species inhabits an extensive network of water-filled interstitial cracks and crevices leading to and from its resident pool.

4.5.3 Pinapinao (*Megalagrion xanthomelas*) or Orange-black Hawaiian Damselfly

Historically, the pinapinao was Hawaii's most abundant species of damselfly, and it utilized a variety of aquatic habitats for breeding sites. In 1913, Perkins described it as "a common insect in Honolulu gardens and in lowland districts generally, not usually partial to the mountains, though in the Kona district of Hawaii it is common about stagnant pools up to an elevation of about 3,000 ft. It is very numerous in individuals under conditions totally changed from natural."

Until recently, the last report of the pinapinao on O'ahu was in 1935 and it was believed extirpated on this island (Polhemus 1996). In 1993, a very small population was discovered existing in pools of an intermittent stream at the Tripler Army Medical Facility (Englund 2000). This is the only known population of this species on O'ahu. Populations are known from Moloka'i, Lana'i, Maui, and Hawai'i, with the latter having the greatest numbers.

Like the 'ōpae 'ula, this species is threatened by present and threatened destruction, alteration, or curtailment of its habitat and range, and the threat of predation by nonnative fish and nonnative invertebrates. It was listed as a candidate species under the Endangered Species Act in 2005.

Based on data collected from restored anchialine pools at Kalaeloa, there is a high potential for successful translocation of eggs and/or larval forms of the pinapinao to the Refuge, thus creating a second population and perhaps reducing the need to list the species as threatened or endangered.

4.6 Endangered Plants

The State of Hawai'i has 354 plant species that are federally listed as threatened and endangered. A total of 121 listed plants are found on the island of O'ahu. Two endangered plant species occur on the Kalaeloa Unit. A recovery plan for 'Ewa hinahina and 'akoko was developed by the Service in 1994.

4.6.1 'Ewa Hinahina *Achyranthes splendens* var. *rotundata*

The endemic 'Ewa hinahina or round-leafed chaff-flower was listed as a federally endangered plant species in 1986. The species was originally listed as *Achyranthes rotundata* and subsequently renamed (USFWS 1994). *A. splendens* var. *rotundata* is a shrub of the Amaranthaceae family, which grows to a height of 2-6 ft. The elliptic leaves of 'Ewa hinahina have dense, light-colored hairs that produce a silvery color. The tiny flowers are closely spaced on long, unbranched spikes. The shrub is characterized from the other variety of this species (*Achyranthes splendens* var. *splendens*) by shorter sepals and bracts; its sepals measure 0.26-0.35 in long and bracteoles have a length of 0.14-0.2 in (Wagner et al. 1999).

'Ewa hinahina is endemic to low altitude sites up to 100 ft in elevation on O'ahu, Moloka'i, and Lana'i; however, its current distribution is limited to only small areas on O'ahu. Historically, the species was reported from several areas on the island of O'ahu including Wai'anae, Ka'ena, Kalaeloa, and Mākua at the northwest tip of the island. The former distribution and population sizes reported in earlier botanical surveys are summarized in Table 4-6 (Tabata 1980, USFWS 1994, Wagner 1999).

Char and Balakrishna (1979) recorded three colonies of this species on the 'Ewa Plain. Two colonies were located within the Campbell Industrial Park between the strand vegetation and the kiawe forest and consisted of roughly 1,100 plants. The third colony was found in the abandoned Malakole Military Reservation, near the Chevron Oil Refinery. Tabata (1980) reported that although a few individuals were seen at Ka'ena, the bulk of the colonies were located at Barbers Point. In 1991, the Campbell Industrial Park population was estimated at 1,187 plants (USFWS 1994) and approximately 86 individuals occurred in the southwest corner of the Barbers Point Naval Air Station (NAS) (NAVFACENGCOM 1998). In addition to the 'Ewa Plain populations, three populations of 'Ewa hinahina were identified at Ka'ena, totaling approximately 70 plants. These plants occurred on State-owned land near the base of the talus slopes just south of Ka'ena Point (USFWS 1994).

Currently, the largest native remnant stand of 'Ewa hinahina occurs at the Kalaeloa Unit of the Pearl Harbor NWR. Restoration efforts have increased the number of 'Ewa hinahina to over 1,000 individuals. Seeds of *A. splendens* var. *rotundata* are reported to have a 50 to 90 percent germination rate (USFWS 1994); however, following initial rapid growth after planting, outplantings of 'Ewa hinahina at Kalaeloa have not been as successful as other planted species. Poor survivorship may be due to altered soil types, ocean salt spray, or the very short lifespan of the plant (USFWS 2002). A natural population of the species no longer exists at Ka'ena and the number of outplanted individuals at this site is unknown. NatureServe (2007) estimates the current total population for 'Ewa hinahina as less than 2,000 individuals.

'Ewa hinahina prefers limestone substrate covered with a thin surface layer of soil and pockets of humus. The species typically occurs in open or closed kiawe forests, as well as in open shrub communities characterized by other nonnative species such as koa haole, pickleweed, and *Pluchea* spp. The endangered shrub has also been noted in association with two native species, maiapilo and naio. Critical habitat was not designated at the time of listing due to the concern for potential issues of vandalism or unauthorized collection (Kimura and Nagata 1980, USFWS 1994).

Similar to other shoreline areas on O'ahu, the declined historic range of 'Ewa hinahina is attributed to development for industrial, agricultural, residential, and recreational uses. Existing populations are threatened by competition or habitat encroachment of nonnative plants. The parasitic native vine kaunaʻoa, which is common at Kalaeloa, may also be a threat. This vine covers shrubs and smaller plants and leaves them vulnerable to diseases and predation. Additional threats to the species include wildfires, environmental contaminants, natural disasters, overcollection, and pedestrian or vehicle trampling. Infestation by damaging insects is another hazard to its survival. Unidentified scales and mites have been noted on ʻEwa hinahina, as well as several nematodes (USFWS 1994, 1999).

Current restoration efforts at Kalaeloa, including nonnative vegetation removal and the planting of native species, are intended to promote the increase of the ʻEwa hinahina population. According to the Draft Recovery Plan (1994), the recovery criteria that would allow for the species to be downlisted to threatened status includes the following: (1) in each geographic region, at least three self-reproducing populations with a minimum of 1,000 reproductive plants per population; (2) populations are stable or growing beyond the minimum size; (3) threats are removed or controlled for at least 10 years; and (4) buffers of 100-490ʻ are established around the expanded population.

4.6.2 ʻAkoko *Chamaesyce skottsbergii* var. **skottsbergii**

The endemic ʻakoko subshrub was originally listed as an endangered plant species under the name *Euphorbia skottsbergii* var. *kalaeloana* in 1982. The stems of this subshrub are prostrate or erect, reaching a maximum height of 6.6 ft. Each flower cluster is situated separately in a leaf axil. The elliptic to ovate leaves are less than 0.79 in long and have a hairless upper surface. *Chamaesyce skottsbergii* var. *skottsbergii* can be distinguished from a closely related variety on Molokaʻi (var. *vaccinoides*) by its smaller size and wider, often toothed leaves (Wagner et al. 1999, Morden and Gregoritza 2005).

The ʻakoko produces an abundance of seeds that are discharged from a mature, dried capsule due to uneven shrinkage of the capsule. The species is pollinated by nonnative, generalist insects and there is no means of long-distance seed dispersal. Seed coats do not have germination inhibitors, and germination is not dependent on exposure to sunlight; however, seed germination rates of the ʻakoko have been reported as low (Char and Balakrishna 1979, USFWS 1994).

Assuming the taxonomic classification of Morden and Gregoritza (2005), *Chamaesyce skottsbergii* var. *skottsbergii* is restricted to calcareous soils in dry coastal strand or shrubland habitats on the ʻEwa Plain at the southwestern tip of Oʻahu. *C. skottsbergii* var. *audens* on the northwestern coast of Molokaʻi currently occurs in two highly localized populations (Moʻomomi and Puʻu Koaʻe) containing several hundred individuals each.

Historical accounts on Oʻahu recorded the ʻakoko species only on the ʻEwa Plain from Barbers Point to Pearl Harbor. It was presumed extinct for 40 years until it was spotted in the vicinity of the deep-draft harbor in 1976. Estimates in 2006 counted 1,354 natural and outplanted individuals, with 451 at the Kalaeloa Unit (USFWS 2006).

ʻAkoko occupies a habitat similar to ʻEwa hinahina; the species prefers coralline rock substrate with no or very shallow soil and partial to full sun (Char and Balakrishna 1979). However, ʻakoko favors more landward calcareous substrate and higher elevations. ʻAkoko exists in open or closed disturbed forests dominated by kiawe and other weedy species such as feathery pennisetum, Australian saltbush, swollen fingergrass, pluchea, and false mallow. Critical habitat for ʻakoko was not designated at the time of listing because no suitable, unaltered habitat was known at the time (USFWS 1996).

The recovery criteria for 'akoko are the same as the endangered 'Ewa hinahina, per the Draft Recovery Plan. One additional criteria necessary for the downlisting of the 'akoko was to maintain the population containing 30,000 *Chamaesyce skottsbergii* var. *skottsbergii* plants on Moloka'i. In 2005, the two Moloka'i populations contained several hundred individuals each (Morden and Gregoritza 2005).

4.6.3 Ko'oloa'ula *Abutilon menziesii*

The endangered shrub ko'oloa'ula grows in the dry forest of Lana'i, Maui, O'ahu, and Hawai'i. Approximately 800 ko'oloa'ula plants were propagated and planted throughout the island by the Department of Land and Natural Resources (DLNR) and 70 of these were outplanted at two different locations on the Honouliuli Unit of the Pearl Harbor NWR (Choy 2007). Ko'oloa'ula plants at the unit appear to be very stable and healthy.

4.7 Other Native Plants

Native Hawaiian plants arrived to the archipelago via natural means such as wind, water, or birds. According to Wagner et al. (1999), the native Hawaiian flora is comprised of roughly 956 species within 87 families. Approximately 89 percent of these species are endemic (found only in Hawai'i), while the remainder are indigenous (naturally found in Hawai'i and elsewhere). Since their establishment, populations of Hawai'i's native vegetation have greatly declined. Few native plants have escaped the impacts of urbanization and agriculture on the coastal and lowland habitats. As a result, recent surveys conclude that 75 percent of the native plant communities in these habitats are considered to be rare. Coastal alteration such as agriculture, residential developments, recreational parks, military installations, golf courses, and roads have permanently displaced much of the native flora (Cuddihy and Stone 1994).

The purpose of the Kalaeloa Unit is to recover and restore native Hawaiian plant species that once dominated the 'Ewa Plain. This area is "considered one of the best examples of the coastal plant ecosystem in the state" (HCDA 2006). Plants that exist in this region can tolerate high amounts of salt spray and intense sunlight. Through the efforts of Federal and State agencies; conservation groups; and volunteers, several native coastal plants now flourish within the 37-acre Kalaeloa Unit.

Native species planted at the Kalaeloa Unit include 'Ewa hinahina, maiapilo, 'akoko, wiliwili, pā'ūohi'iaka, 'ōhelo kai, naio, 'iliahialo'e, 'ilima, and 'akulikuli. Survivorship of these plants varies depending on species. Total survivorship from November 1997 - January 2002 was calculated to be 56 percent. Of the approximately 139 native plants outplanted in 2002, roughly 83 percent survived the following year. Native plant monitoring programs report 'ōhelo kai as having the highest survivorship, while 'Ewa hinahina had the poorest survivorship. Recently, large naio individuals have been successfully growing in the southwest portion of the parcel. A low growing, pubescent form of naio was common along the 'Ewa coastal plain in historic times. The indigenous species has proven to be a strong competitor against alien grasses that typically invade Hawaiian ecosystems (Wagner et al. 1999).

Although the Waiawa and Honouliuli Units were designed to protect waterbirds, native plant species do occur at these areas. Several restoration efforts have contributed to native plant populations in these areas. The endangered shrub 'Ewa ko'oloa'ula was outplanted at two different locations on the Honouliuli Unit. In 2002, four native sedge species and three native groundcover species were planted at the Honouliuli Unit. Outplanted species include the following: kaluhā, 'ahu'awa, makaloa, manyspike flatsedge, 'akulikuli, pā'ūohi'iaka, and 'aki'aki. A total of 2,100 seedlings were transplanted and survival rate varied according to species. 'Alae'ula and 'alae ke'oke'o have been observed feeding on several of these species or using the plants as nesting material (Brimacombe 2003). Table 4.2 lists the native plant species found in each unit of Pearl Harbor NWR.

Table 4.2. Native Plant Species (K=Kalaeloa, H=Honouliuli, W=Waiawa)

Scientific Name	Common Name	Origin	K	H	W
Sesuvium portulacastrum	'Akulikuli, sea purslane	Ind.	X		X
Achyranthes splendens var. splendens	'Ewa hinahina	End.	X		
Heliotropium anomalum var. argenterum	Hinahina	Ind.	X		
Heliotropium curassavicum	Seaside heliotrope	Ind.	X	X	X
Chenopodium oahuense	'Āheahea	End.	X		
Capparis sandwichiana	Maiapilo, pua pilo	End.	X		
Ipomoea imperati	Hunakai	Ind.	X		
Ipomoea indica	Koali'awa	Ind.	X		
Jaquemontia ovalifolia	Pā'ūohi'iaka	Ind.	X	X	X
Sicyos sp.	'Ānunu	End.	X	X	
Cuscuta sandwichiana	Kauna'oa	End.	X		
Bolboschoenus maritimus	Kaluhā	Ind.		X	X
Mariscus javanicus	'Ahu'awa	Ind.		X	
Chamaesyce skottsbergii var. skottsbergii	'Akoko	End.	X		
Erythrina sandwicensis	Wiliwili	End.	X		
Abutilon menziesii	Ko'oloa'ula	End.		X	
Sida fallax	'Ilima	Ind.	X		
Thespesia populnea	Milo	Ind.		X	X
Cocculus trilobus	Huehue	Ind.	X		
Myoporum sandwicense	Naio	Ind.	X		
Boerhavia repens	Alena	Ind.	X		
Plumbago zeylandica	'Ilie'e	Ind.	X		
Sporobolus virginicus	'Aki'aki	Ind.	X		
Morinda trimera	Noni kuahiwi	End.	X		
Santalum ellipticum	'Iliahialo'e	End.	X		
Bacopa monnieri	'Ae'ae	Ind.		X	
Lycium sandwicense	'Ōhelo kai	Ind.	X		
Solanum americanum	Popolo	Ind.	X		
Waltheria indica	'Uhaloa	Ind.	X		X
Vitex rotundifolia	Pōhinahina	Ind.	X		

The taxonomy and nomenclature of the plants are in accordance with Wagner et al. (1999).

4.8 Invasive Species

An invasive species is defined as a species whose migration and growth within a new range is causing detrimental effects on the native biota in that range (Pattison et al. 1998). Mammals, amphibians, invertebrates, and plants can all be considered invasive. These species become invasive because their population and growth are no longer balanced by natural predators or biological processes that kept them in balance in their native ecosystems. In the absence of these restraints, invasive species have the potential to compete with native species for limited resources, alter or destroy habitats, shift ecological relationships, and transmit diseases (Ikuma et al. 2002). Invasive species are one of the most serious problems in conserving and managing natural resources (Middleton 2006). In particular, the ecological integrity of Pacific Island environments is greatly threatened by invasive species. Hawai'i, which existed in isolation for millions of years, is an exceptionally ideal environment for invasive species. Most native species lost their natural defense mechanisms and are more vulnerable to introduced species (Ikuma et al. 2002).

4.8.1 Mammals

Predator control for invasive mammals is conducted year-round at the Waiawa and Honouliuli Units. Both live traps and rodenticide bait stations are used to control mammal populations in order to increase native bird populations. Currently, there are 16 live traps and 16 bait stations at the Waiawa Unit; and 22 live traps and 23 bait stations at the Honouliuli Unit. On a weekly basis, each bait station is checked and filled with diphacinone rodenticide. Live traps are inspected daily. Approximately 250 1-oz. diphacinone bait blocks are used annually to control invasive mammals on the Refuge.

Rats (*Rattus* spp.)

Three nonnative rat species are found throughout the Hawaiian Islands. Polynesian rats arrived from the central Pacific approximately 1,500 years ago with the Polynesians who settled Hawai'i; Norway rats reached the Hawaiian Islands after the arrival of Captain Cook in the 1770s; and black or roof rats most likely arrived in the 1870s. It is estimated that these three species have populated nearly 82 percent of the major islands and island chains throughout the globe (Tomich 1986, Tobin and Sugihara 1992). Black and Polynesian rats have a

USFWS/@Jack Jeffrey

large distributional range and can be found from sea level to nearly 10,000 ft. Norway rats are restricted to areas below 6,000 ft (Tomich 1986). Polynesian rats and Norway rats nest exclusively in terrestrial habitats, while black rats are arboreal nesters. This nesting difference may contribute to a larger population of black rats in Hawai'i due to the presence of nonarboreal mongoose predators (Hays and Conant 2007).

Globally, introduced *Rattus* species have caused the decline, extirpation, or extinction of insular bird species. In the main Hawaiian Islands, Atkinson (1977) suggested that black rats caused the accelerated decline or extinction of many native forest birds between 1870 and 1930. Polynesian rats are speculated to have been a contributing factor in the large-scale extinctions of Hawaiian bird species during Polynesian occupation prior to European contact. Rats continue to be a major threat to waterbirds, seabirds, and forest birds in the Hawaiian Islands. All three species in Hawai'i are known predators of eggs, nestlings, young, and occasionally adults of endangered waterbirds, seabirds, migratory shorebirds, and forest birds. Ground and burrow-nesting seabirds are particularly vulnerable to rat predation, even by the arboreal black rat. Rats also consume plants, insects, mollusks, herpetofauna, and other invertebrates. Because these species are eaten by birds, a reduction in these populations may indirectly affect avian populations (Olson and James 1982, Harrison et al. 1984, Brisbin et al. 2002, Engilis et al. 2002, Mitchell et al. 2005).

The use of snap traps and ground-based application of diphacinone rodenticide to control rats in the main Hawaiian Islands has shown a positive effect in native bird survival. Rat control is conducted year-round through the use of rodenticide placed in bait stations at the Honouliuli and Waiawa Units of the Pearl Harbor NWR. Snap traps are not currently in use at these units.

Mongooses (*Herpestes javanicus*)

The small Indian mongoose was intentionally introduced to numerous island ecosystems during the 1800 and 1900s and has since expanded to large portions of Asia, Africa, Europe, Oceania, and the Americas (Hays and Conant 2007). In 1883, the species was introduced to the main Hawaiian Islands as a biocontrol agent against rats in sugarcane fields. The mongoose inhabits all habitat types from sea level to nearly 10,000 ft on the islands of Hawai'i, Maui, O'ahu, and Moloka'i (Tomich 1986, Staples and Cowie 2001). In other

Mongoose on the prowl / Photo C.Babbitt

areas of the world, mongooses appear to avoid wet areas; however, in Hawai'i, dense populations of mongooses are concentrated in wet habitats. The mean home range of a female in Hawai'i is approximately 3.5 acres, and the main reproductive period occurs February-August. The high density of mongooses in the Hawaiian Islands is due to abundant food and the lack of natural predators (Hays and Conant 2007).

Mongooses are voracious omnivores, consuming insects, reptiles, mammals, amphibians, crabs, plants, and birds. In Hawai'i, mongooses are diurnal predators that primarily eat invertebrates and secondly small mammals (Hays and Conant 2007). They are a major threat to any ground dwelling and nesting species in Hawai'i. These mammals are known to eat eggs, young, and adults of the four endangered Hawaiian waterbirds, various seabirds, and migratory shorebirds (Tomich 1986, Staples and Cowie 2001, Brisbin et al. 2002, Engilis et al. 2002, USFWS 2004a, Mitchell et al. 2005, USFWS 2005a). In addition, mongooses are known to consume young sea turtles (Hays and Conant 2007).

Mongoose populations are managed using traps and diphacinone rodenticide. Since mongooses are a constant threat to waterbirds, year-round control has been conducted on both O'ahu wetland refuges since 2004. Figure 4.6 depicts mongoose control data from 2004 to 2009.

Figure 4.6 Small Indian mongoose control

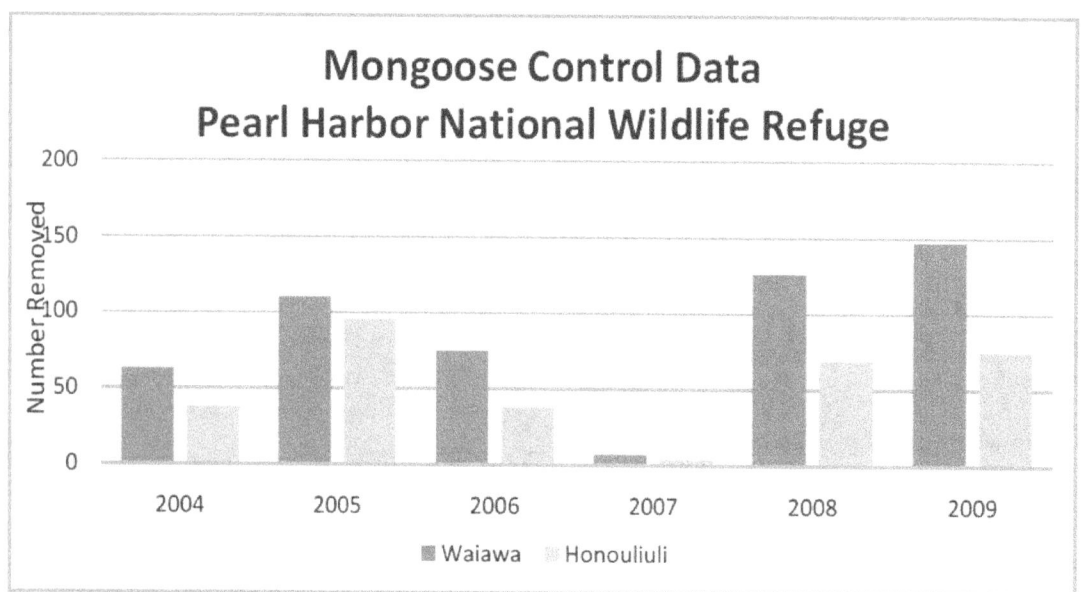

Cats (*Felis catus*)

Cats are found on all the main Hawaiian Islands from sea level to nearly 10.000 ft (Tomich 1986). Food habits of feral cats in Hawai'i include insects. centipedes. marine crustaceans. lizards. mice. rats. bird eggs. birds (young and adults). 'ōpe'ape'a (Hawaiian hoary bat). grasses. and seeds. Feral cats have a universally damaging effect on insular forest birds and nesting seabirds. In Hawai'i. cats can prey on waterbirds. migratory shorebirds. nesting seabirds. and forest birds (Snetsinger et al. 1994. Smucker et al. 2000. Brisbin et al. 2002. Engilis et al. 2002. Mitchell et al. 2005).

There are many "managed" feral cat colonies on O'ahu with 19.786 feral cats sterilized and released between 1993 and 2002. Cat colonies near seabird colonies have been very detrimental to nesting birds with the loss of adult and chicks of ua'u kani on Maui and O'ahu (Smith et al. 2002). Currently. there is a cat colony on the Pearl Harbor Historic Trail adjacent to the Honouliuli Unit of the Pearl Harbor NWR (Winter 2003). Due to the threat of cats adjacent to the Honouliuli Unit and the presence of free roaming feral cats across O'ahu. cat control has been conducted year-round at both wetland units since 2004.

Cat with 'alae ula – Honouliuli Unit / Photo M.Walther

Figure 4.7 Cat control at Pearl Harbor NWR.

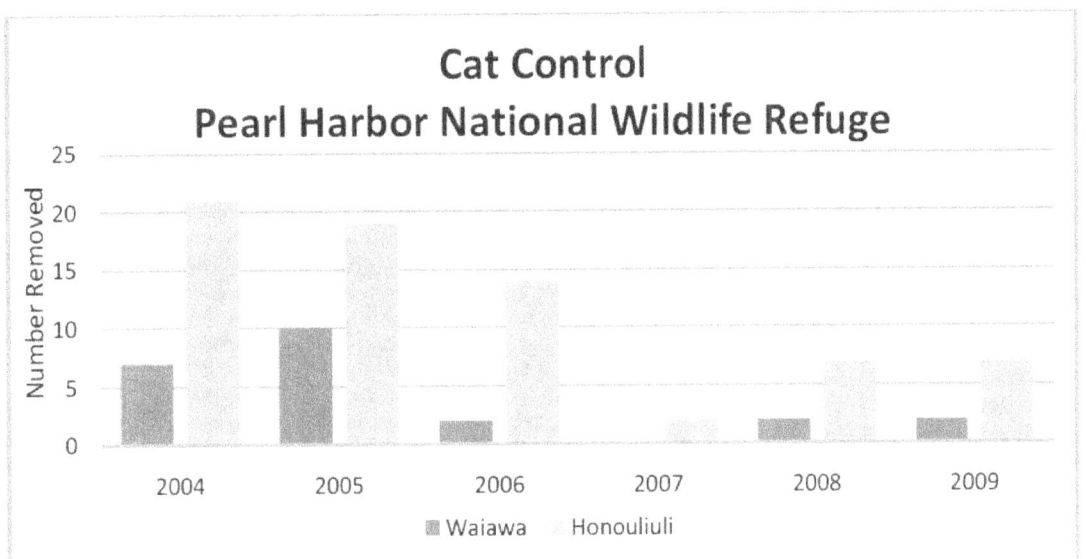

4.8.2 Birds

The cattle egret (*Bubulcus ibis*) is an introduced species common in the main Hawaiian Islands. It was introduced from Florida for insect control associated with cattle ranching and has become widespread. Their diet primarily consists of grasshoppers, crickets, spiders, flies, frogs, and nocturnal moths, but the bird will also consume prawns, mice, crayfish, and the young of native waterbirds. Cattle egrets have been observed eating endangered ae'o and 'alae ke'oke'o young and are suspected of possible predation pressure on 'alae'ula. In addition, egrets may compete with waterbirds for food and nesting resources. The USDA conducted cattle egret removal in both the Waiawa and Honouliuli Units of Pearl Harbor NWR from 1998 to 2009 (Figure 4-8). Cattle egret survey count numbers remained relative low during the control years, but count numbers significantly increased after control efforts ceased. (Robinson et al. 1999, Brisbin et al. 2002, Engilis et al. 2002, Hawaii Audubon Society 2005, USFWS 2005a).

Figure 4.8 Monthly survey data for cattle egrets 1989 -2008.

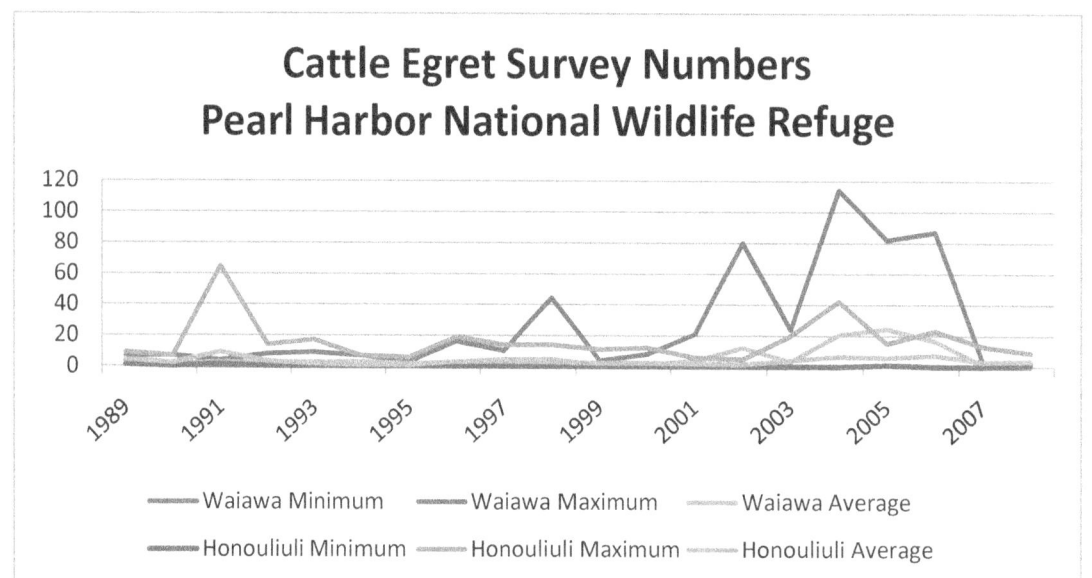

4.8.3. Amphibians

Invasive amphibians also have a negative effect on native Hawaiian species. Recent radio transmitter studies at James Campbell NWR provide conclusive evidence that certain nonnative amphibians are key predators of juvenile Hawaiian waterbirds.

Cane toad (*Bufo marinus*)

Cane toads or Pacific giant toads, which are native to Latin America, have a broad geographic range that includes a majority of the Pacific region. The toads were brought to the Hawaiian Islands in 1932 to control insect pests (Yamamoto and Tagawa 2000). Both wetland units are infested with cane toads. *B. marinus* are more terrestrial than bullfrogs, preferring yards and gardens. The adults only require water for breeding, an event which results in thousands of eggs per mating occurrence (Yamamoto and Tagawa 2000). Cane toads are active at night and primarily feed on cockroaches, crickets, grasshoppers, grubs, earthworms, slugs, spiders, centipedes, and snails. In addition, these highly invasive amphibians could be a potential predator of endangered waterbird eggs and young (McKeown 1996, Yamamoto and Tagawa 2000, Staples and Cowie 2001).

4.8.4 Invertebrates

Although the Hawaiian Islands support a large number of native invertebrates, wide arrays of nonnative invertebrates have invaded marine and freshwater habitats. Between 20 and 30 species of introduced snails are believed to have established themselves on the Hawaiian Islands (Staples and Cowie 2001). Aquatic nonnative snails occur in wetland units, but are used for food by waterbirds and have not been shown to be a threat to endangered waterbirds and native plants.

4.8.5 Plants

Invasive species are recognized as a major threat to native ecosystems and to the survival of threatened and endangered species (Pimental 2005). At the ecosystem level, invasive plants have been shown to be capable of changing fire regimes (D'Antonio and Vitosek 1992), altering nutrient cycling patterns, (Vitousek 1990) and modifying the surface runoff of water. Invasive plants can physically displace native species, and/or supersede them by competition for water, nutrients, or other limited resources. Nonnative plants can also be vectors and hosts for introduced pests and diseases to which the native species lack natural defenses (Jui Min et al. 2007). Furthermore, compared to native plants, introduced plants lack their natural enemies in the introduced range, which again gives them a competitive edge over native species. Invasive plants are also reported to be faster growing and can therefore easily and quickly colonize, establish, and displace native species (Blossey and Notzold 1995).

Island ecosystems particularly have been reported to be more vulnerable to biological invasions (Loope and Muller-Dombios 1989). Almost half the flora of the Hawaiian Islands is comprised of naturalized introduced plants, approximately 1,100 species. In spite of a multitude of naturalized introduced plants, only a small percent of them are invasive and have a negative impact on the native habitats. According to the Hawai'i Department of Land and Natural Resources, only about 1 percent (130 out of 13,000 species) of the plant species that have been introduced to Hawai'i have become invasive; however, it is anticipated that an additional 200 to 300 species already present in the State may become problems in the future.

Invasive plants are successful in island ecosystems due to a multitude of traits. According to Staples et al. (2000), invasive plants in Hawai'i share the following biological and reproductive characteristics:

- Adaptable to and capable of thriving in different habitats
- Tolerant of variable conditions (such as light, temperature, moisture)
- Fast growing
- Tolerant of disturbance
- Easily dispersible to new localities by seeds, fruits, spores, or vegetative parts
- Produce small seeds/spores early in life
- Long reproductive periods
- Dispersed by animals and with no special germination requirements

The control and eradication of introduced weeds has been the top priority of natural resource managers in Hawai'i. In the wetland habitats of the Refuge, invasive plant species can drastically reduce the value of wetland habitat to native species. Nonnative species outcompete more desirable plant species here, as well as absorb open water and mudflat habitats. In addition, the high biomass amounts characteristic of invasive grasses produces a high amount of fuel for fire. In dry areas such as Kalaeloa, invasive plant species become fire threats to nearby residential, commercial, and military land uses. In Hawai'i, plants grow year round; thus, the Service has a full time task of maintaining the habitat by weeding. At Pearl Harbor NWR, a combination of control techniques are employed for alien invasive plant removal including chemical, mechanical (hand and tractor), and water level manipulations. For the Waiawa and Honouliuli Units, invasive plant management costs were estimated at $1,000 and $36,000, annually (Denslow 2005). The following five introduced plant species are of major concern on the O'ahu Refuges.

California grass (*Brachiaria mutica*)

California grass (Family –Poacaeae) is a sprawling perennial with culms up to 19.7 ft long and rooting at the nodes. Stolons and leaf sheaths are densely hairy. It occurs pantropically as a pasture grass and its native range is unknown, although it is suspected to have originated in sub-Saharan Africa. California grass occurs in aquatic environments such as the openings of wet forests, marshes, and other open water areas. It is reported to be well adapted to a wide range of soil conditions (sandy to clay) and tolerates moderate shade but prefers full sun (Tropical Forages 2005).

In Hawai'i, California grass occurs between sea level and 2,297 ft on the five main Hawaiian Islands. The grass can form monotypic stands reaching 5 feet in height, with rooting runners up to 18 ft in length. Throughout the State it has been reported to grow in a wide range of moisture conditions. It grows prolifically in wet swampy habitats, but it can also withstand severe drought (Haselwood and Hirano 1983). In addition to displacing native plants, California grass alters and destroys aquatic environments, causing a reduction in bird habitat. The grass also interferes with stream flow and poses a nuisance to marine navigation when rafts of the grass float out to sea (Stone et al. 1999, Motooka et al. 2003). The Hawai'i-Pacific Weed Risk Assessment is a research project conducted by the University of Hawai'i and the USDA Forest Service to identify plants that pose a high risk in Hawai'i and other Pacific Islands. The assessment score of 12 for California grass reflects its invasion potential. It also designates the species as H (Hawai'i), meaning the species is "documented to cause significant ecological or economic harm in Hawai'i, as determined from published information on the species."

Khaki weed (*Alternanthera pungens*)

Khaki weed (Family – Amaranthaceae) is a perennial prostrate herb, sometimes rooting at the nodes. Flowers are sessile, bracts are approximately 0.16 in long, tipped with a 0.08-0.12 in long spine (Wagner et al 1999). Khaki weed is native to portions of southern America, such as Venezuela, Brazil, Peru and Ecuador, and is widely naturalized elsewhere in the world (USDA, GRIN Online Database).

In Hawai'i it was first recorded on O'ahu in 1959 and has become naturalized on O'ahu, Moloka'i, and Hawai'i. It is common in beach parks and other low elevation dry disturbed areas (Wagner et al. 1999). Khaki weed is easily dispersed by numerous spiky, straw colored burrs that are transported by animals, machinery, or water. The large and deep woody taproot allows the plant to tolerate drought and makes control difficult. These traits contribute to the plant's invasive ability (Animal and Plant Control Commission of SA 2002, Smith 2002).

Currently, this weed grows on all three units of the Pearl Harbor NWR. Char and Balakrishnan (1979) recorded this weed at recreational areas throughout the 'Ewa Plain. Their surveys found khaki weed to be common on sites with repeated disturbance such as pedestrian or vehicle trampling.

Pluchea spp.

Pluchea spp. (Family – Asteraceae) is comprised of two shrub species in Hawai'i- *P. indica* or Indian fleabane (*P. indica*) and sourbush (*P. carolinensis*, synonym: *Pluchea symphytifolia*) - and a hybrid species. *Pluchea indica* readily hybridizes with *P. carolinensis* to form the intermediate plant *P. x fosbergii*. The leaves of this hybrid species are usually more similar to *P. indica*, while the inflorescence more closely resembles *P. symphytifolia*. *Pluchea* x *fosbergii* can be found in any instance where the two species occur together (Wagner et al. 1999).

Pluchea indica is an erect shrub up to 6.6 ft tall. It is native to temperate and tropical Asia and northern Australia and is naturalized elsewhere (USDA, GRIN Online Database). In Hawai'i, *P. indica* occurs in lowland, coastal habitats such as wetlands and fishponds. Initially recorded on O'ahu in 1915, *P. indica* has been identified on Maui, O'ahu, Kaua'i, and Niihau. It prefers marshes and saline soils (Wagner et al. 1999, Motooka et al. 2003).

Pluchea carolinensis is an erect aromatic shrub native to parts of North and South America (USDA, GRIN Online Database). The species has naturalized in Hawai'i, Guam, Taiwan, Africa, and other tropical and Pacific areas. It can grow in poor soil conditions; however, it cannot withstand shade and severe competition from brush and grass. In dry habitats, the fast-growing shrub can form thickets. In Hawai'i, *P. carolinensis* has spread to all the main islands since its arrival in the 1930s. This shrub is able to grow in a wide array of habitats, ranging in distribution from dry coastal areas to open forests at 2,953 ft elevation. It usually invades abandoned fields and burned areas, but being an early successional species, it is soon replaced by other species. The plant seeds prolifically and the seeds are easily dispersed by wind (Mueller-Dombois and Fosberg 1998, Wagner et al. 1999).

All species of *Pluchea* (Indian fleabane, sourbush, and the hybrid) can be found at the Kalaeloa Unit. During invasive plant removal programs in 2002, the majority of the 87 truckloads consisted of *Pluchea* species. The rapid growth of *Pluchea x fosbergii* has threatened the existence of the 'Ewa hinahina at the the Kalaeloa Unit. In addition, because the Kalaeloa area receives minimal rainfall, thick vegetation of invasive species such as *Pluchea* spp. creates a severe fire hazard. Removal of *Pluchea* spp. and revegetation with native species has been funded through the Wildland Urban Interface (WUI) project (USFWS 2003c). While conducting native plant outplantings in the Honouliuli Unit, Brimacombe (2004) found that initially native species such as 'ae'ae (*Bacopa monnieri*), kahulā (*Bolboschoenus maritimus*) and kīpūkai (*Heliotropium curassavicum*) responded well to the removal of *Pluchea* species.

Extensive growth of *Pluchea* species also destroys habitat for water birds. Growth of *Pluchea* spp. outcompetes more desirable wetland plant species. At Honouliuli, *Pluchea* spp. occur in very limited numbers within the wetland impoundments and 'alae 'ula have been documented nesting successfully in them. Although large stands of *Pluchea* can be found outside of the Waiawa Unit fence line, only small amounts of *Pluchea* occur on northwest side of unit. This unit is too salty for excessive growth of *Pluchea*.

Blutaparon vermiculare

Blutaparon vermiculare (often refered to as Silverhead or Samphire) is a perennial herb in the Amaranthaceae family. It is native to Africa, the southern states of North America, and South America (USDA, GRIN Online Database). This species is perennial or occasionally annual with prostrate stems and ascending branches that flower year round. *B. vermiculare* have spikes greater than 0.2 in, opposite leaves greater than 0.39 in in length, and the flower stalk is not inflated (Wagner and Herbst 1994).

4.9 Habitats

The units of Pearl Harbor NWR are located on lowland coastal areas. On the island of Oʻahu, these habitats have been severely altered by a variety of factors including invasive species introductions and land use changes. Continued threats to these habitats remain and conservation efforts are needed to improve habitat conditions.

4.9.1 Coastal Strand

Coastal habitats are lands between 0 and 985 ft in elevation that are typically vegetated with salt-tolerant species that are dispersed by currents and waves but are incapable of terrestrial migration. Strand species are highly influenced by the sea due to their location on the shoreline and adjacent areas. Strand environments can be harsh due to salt spray, constant wind, low rainfall, intense sunlight, high evaporation, high temperatures, and unstable sands. As a result, strand plants have developed a variety of adaptations to deal with these conditions including moist stems, prostrate growth forms, thick cuticles, and small leaves that are succulent, hairy, or rosette. Because of these harsh conditions, species diversity is usually low in this habitat (Char and Balakrishna 1979, Tabata 1980, Wagner et al. 1999).).

According to Wagner et al. (1999), the Kalaeloa Unit supports strand vegetation characteristic of a coastal dry shrubland community. Strand species in this community are typically dominated by nonnative trees such as kiawe, which is able to tap brackish groundwater, or koa haole. Char and Balakrishna (1979) listed the following as typical native strand species occurring on the coastal ʻEwa Plain: ʻakiʻaki, hunakai, pōhuehue, nohu, ʻakulikuli, hinahina, pōhinahina, and naupaka. In addition, the following weedy species are noted to occur on the coastal ʻEwa area: Bermuda grass, golden crownbeard, hairy spurge, swollen fingergrass, and false mallow (Char and Balakrishna 1979).

Coastal Strand Vegetation -Kalaeloa / Photo L.Beauregard

4.9.2 Freshwater Emergent Wetlands

Wetlands typically have three distinguishing characteristics: (1) hydrological conditions that exhibit inundation or saturation, (2) unique hydric soil conditions, and (3) support hydrophyte vegetation that is adapted to wet conditions. Although wetlands typically share these common characteristics, the precise definition of a wetland varies among managers, landowners, and agencies. The Service defines wetlands as "lands transitional between terrestrial and aquatic systems where the water table is usually at or near the surface or the land is covered by shallow water" (Erickson and Puttock 2006). According to this definition, unvegetated areas including beaches, mudflats, and ponds can be considered wetlands. The U.S. Army Corps of Engineers (USACE), U.S. Environmental Protection Agency, and State Department of Health define wetlands as "those areas that are inundated or saturated by surface or groundwater at a frequency and duration sufficient to support, and that under normal circumstance do support, a prevalence of vegetation typically adapted for life in saturates soil conditions." Because of these varied definitions, three indicators are used to assess whether an area is considered a wetland: hydrology, vegetation, and soils (Mitsch and Gosselink 1993, Erickson and Puttock 2006).

Estimates of wetland areas in the State range between 52,000 and 110,000 acres (Levin and 'Onipa'a Nā Hui Kalo 2006). In the coastal plain areas of the main Hawaiian Islands, USFWS (1996) estimates a total of 22,474 acres of wetlands. A USACE wetland study conducted in 1999 estimated approximately 456.41 acres of wetland in the entire Pearl Harbor area. The wetland areas in Pearl Harbor are comprised of mudflats, shallow ponds, and coastal wetlands. The majority of these wetland areas (288.39 acres) are identified as mangroves, while freshwater wetlands comprised 86.02 acres. The Pearl Harbor wetlands are considered one of the most unique and significant natural resources in the Hawaiian archipelago (Department of Navy 2001).

In Hawai'i, wetland habitat is necessary for the persistence of six endemic waterbirds that are federally listed as endangered. These waterbirds include the nēnē or Hawaiian goose, Laysan duck, koloa,'alae 'ula, 'alae ke'oke'o, and the ae'o. These endangered Hawaiian waterbirds use a variety of wetland types and forage on various wetland plants. Wetland plants known to be eaten by these species include sedges, grasses, forbs, and legumes. In addition, the native 'auku'u uses a variety of wetland habitats throughout the State (Erickson and Puttock 2006). A more detailed discussion on the habitat and diet of waterbirds, waterfowl, and shorebirds is provided in the beginning of this chapter. Wetlands also provide breeding and feeding grounds for fish and crustaceans that are part of the food chain.

In addition to providing habitat, wetlands are critical components of an area's hydrology by serving as detention areas for flood waters. These areas help reduce the velocity of water and decrease erosion through sediment attenuation. Reduced siltation results in decreased turbidity of ports, harbors, and rivers (USFWS 1984). Another value that wetlands provide is trapping pesticides and fertilizers, such as phosphate and nitrates. By filtering these pollutants, wetlands improve water quality in streams and marine areas. Wetlands also function as a groundwater recharge area for potential human use (Erickson and Puttock 2006). Finally, the aesthetic qualities of wetlands offer recreation and leisure areas for tourists and local residents.

Wetland habitat has declined in area by 12 percent in the Hawaiian Islands over the last 200 years. Freshwater wetland areas on O'ahu have been severely reduced by a myriad of factors. This decline is due in part to the encroachment of invasive alien vegetation which alters water depths and soils, and competes with native vegetation. Wetland vegetation must be salt tolerant and able to withstand periods of inundation. These requirements create a harsh environment where often monotypic stands of highly competitive species occur. Groundwater pumping has also had an impact on O'ahu's wetlands. Groundwater wells have drained the existing water table, changing salinities and lowering water levels within wetland areas. Many wetlands have been filled to accommodate development or were used as a convenient disposal site for dredged materials . Intense agricultural activities during the early 1900s have also contributed to the degradation and dewatering of former wetland areas (Char and Balakrishna 1979, Department of Navy 2001).

Manipulation of water levels is an important component of managing wetlands for Hawaiian waterbirds. Controlling water levels can help restrain encroachment of nonnative vegetation, as well as provide proper waterbird habitats during the reproductive season.

4.9.3 Anchialine Pools/Coastal Coralline Shelf

Karst topography is formed when rainwater dissolves limestone landscapes leaving subterranean tunnels, caves, or sinkholes, due to dissolution or collapse of the surface openings. The ʻEwa Karst is the largest network of karsts (pit caves or sinkholes) on the island of Oʻahu. The karst in this area is estimated to cover roughly 31 square miles. Surveys conducted in the late 1970s termed these karst features as wet or flooded sinkholes; however, the spatial extent of these features is not entirely known (Halliday 1998).

Sinkholes are a type of karstic structure that is formed by the dissolution of the consolidated and cemented hard limestone. Sinkholes in hard limestone are openings into the hypogeal water table and often contain anchialine ponds in Hawaiʻi. Anchialine pools are exposed portions of the groundwater table that have a subsurface connection to the sea. The Hawaiʻi Administrative Rules Title 11, Department of Health Chapter 54, Water Quality Standards, April 17, 2000, defines anchialine pools as "…coastal bodies of standing waters that have no surface connections to the ocean but display both tidal fluctuations and salinity ranges characteristic of fresh and brackish waters, indicating the presence of subsurface connections to the water table and ocean." (Char and Balakrishna 1979, Maciolek 1983, Craft et al. 2008)

Anchialine pools are typically found on geologically young and porous lavas within the coastal tropics and subtropics (Chai et al. 1989). The largest number of anchialine ponds in Hawaiʻi occurs along the Kona Coast from Kawaihae to South Point. Maciolek and Brock (1974) conducted extensive biological surveys of the anchialine pond ecosystems along the Kona Coast. At Kalaeloa on Oʻahu, ponds are scattered within the limestone remnants of the fossil reef system that comprises the ʻEwa Plain. Anchialine ponds have been reported as one of the most threatened aquatic ecosystems in the State of Hawaiʻi.

These habitats represent a unique coastal ecosystem dominated by bacterial mats, algae, emergent aquatic plants, mollusks, and crustaceans under natural, undisturbed conditions (Maciolek and Brock 1974). Anchialine ponds are considered to be windows into a far more extensive subterranean brackish water ecosystem that is home to a unique assemblage of native species. They harbor at least four species of endemic anchialine shrimp that are listed as candidate endangered species by the Service: *Metabetaeus lohena, Vetericaris chaceorum, Palaemonella burnsi, and Procaris hawaiiana*. Of these four only *Metabetaeus lohena* has recently (2010) been documented on the Refuge. The biology of these species is discussed in by Maciolek (1983), Bailey-Brock and Brock (1993), and Santos (2006).

In 2004, ʻōpaeʻula were discovered in a recently restored anchialine pool at the Kalaeloa Unit. In addition, a natural sinkhole with these shrimp is found near Chevron's Rowland's Pond preserve (Oceanit et al. 2007). In addition to supporting rare invertebrate populations, these sinkholes may contain cultural or paleontological remains (USFWS 1999). Thirteen additional anchialine pools have successfully been restored since 2008. Anchialine ponds on the ʻEwa Plain are threatened by invasions of alien species and poor water quality. Structural modification and filling due to development activities on the ʻEwa Plain have also impacted anchialine pools.

Chapter 5. Outdoor Recreation, Social, and Economic Factors

5.1 Outdoor Recreation

The climate and geography of Hawai'i make the islands a perfect location for outdoor recreation activities. The State Comprehensive Outdoor Recreation Plan (2008) was developed to guide planning, development, and management of these outdoor recreation resources. In addition, the eight regional Development Plans/Sustainable Communities Plans throughout the island identify local recreational goals.

As identified in the National Wildlife Refuge System Administration Act, as amended, the Service identifies six general wildlife-dependent uses on national wildlife refuges: hunting, fishing, wildlife observation, photography, interpretation, and environmental education. Similar opportunities are available on lands managed by the State and City and County of Honolulu.

This section describes recreational opportunities in the areas surrounding Pearl Harbor NWR, as well as recreational activities currently occurring at the refuge units. Islandwide recreational demands and potential recreational opportunities are also discussed.

5.1.1 Federal, State, and County Recreational Parks

State parks are administered by the Hawai'i Department of Land and Natural Resources (DLNR), Division of State Parks. The State park system on O'ahu encompasses 22 parks covering approximately 9,900 acres. Special use permits are required for certain activities including group activities, pavilion usage, meetings, weddings, shows, community events, scientific research, and gathering of forest products.

The City and County of Honolulu, Department of Parks and Recreation (DPR) administers an additional 282 parks throughout O'ahu comprising 5,314 acres (DBEDT 2009). These parks are divided into two groups: Island-Based Parks and Community-Based Parks. The largest and most specialized parks (such as regional parks, beach and shoreline parks, beach and shoreline rights-of-way, nature parks and reserves, botanical gardens, golf courses, and zoological parks) are classified as Island-Based Parks. These parks are intended to serve the needs of all O'ahu residents. The DPR suggests 8 acres of Island-Based Parks for every 1,000 persons. Community-Based Parks are smaller parks designed to provide recreation for more localized populations. These parks include district parks, community parks, neighborhood parks, and mini parks. The DPR uses a standard of 2 acres of Community-Based Parks for every 1,000 persons (DPP 2000).

The World War II Valor in the Pacific National Monument at Pearl Harbor, which is managed by the National Park Service, is located within 5 miles of the Waiawa and Honouliuli Units. Included within the Monument are the USS Arizona Memorial and several sites on Ford Island: the USS Oklahoma Memorial, USS Utah Memorial, and several historic Battleship Row mooring quays. This 11-acre park is located on the Pearl Harbor Naval Base. The USS Arizona Memorial is one of the most popular attractions in the State. The Monument site offers a visitor center, theater, museum, and gift shop. Three other privately operated visitor destinations affiliated with the Monument are nearby: the Pacific Submarine Memorial Association Museum and the USS Bowfin, a World War II submarine; the Battleship Missouri Memorial; and the Pacific Aviation Museum.

Two State parks are located east of the Waiawa Unit of Pearl Harbor NWR. The 'Aiea Bay State Recreation Area is located along the banks of Pearl Harbor's East Loch. This park offers picnic tables and aesthetic views from 6:00 a.m. to 6:45 p.m. (Division of State Parks 2008). The City and County of Honolulu's Department of Public Works maintains a

The USS Arizona Memorial at Pearl Harbor/
NPS photo Brett Seymour

paved, public bicycle/jogging path, the Pearl Harbor Historic Trail, that crosses through the 'Aiea Bay State Recreation Area. The path follows the perimeter of the East Loch of Pearl Harbor and extends from Halawa Stream westward for approximately 5 miles to Waipio Point Access Road. The path is heavily used by joggers, walkers, skaters, and bicyclists. Keaīwa Heiau State Recreation Area is a 384-acre park with campgrounds, picnic areas, an archaeological heiau (Hawaiian temple), and a trailhead for the 'Aiea Loop Trail (Division of State Parks 2008).

Regional parks in the vicinity of Pearl Harbor NWR include Central Oʻahu Regional Park (Waiola Regional Park), Waipahu Cultural Garden, Kapolei Regional Park, and Kalaeloa Regional Park. The 269-acre Central Oʻahu Regional Park includes baseball and softball fields, tennis courts, an archery range, a skateboard park, and other facilities. The Waipahu Cultural Garden is a 49-acre park owned by the City and County of Honolulu with a picnic area, an ethnobotanical garden, and an educational building with a crafts room (DPP 2002). In addition, the Waipio Peninsula Sports Complex is a 288-acre recreational park located on the peninsula between the Waiawa and Honouliuli Units. This complex has 19 regulation soccer fields and a 5,000 seat stadium. The Kapolei Regional Park is a 73-acre park area within easy walking distance of both the City Center and the Villages of Kapolei that provides picnicking and occasional family events. Kalaeloa Regional Park will eventually provide 484 acres of ocean/beach recreation area.

5.1.2 Historical/Cultural Sites

Oʻahu has 151 State historic sites and 68 sites on the National Register of Historic Places. These resources have the potential to be recreational areas for local residents and tourists. Historic features of recreational interest in the 'Ewa Region include Lanikuhonua, Oʻahu Rail & Land Company (OR&L) Historic Railway, 'Ewa Villages, and the Pearl Harbor National Historic Landmark. Native Hawaiian and archaeological sites include the Barbers Point Archaeological District and One'ula Archaeological District (DPP 2000).

The Kalaeloa Unit is located on the former Naval Air Station (NAS) Barbers Point, named for Henry Barber, master of *Arthur*, a 100-ft British brigantine that ran aground on the point of Oʻahu during a storm in 1796. Captain Barber, determined to get underway despite the storm, hoisted anchor on his 100-foot brig on October 31, 1796. All other captains held their ships in port while Arthur was deluged by wind, rain and pounding surf. The ship went down taking with it all but six crewmembers and its captain. The seven survivors struggled ashore near Kalaeloa, a legendary birthplace of Hawaiian Kings. Kalaeloa subsequently became known as Barbers Point.

In the early 1930s, the Navy leased land from the Estate of James Campbell to be used as a mooring location for the dirigible, *Akron*. In September 1940, 3,500 acres were purchased from the Campbell Estate for the Marine Corps Air Station 'Ewa. The site, chosen for its ideal peacetime air training atmosphere, was completed in early 1941. Concurrently with the groundbreaking, plans were already being developed for an expansion of naval aviation facilities at Barbers Point. Base construction was well underway by December 7, 1941, when the Japanese attacked U.S. forces in Hawai'i, marking the United States' entrance into World War II. Although much of the attack was concentrated at Pearl Harbor, Wheeler Air Force Base, Hickam Field, the 'Ewa Marine Corps Air Station (and its supporting equipment) sustained a great deal of damage. The Pearl Harbor attack, along with the increasing need for additional facilities to train pilots, led to an extensive construction project.

Barbers Point was established as a naval air station on April 15, 1942, and became a hub of aviation activity as the Navy amassed forces in Hawai'i to carry the war across the Pacific. Base operations centered on working up carrier air groups and squadrons for deployment to combat operations farther west. With more than 3,800 acres and up to 6,500 military, family members, and civilian employees, NAS Barbers Point served as the largest naval air station in the Pacific theater. It was disestablished in July 1999, closing out 57 years of service.

World War II pillbox at Kalaeloa / photo L.Beauregard

Forty acres were transferred to the Service in 2001 to protect and enhance habitat for endangered coastal dryland plants. During restoration work on the new Kalaeloa Unit, Refuge staff discovered several military concrete structures from the World War II era that had been hidden by a dense thicket of invasive kiawe trees. Refuge management actions will preserve these artifacts.

5.1.3 Ocean Recreation

Ocean recreation in Hawai'i supports an $800 million industry. The Hawai'i Division of Boating and Ocean Recreation manages 14 small boat harbors, 1 deep draft harbor, and 4 launching facilities on the island of O'ahu. The Iroquois Point Harbor and the Ko 'Olina Ocean Marina are the closest small boat harbors to the Pearl Harbor NWR Units. The Barbers Point Deep Draft Harbor, located adjacent to the Ko Olina Ocean Marina, is restricted to State and County commercial uses. An additional recreational marina is being constructed on 1,110acre-Ocean Point, between 'Ewa Beach and Kalaeloa about 2.6 miles east of the Kalaeloa Unit. The 120-acre 'Ewa Marina would support 1,400 boat slips, marine haul-out and other repair facilities, and a public boat ramp. It is planned to be the region's principal recreational marina destination for local residents and visitors, as well as provide substantial public areas through shoreline and waterfront access (DPP 2002).

5.1.4 Wildlife Observation, Photography, Interpretation, and Environmental Education

The 18 wildlife sanctuaries and refuges on Oʻahu consist of 700 acres (DBDT 2009). Opportunities for wildlife observation, photography, and environmental education are available at most of these areas, and private tour operators provide interpretation at some sites. One of the closest such sanctuaries to Pearl Harbor NWR is Pouhala Marsh, a remnant fishpond and coastal marsh in the western loch of Pearl Harbor. Pouhala is owned by the City and County of Honolulu and the State of Hawaiʻi; a land-lease agreement with the City allows the State to manage the entire area as a wildlife sanctuary. A multiagency cooperative restoration project is in progress to restore nearly 70 acres of this wetland area.

Although Oʻahu is the most populated and visited island in the State, there are very few visitor opportunities on the national wildlife refuges. Access is occasionally provided via environmental education, special events, and special use permits. Individuals from the public, conservation groups, schools, and commercial tour operators and photographers request access to these areas via a Special Use Permit.

The units of Pearl Harbor NWR offer a minimal amount of wildlife watching and environmental education for schools and other groups. Public use is highly restricted at all units due to access issues and sensitivity of the species located on the Refuge. During the 2009 aeʻo nonnesting season (September through February), five Special Use Permits were granted to access the Refuge for these activities.

Although access is completely prohibited during the stilt nesting season, organized public service programs do occur during other times of the year. Since 1993, the Hawaiʻi Nature Center has operated the third grade Wetlands Education Program at the Honouliuli Unit September-mid-December. This nonprofit organization educates third graders about Hawaiʻi's wetland areas including food chains, wetland species and behavior, and plant adaptations. This highly demanded program is available to all schools on Oʻahu. In 2009 the Hawaiʻi Nature Center brought 1,750 students to the Honouliuli Unit (USFWS, unpubl. data). Other organized groups that have participated in invasive vegetation removal, outlet ditch clearing, and fence repairs include the Hawaiʻi Youth Conservation Corps and Ducks Unlimited.

A handicapped-accessible overlook is planned at the Honouliuli Unit that will allow the public to observe and photograph wildlife within the Refuge without entering the fenced portion of the unit. This overlook will be a memorial to Betty Nagamine Bliss, a volunteer with the Hawaiʻi Audubon Society, who lobbied to create Pearl Harbor NWR during construction of the Honolulu Airport's Reef Runway. The overlook, which is part of the State's Pearl Harbor Historic Trail Project, will also have interpretive signage.

Wildlife observation and environmental education are more common at the Kalaeloa Unit of the Pearl Harbor NWR. Numerous volunteer groups have contributed to native planting and invasive plant removal programs at the Kalaeloa Unit. Some of the groups that have annually participated include the Hawaiʻi Youth Conservation Corps, Waiʻanae High School, Mililani High School, Leeward Community College, Brigham Young University, Kapolei Eagle and Cub Scouts, and Kaʻala Farms.

5.1.5 Fishing

Recreational fishing is administered by the Division of Aquatic Resources within DLNR. Fishing is restricted in all military bases, national wildlife refuges, State natural area reserves, and harbors; however, the public is allowed to fish along the State-owned shorelines. Virtually the entire Pearl Harbor shoreline is owned by the U.S. Navy. The Navy suspended the issuance of recreational fishing permits in Pearl Harbor in 1998 due to public health concerns. Although recreational fishing in Pearl Harbor is restricted and generally discouraged by the U.S. Navy, the public does participate in recreational fishing on the shores and around the margins of Pearl Harbor. Rod and reel poles and cast nets are used to catch finfish such as the striped mullet, Hawaiian flagtail, surgeonfish, ulua, pāpio, weke, and tilapia. Crustaceans are also caught in the area using nets. Typical crustacean species caught within the Pearl Harbor area may include the mangrove or Samoan crab, the white crab, and the slipper lobster.

Shoreline fishing at Pearl Harbor NWR occurs most frequently off the coastal portion of the Kalaeloa Unit. Access to this coastal area is difficult due to nearby military security; however, the beach area is accessible from the western side of the Refuge unit.

5.1.6 Hunting

On Oʻahu, hunting is permitted in 12 public hunting areas, covering 25,000 acres. The main species hunted are feral goats and pigs. Non-native game birds are also hunted including the Ring-necked pheasant, Japanese quail, three francolin species, and several dove species. Personnel engaging in hunting must possess a valid State of Hawaiʻi hunting license. A total of 8,249 hunting licenses were issued throughout the State in 2008 (DBEDT 2009). There are no game species within the Refuge and it is closed to the public for hunting.

5.2 Social and Economic Conditions

The purpose of this section is to address the local economy and social environment surrounding the Pearl Harbor NWR, including population estimates and economic indicators. The Refuge is located within the City and County of Honolulu.

5.2.1 Population

The total resident population of the Hawaiian Islands in 2009 was 1,295,000. The Island of Oʻahu is home to 73 percent of this total. According to the Hawaiʻi Department of Business, Economic Development and Tourism (DBEDT), roughly 43 percent of the Hawaiʻi population was born outside of the State of Hawaiʻi. The ethnic composition of the City and County of Honolulu is diverse. In 2005, the City and County of Honolulu was comprised of 21.7 percent Caucasian, 20.3 percent Hawaiian or part Hawaiian, 19.2 percent Japanese and 11.3 percent Filipino. Approximately 20.2 percentof the population identified themselves as having a mixed ethnic background (DBEDT 2009).

Pearl Harbor NWR is located within the State District of ʻEwa and the City and County ʻEwa Development Plan Area. Four neighborhood areas, as defined by the City and County of Honolulu, surround the Refuge. These include the neighborhood areas of Pearl City, Waipahu, ʻEwa, and

Makakilo/Kapolei/Honokai Hale. Much of the population increase on the island has been concentrated in the 'Ewa District, which experienced a 27.9 percent population increase 2000-2008 (DBEDT 2009). The 'Ewa region has recently developed into O'ahu second urban center supporting approximately 70,000 people. This region is expected to see a large population growth, increasing to 125,000 by 2020. Compared to the island-wide population increase of 1.6 percent annually, the 'Ewa region is projected to increase 3.6 percent per year (HCDA 2006). In particular, the community of Kalaeloa, which encompasses 3,700 acres, has been designated as one of the primary urban growth areas of the island (HCDA 2005).

5.2.2 Education

Educational attainment is slightly higher on the island of O'ahu compared to the rest of the State. In 2000, approximately 84.8 percent of the O'ahu population 25 years and over had received a high school diploma. Furthermore, approximately 27.9 percent reported to have a Bachelor's degree or higher. The State averages during the same year were 84.6 and 26.2 percent, respectively (DBEDT 2009).

Within the University of Hawai'i system (UH) are five community colleges and two universities on O'ahu. In 2008, enrollment at UH Mānoa was 20,169 and at the West O'ahu Campus was 1,140 students. Approximately 21,169 students were enrolled in the community colleges throughout O'ahu. Total enrollment in private universities on O'ahu (including Brigham Young, Hawai'i Pacific, and Chaminade) in 2008 was 13,293 (DBEDT 2009).

5.2.3 Economy

Hawai'i is economically dynamic with diversified agriculture and manufacturing; strategically important to the global defense system of the United States; a Pacific Basin transportation center; and a major tourism destination. The health of the State's economy depends significantly on conditions in the overall U.S. economy and key international economies, especially Japan. State taxes are collected under a centralized tax system. The chief sources of the State's revenue are a general excise tax, individual income taxes, and federal grants-in-aid. The second largest source of income in Hawai'i is the Federal government, primarily through defense expenditures.

Tourism is Hawai'i's largest industry with the majority of visitors coming from the U.S. mainland, Canada, Australia, and countries of the Far East, particularly Japan. Most visitors to Hawai'i travel by air. The Honolulu International Airport, on O'ahu; General Lyman Field at Hilo on Hawai'i; and the Kahului Airport on Maui, are the major civilian airports capable of serving large-jet traffic. There are several smaller airports among the islands and a number of small private airfields and military airports throughout the State. Oceanic passenger ships also carry visitors through Honolulu, and there is one interisland cruise line.

Hawai'i's mild, year-round climate sustains many different types of agriculture. Approximately 40% of land in Hawai'i is farmland. Significant crops include sugarcane, pineapple, macadamia nuts and coffee. Helping to sustain the agricultural economy are ginger, banana, onions, sweet potato, lettuce and seed crops. There has been a slow but steady growth of diversified agriculture, including grain sorghum, corn, flowers, and nursery products. Livestock, poultry, and dairy production, together with some commercial fishing, are other important sources of income.

Hawai'i has several hundred companies engaged in diversified manufacturing. Heavy-manufacturing plants, using raw materials for the most part imported from the U.S. mainland, include an oil refinery that produces a variety of petroleum products and chemical compounds, a steel mill manufacturing reinforcing bars, several cement plants, a concrete-pipe plant, and an aluminum-extrusion plant. Manufacturing is confined mainly to the island of O'ahu. Most building lumber is imported from the mainland. A number of garment manufacturers, largely situated in Honolulu, produce printed fabrics and apparel marketed locally, nationally, and abroad.

Ocean-surface transportation is Hawai'i's lifeline, and Honolulu Harbor is the primary shipping center. A large percentage of the cargo ships traverse between Hawai'i and California ports, a few between Hawai'i and the East Coast of the United States via the Panama Canal, and others from western Pacific ports. Around-the-world passenger ships carry visitors through Honolulu, and there is an interisland luxury cruise line. Tug-pulled barges and small freighters transport goods from Honolulu to the outer islands, returning with agricultural crops and livestock.

A major concern is the high cost of living, due in large part to the dependence on imports. The State imports 85 percent of the food consumed in Hawai'i. Transportation costs are included in the prices of nearly all consumer goods. As the population increases, housing grows increasingly difficult to acquire, and it is disproportionately expensive when compared with housing costs in many of the mainland States. Building materials, most of which are imported, are expensive. Residential land is limited and highly priced, since much of the property is owned by corporations and trusts. More than half the land in the State is owned by private individuals or corporations, although the State itself, holding more than one-third of the land, is the largest single landowner. State and county governments are major employers. Honolulu is the regional headquarters of the Federal government, which owns one-sixth of the land (Hawai'i Travel Guide).

5.2.4 Refuge Contribution

Because the units of Pearl Harbor NWR are generally not available to the public, the Refuge contribution to the local economy through recreational expenditures is small. Based on Fiscal Year 2010, the budget for the Pearl Harbor NWR is $169,939, of which $100,349 is for employee salaries. The remaining $69,590 is for local expenditures.

In addition to recreational expenditures, the Refuge contributes money to the local economy through the Refuge Revenue Sharing Act of 1978 (16 U.S.C. 715s). This Act authorizes Federal payments to be transferred to the County of Hawai'i annually in lieu of discontinued taxation of private property. The amount compensated is approximately 0.75 percent of the fair market value of fee lands. In 2009, $1,264 was paid to the City and County of Honolulu for the Kalaeloa Unit of Pearl Harbor NWR. Lands administered in the Honouliuli and Waiawa Units are managed under a cooperative agreement with the U.S. Navy and are not owned in fee title by the Service.

Chapter 6. Environmental Effects Analysis

6.1 Overview of Effects Analysis

The effects analysis was developed by identifying resources associated with the physical, biological, and human environment identified in Chapters 3 through 5 of the Draft CCP/EA that may be impacted by the various alternative strategies presented in Chapter 2. The potential effects to those resources as a result of implementing the strategies described under each alternative were then assessed.

The information used in this Draft CCP/EA was obtained from relevant scientific literature, existing databases and inventories, consultations with other professionals, professional knowledge of resources based on field visits, and experience. Subheadings have been included to guide the reader in understanding which types of management strategies are likely to affect each resource as not all management strategies affect each resource.

Cumulative impacts, including impacts to Refuge resources from reasonably foreseeable events and impacts resulting from interaction of Refuge actions with actions taking place outside the Refuge, are addressed in the final section of this chapter. That discussion includes a brief discussion on potential impacts of climate change to Refuge resources.

6.2 Terminology

Effects were assessed for scope, scale, and intensity of impacts to resources. Effects may be identified further as beneficial or negative as well as long-term or short-term.

- **Negligible.** Resources would not be affected, or the effects would be at or near the lowest level of detection. Resource conditions would not change or would be so slight no measurable or perceptible consequence to a population, wildlife or plant community, recreation opportunity, visitor experience, or cultural resource would occur.

- **Minor.** Effects would be detectable but localized, small, and of little consequence to a population, wildlife or plant community, recreation opportunity, visitor experience, or cultural resource. Mitigation, if needed to offset adverse effects, would be easily implemented and successful.

- **Intermediate.** Effects would be readily detectable and localized; with consequences to a population, wildlife, or plant community; recreation opportunity; visitor experience; or cultural resource. Mitigation measures would be needed to offset adverse effects and would be extensive, moderately complicated to implement, and probably successful.

- **Major.** Effects would be obvious and would result in substantial consequences to a population, wildlife, or plant community; recreation opportunity; visitor experience; or cultural resource within the local area and region. Extensive mitigating measures may be needed to offset adverse effects and would be large scale in nature, very complicated to implement, and may not have a guaranteed probability of success. In some instances, major effects would include the irretrievable loss of the resource.

Time and duration of effects have been defined as follows.

- **Short-term or Temporary.** An effect that generally would last less than a year or season.

- **Long-term.** A change in a resource or its condition that would last longer than a single year or season.

6.3 Summary of Effects for Pearl Harbor National Wildlife Refuge

A summary of the effects analysis is presented in Table 6.1. Current management (Alternative 1) does benefit wildlife and habitats; however, effects are described in terms of the change from current conditions. Therefore, Alternative 1 generally has negligible, if any, effects because little or no change to management programs occurs under this alternative. Effects from Alternative 2 are summarized in the table using the above definitions to describe the magnitude of change from the current condition.

Table 6.1 CCP Alternatives Summary of Effects for Pearl Harbor Refuge

	Alternative 1	Alternative 2
EFFECTS TO WILDLIFE AND HABITAT		
Effects on Endangered Waterbirds	This alternative would continue to provide for stable numbers of all four endangered waterbirds occurring on the Refuge and contribute to recovery.	Moderate positive effect to provide for increasing numbers of all four endangered waterbirds occurring on the Refuge and contribute to recovery.
Effects to endangered ae'o	Neutral effect. No change from current management. High quality wetlands supporting loafing, foraging, nesting, and chick rearing provided appropriate to the life-history needs of the species.	Moderate positive effect. Increased predator control efficiency through monitoring and construction of predator-proof fence will result in decreased predation on young and adult birds yielding a greater number of young fledged. Increased water level pulsing will result in increased production of suitable food for chicks and adults throughout the year resulting in healthier birds and increasing the carrying capacity of the Refuge.

	Alternative 1	Alternative 2
		Possible minor positive effects resulting from mangrove removal at Honouliuli are increasing intertidal foraging area.
Effects to endangered 'alae 'ula	Neutral effect. No change from current management. High quality wetlands supporting loafing, foraging, nesting, and chick rearing provided appropriate to the life-history needs of the species.	Moderate positive effect. Increased predator control efficiency through monitoring and construction of predator-proof fence will result in decreased predation on young and adult birds yielding a greater number of young fledged. Increased water level pulsing will result in increased production of suitable food for chicks and adults throughout the year resulting in healthier birds and increasing the carrying capacity of the Refuge.
Effects to endangered 'alae ke'o ke'o	Neutral effect. No change from current management. High quality wetlands supporting loafing, foraging, nesting, and chick rearing provided appropriate to the life-history needs of the species.	Slight positive effect. Increased predator control efficiency through monitoring and construction of predator-proof fence will result in decreased predation on young and adult birds yielding a greater number of young fledged. Increased water level pulsing will have slightly negative effects due to less nesting area for 'alae ke'o ke'o at lower water levels.
Effects to endangered plants 'Ewa hinahina and 'akoko	Neutral effect. No change from current management. 'Ewa hinahina and akoko habitat is managed through control of nonnative invasive plants and minimal outplanting.	Moderate long-term positive effect resulting from increased invasive plant control, removal of up to 12 acres of kiawe and koa haole, and additional outplantings of 'Ewa hinahina and 'akoko.

	Alternative 1	Alternative 2
		Foot trail system will further protect endangered plants from inadvertent trampling.
Effects to endangered koʻoloaʻula plants	Neutral effect. No change from current management. Partnership with State DLNR provides protection for koʻoloaʻula.	Neutral effect. No change from current management. Partnership with State DLNR provides protection for koʻoloaʻula.
Effects to candidate T&E species	Neutral effect. No change from current management. Anchialine pool habitat is provided for *Metabetaeus lohena*.	Minor long-term positive effects if additional anchialine pools are restored for *Metabetaeus lohena* habitat. Moderate long-term positive effect on pinapinao by providing habitat for possible translocation to expand current range and protection.
Effects to wetland habitats and associated resident wildlife	Neutral effect. No change from current management.	Slight positive benefits to migratory and resident wetland bird species due to reduction in predation within Refuge. Pulsing water will have minor positive effect by stimulating germination of native plants, thereby increasing plant diversity and additional foraging habitat.
Effects to migratory waterbirds	Neutral effect. No change from current management.	Pulsing water will have minor positive effect by stimulating production of invertebrates and seeds, thereby increasing foraging area and food abundance for shorebirds. Possible minor positive effects resulting from mangrove removal at Honouliuli increasing intertidal foraging area.
Effects to native fish	Neutral effect. No change from current management.	Negligible effects from water pulsing due to intermittent occurrence of native fish (awa) in the Refuge.

	Alternative 1	Alternative 2
PHYSICAL ENVIRONMENTAL EFFECTS		
Effects to air quality	Neutral effect. No change from current management.	Negligible short-term effects from equipment associated with potential overlook (Waiawa) construction, mangrove removal project, and anchialine pool restoration. Long-term minor positive effects resulting from reduced transportation needs and reduction of carbon footprint size from shed construction.
Effects to water quality	Neutral effect. No change from current management.	Negligible short-term effect during mangrove removal associated with turbidity, mitigated through timing removal action with low tides.
Effects to soils	Neutral effect. No change from current management.	Minor short-term erosion effect mitigated by placement of riprap timed to coincide with mangrove removal. Long-term positive effect by reducing dike erosion.
SOCIAL EFFECTS		
Opportunities for wildlife observation and photography	Current management plan includes construction of overlook at Honouliuli which will provide new opportunities for wildlife observation and photography.	Construction of overlook at Honouliuli will provide new long-term opportunities for wildlife observation and photography. Additional minor increase in opportunities may be provided if an overlook is constructed at Waiawa.
Opportunities for environmental education	Neutral effect. No change from current management. The Refuge currently hosts environmental education opportunities for 2,500 students at Honouliuli and 100 students at Kalaeloa.	Additional resources may enable the Refuge to provide environmental education opportunities for up to 3,500 students at Honouliuli and 1,500 students at Kalaeloa.
Opportunities for interpretation	Neutral effect. No change from current management.	Information gleaned from avian paleontological survey

	Alternative 1	Alternative 2
	The Betty Bliss Memorial Overlook will provide new interpretive opportunities.	will provide insight into historical plant and animal communities at Kalaeloa, thereby enhancing interpretive opportunities. Installation of entrance signs will enhance recognition of Refuge presence. The Betty Bliss Memorial Overlook and potential Waiawa overlook will provide new interpretive opportunities.
Economic effects	Neutral effects expected from current level of Refuge expenditures.	Negligible beneficial effects expected from increased Refuge expenditures.
Environmental justice	No effects.	No effects.
FACILITIES		
Equipment Shed	Not included in alternative.	Negligible to minor short-term disturbance to wildlife may result from construction of small equipment shed or installation of equipment container.
EFFECTS TO NONNATIVE PREDATORS		
Effects to target predators	Neutral effect. No change from current management. Minor localized reduction of mongooses, cats, rats, and mice.	Minor localized reduction of mongooses, cats, rats, and mice; improved efficiency with modified techniques. Potential to reduce the need for lethal predator-control efforts by installation of predator-proof fences.
Effects to nontarget species	Neutral effect. Nontarget species are released unharmed at capture site. No recorded incidents of non-target species killed as a result of Refuge bait stations.	Neutral effect. Nontarget species are released unharmed at capture site. No recorded incidents of nontarget species killed as a result of Refuge bait stations.

6.4 Effects Analysis

The following analysis describes the anticipated effects of implementing the Refuge management strategies described in Chapter 2 on the physical, biological, and social environment, the attributes of which were described in detail in Chapters 3, 4, and 5.

6.4.1 Water Pulsing and Management

Incremental raising and lowering of water levels is referred to as "pulsing" and is used as a habitat modification tool. The timing, duration, and degree of pulsing affects plant germination and growth, invertebrate production, and food accessibility to foraging shorebirds and endangered waterbird chicks.

Pulsing just prior to chicks being produced stimulates increased production of invertebrates used by the endangered ae'o, 'alae ke'oke'o, and 'alae 'ula. This assists managers in providing ample food to help maximize fledglings and increase populations. Invertebrates range from small insects the size of midges to macroinvertebrates like crayfish. All are important food items in various life stages of Hawai'i's endangered waterbirds. Pulsing also creates suitable substrate, moisture, and temperature conditions to favor wetland plant germination. Many wetland plants provide food, cover, or nesting habitat/structure for nesting endangered Hawaiian waterbirds.

Pulsing is currently used as an endangered species management tool. The frequency of pulsing is currently limited due to staffing shortage and workload. Under Alternative 2, pulsing would be increased to maximize its use as a method to enhance habitat and moderately improve endangered waterbird recovery potential on the Honouliuli and Waiawa Units.

The effects of increased pulsing include potential increases in fledged waterbirds chicks, and additional suitable nesting and foraging/loafing habitat. Throughout the summer there is an increased risk of botulism, and when pulsing, a flow of water is allowed to continually flow over boards in water control structures. This helps keep water temperatures lower by circulating cooler groundwater and reduces the potential for botulism. This flow of water results in a moderate increase in water consumption seasonally. To offset this, water usage is continually monitored and when rainfall levels permit, groundwater is not utilized. This water-saving measure is utilized throughout the year.

During the cooler fall and winter months it is often not necessary to provide a continual flow of water through wetland impoundments, but this is partially dictated by weather conditions. During this period evapotranspiration can be used to assist pulsing.

Increased pulsing is expected to increase water use by a minor amount on a yearly basis. On the Waiawa Unit this water is drawn from a brackish (7-8 ppt) aquifer, not suitable for potable water. Honouliuli Unit uses water from a fresher aquifer. The increased water use anticipated is expected to be minor, but result in moderate positive benefits to endangered, migrant, and other waterbirds utilizing the Refuge. An increase in improved habitat would support larger population of waterbirds and contribute to recovery of endangered waterbirds for which the Refuge was established. An increase in number of native wetland plant species and a greater distribution in the wetlands is also a potential with more regular pulsing. If increased water use results in the Refuge exceeding State water use allocation, then a modification to increase the existing allocation will be submitted.

6.4.2 Mangrove Removal and Associated Dike Stabilization

This project, if undertaken, is anticipated to result in negligible short-term negative impacts to the environment. The impacts will result from disturbance to wetland related species during the removal process from noise and equipment operation. Equipment will be outfitted with mufflers to minimize effects to wildlife and nearby communities. Seasonal timing will be set to minimize effects on native wildlife, including endangered species. Work will only be conducted during daylight hours.

Additionally, removal of the mangroves will result in negligible short-term decrease in water quality in harbor waters near the Refuge resulting from soil disturbance. Seasonal timing will be used to minimize this effect. Removal will be limited to periods of outgoing low tide when water is below the elevation of the removal site. This will allow a period of at least 6 hours for soil consolidation to occur before the incoming tide. The slow wetting by the incoming tide is also expected to allow sediment consolidation and minimize silt transmittal to harbor waters.

Long-term wetland dike stabilization and dike deterioration prevention will be achieved by placing appropriate size rip-rap along the harbor side of the dike. This will also prevent sediment from entering the harbor in the long term. Effects to visitor use programs are not expected. The environmental education program operates September-early December and does not occur in the area where mangrove would be removed.

Long-term positive effects will be increased with additional intertidal mudflat area for endangered, other resident and migratory waterbird foraging. Expanded foraging areas for endangered waterbirds will help meet recovery goals with increasing habitat to support increased waterbird populations. Native fish species might also benefit from the more open accessible shoreline.

6.4.3 Predator Control

Predator control is currently conducted on the Honouliuli and Waiawa Units of the Refuge as part of endangered species recovery efforts through Refuge management. Control might be implemented on the Kalaeloa Unit to minimize predation from rodents and mongooses on endangered and native plant vegetation, fruit, and seed.

The Second Draft Revised Recovery Plan for Hawaiian Waterbirds, Second Revision (May 2005) identifies the Honouliuli and Waiawa Units as Core Wetlands as related to recovery of Hawai'i's waterbirds. In accordance with the plan, these sites must be protected and managed to recover Hawai'i's waterbirds. Eliminating or controlling predation is a listed objective in the plan as a tool for increasing endangered waterbird numbers and potentially making areas suitable for successful reintroduction of other native or endangered species such as nēnē.

Predator control presently consists of fencing, habitat manipulation, live trapping and euthanasia, and diphacinone bait stations. Live traps are used to control mongooses and cats, while bait stations are used primarily to control mice, rats, and mongooses within the Refuge.

Fencing

Chain-link fence topped with strands of barbed wire is currently used as a mammalian predator and human deterrent to minimize unauthorized access to the Refuge. Chain-link fence will not prevent mammals from entering the Refuge. Small mammals such as mice, rats, and mongooses can move through the fence. Cats and potentially dogs can climb over the fence. Monitoring of fences for breaches such as cuts made by humans; digging by animals; and damage from falling trees and limbs, is ongoing and time consuming. The presence of cats and dogs has been documented on the Refuge. This type of fencing provides minimal protection against mammalian predation and other negative impacts to endangered and native wildlife species.

Under consideration on one or more of the Refuge units is a predator-proof fence. These fences are very expensive, but such fences have proven to prevent entry by mammals as small as a mouse. They are designed to prevent digging under and climbing over by animals. They are still not fail-proof because damage from human vandalism and natural causes, such as falling trees and branches, can result in failure. Predator-proof fences have been successfully used on a large scale in New Zealand.

Fence installation results in a short term disturbance to vegetation, soil, air quality, and noise level due to the use of heavy equipment to clear a path for the fence and then construction of the fence. These effects are negligible and short term compared to the benefits gained over the long term by protecting habitats and native wildlife dependent on them, especially endangered species. Predator-proof fencing would reduce the need for lethal control methods and use of other techniques on an ongoing basis. This would also result in long term financial savings.

Live trapping

Currently, Tomahawk Live Traps are used, but other similar devices could be considered for use in the future, if deemed appropriate for the target species. Traps are set and baited with dry pet food, canned foods, and sardines. Sometimes used cooking oils are used to create a different olfactory attractant in an attempt to capture trap-wary animals that might be avoiding certain baits. Trying different baits and rotating through various baits is a part of the program. Walk-in traps are checked daily when set. If traps cannot be checked at this frequency, they are closed.

A cover over each Tomahawk trap provides shade along with an attached water bottle that allows a trapped animal to drink. When a target species is captured, it is euthanized by shooting with a small caliber weapon, generally a .22 caliber rifle or pistol. Carcasses are disposed of according to State and local requirements at an approved location.

Nontarget species are occasionally caught in this type trap. A small number are occasionally found dead, mostly the result of predation by mammalian predators attacking from outside the trap. These nontarget animals are primarily nonnative doves and cardinals that are released unharmed at the capture site. Effects to nontarget species are negligible because they are nonnative and widespread on Oʻahu. The area of effect (Refuge) is infinitesimal compared to the range and numbers of nontargets affected.

Lethal Traps

Currently no lethal traps are being deployed on the Refuge. Under either alternative, however, initiation of this type of trap may be considered to protect endangered species and meet Refuge goals and objectives for management and recovery. Several designs are available that are intended to dispatch animals in a humane manner quickly. A series of traps that has been explored in Hawai'i and used in New Zealand is the Department of Conservation (DOC) series of lethal traps. The kill portion of the trap is enclosed in a sturdy box for safety, and the entrance to the trap is designed to keep out nontarget species. These traps are intended for capturing and humanely killing small mammals up to the size of cats. Traps in the DOC series have either passed draft or final New Zealand National Animal Welfare Advisory Committee standards as a humane kill trap.

Bait Stations

Currently, diphacinone bait blocks are used in approved lockable bait stations on Honouliuli and Waiawa Units. Commonly used throughout the State, the size and design of these bait stations allows entry to animals up to the size of a mongoose. This includes mice and rats. Each bait station is labeled with a contact number and each Refuge entry area is signed with a warning notifying the public that bait stations are in use in the area. Bait is secured in each bait box according to regulations. Bait is checked once weekly, new blocks placed in the box to replace eaten ones, and the data recorded. Small portions of blocks left in the bait box are disposed of according to label requirements.

Exact numbers of target species affected by bait stations are difficult to ascertain from direct observations because target species are relatively small and head to cover after consuming bait. Very few animals are found after they consume the Diphacinone bait. Presently, observation of target animals on the Refuge is the only method used to determine relative presence. Under Alternative 2, implementation of track tunnel monitoring will occur on a quarterly basis. By using track tunnels or a similar device, a more accurate numerical and trend assessment of mice, rats, and mongooses on the Refuge will be possible. The devices allow identification of tracks left by species that walk through a nontoxic ink or other substance that leaves behind a footprint. Track tunnel monitoring will help the Refuge determine the efficacy of ongoing predator control programs and provide information needed to make modifications to improve the program.

Presently, bait stations are not used on the Kalaeloa Unit. Since use of bait stations provides a safe and approved method of controlling rodents and mongooses in Hawai'i, it may be considered for use on the Kalaeloa Unit to reduce and maintain minimal predation on native and endangered plants. Higher seed survival would contribute to enhanced potential for germination and allow for seeds to be banked for future outplanting on the Refuge or other locations within the plants' range. Reduced feeding on new young shoots of native and endangered plants would enhance the potential for greater recovery of restored plant communities on the Refuge.

Shooting

Shooting with small-caliber rifle or pistol and shotgun is a viable tool for controlling difficult to trap individual animals or removing predator species on an opportunistic basis. This tool is very selective, and specific predators can be targeted for removal. This tool is not expected to be frequently used because of the proximity of residential areas and other facilities. Sound reduced weapons will be used, whenever possible, by trained and qualified individuals, to minimize any disturbance and ensure safety of nearby neighborhoods. Animals removed using this technique will be removed from the site so as not to impact human health or adversely impact other wildlife. Very few animals are removed by this method and local populations of such animals are quite numerous, thus no significant adverse effects to predators are expected to result from using this control method.

Predator control activities are confined to the small area of the Refuge encompassing a maximum of 100 acres for all three Pearl Harbor NWR Units. On this limited acreage, control of predators on endangered and other trust resources managed by the Refuge is considered negligible because of the extensive range, large distribution, and other unaffected areas off-Refuge that these species occur on in the immediate vicinity of the Refuge and other parts of O'ahu. The number of target and nontarget species removed resulting from the program is negligible when compared to overall numbers of mongooses, mice, rats, cats occurring in the wild on O'ahu.

The program is expected to have moderate positive effects on endangered and other waterbirds and wetland related native species. The effects of reducing or eliminating predation by utilizing one or more of the above techniques is expected to provide moderate positive benefits to endangered, other resident, and migratory waterbirds. For endangered waterbirds, increased chick survival will move each species closer to the potential for recovery and delisting. The anticipated effects are consistent with the goals of the Regional and Pacific Islands Shorebird Management Plan and the Recovery Plan for Hawaiian Waterbirds. The moderate positive effects are based on the fact limited managed, protected wetlands occur on O'ahu and throughout the State.

6.4.4 Increased Invasive Species Removal

With time comes the introduction of new pests and invasive species of both plants and animals. Ants are a growing concern since they can have negative effects on native and endangered plants and animals. Ants are known to attack and injure or kill young birds. Ants are also implicated in having negative effects on native and endangered plants. Control of ants has potential on all units of the Pearl Harbor NWR to protect trust resources. The Service is currently studying the efficacy of various baits and approved toxins on invasive ants on O'ahu. It is anticipated that the Refuge will adopt methods in the future based on the results of these studies. Future ant control strategies may be subject to a separate environmental compliance process.

6.4.5 Additional Anchialine Pool Restoration

Based on present knowledge, potentially dozens of restorable anchialine pools are within the Kalaeloa Unit. These pools are essential habitat of small native shrimp; some of which are candidates for listing as endangered by the Service.

Past land-use practices resulted in degradation and filling of anchialine pools. Restoration involves removal of rock, rubble, and dirt from the pool sites. A site is deemed restorable if, after removal of debris, a flow of brackish water begins coming into and out of the pool with tidal movement. A small mini-excavator is used to remove the large rocks, rubble, and soil from the opening. Next, removal of finer silt material from the walls of the vertical limestone tube is accomplished using a high pressure water sprayer. Silt-laden water in the open pool is then pumped onto the ground. Removal of the silt is important to allowing subterranean fissures to transport subsurface fresh and sea water to the site to create the unique brackish-water environment of the pools.

It is anticipated throughout the life of this CCP, up to 40 anchialine pools could be restored. The increased number would allow for greater populations of anchialine pool shrimp ('opae 'ula and *Metabetaeus lohena*) to thrive on the Refuge and prevent them from reaching threatened status.

Negligible, short-term effects would include localized disturbance to a small area around the pool being restored. Disturbance would include negligible damage to native and nonnative plants. Threatened and endangered plants would not be damaged or destroyed. Short-term, negligible decrease in air quality would result from operation of mechanized equipment described above.

To minimize effects described above, equipment operation would be reduced to the minimum necessary to accomplish the task. Biologists would determine if threatened or endangered species are present in the work area. If they are, the locations would be delineated and avoided during restoration operations. Once a pool is restored, native plants are expected to naturally revive and others grow, reclaiming the natural look of the area, as has been the case with previous pool restoration on the Refuge.

The short-term negligible negative effects are offset by the long-term intermediate positive effects, including restoration of a unique and limited coastal environment on O'ahu, creating habitat for native anchialine pool shrimp, including *Metabetaeus lohena*, a candidate for listing as endangered. The pinapinao, also considered an endangered species candidate, would benefit since the only population is restricted to one known location.

6.4.6 Pinapinao Translocation

Threats to the pinapinao (orange-black Hawaiian damselfly) include severely altered or loss of water habitats and predation by introduced fish species that feed on the naiads. Predation from introduced fish, crustaceans, and possibly nonnative birds such as bulbuls, cardinals, and mynas may also pose a threat to all life phases of the pinapinao. Based on data collected from restored anchialine pools on the Refuge, there is a high potential for successful translocation of eggs and/or larval forms of this species to the Kalaeloa Unit. A translocation would involve movement of the available life stage from the existing site on O'ahu to the Refuge after a pool is selected that is deemed to have suitable conditions (invertebrate prey to sustain naiads, salinity range, temperature, and accessible by adult pinapino).

Just a small number of eggs and/or naiads would be moved to the Kalaeloa Unit, initially. This would provide the opportunity to monitor and evaluate the outcome of the translocation and determine the potential for future translocations to the site.

The small number of initially translocated life stages would only negligibly affect the overall population at the single site where this species is located on O'ahu. Continued protection and successful natural reproduction at the original site will negate the small number removed for the translocation. A successful translocation to the Refuge would create another population, adding to the security of the overall population. An established population on the Refuge would also allow the potential for expansion into other anchialine pools. A long-term benefit would result if this species can radiate and colonize other suitable habitat on the 'Ewa Plain. Any or all of these effects will aid in sustaining a more stable and geographically dispersed population.

6.4.7 Avian Paleontological Study

The restoration of anchialine pools on the Kalaeloa Unit uncovered hidden treasures that are providing a window to the area's ancient past. While removing the debris, fossilized bird bones – some never before recorded by modern humans – were discovered, preserved by the earthen matrix of the pools. To date, fossilized bones of an extinct hawk (first time reported as a fossil on Oʻahu), long-legged owl, Hawaiian sea eagle, petrel, two species of crow, Hawaiian finches, Hawaiian honeyeaters, and the moa nalo (a turkey-sized, flightless goose-like duck– largest of the native Hawaiian birds) have been identified. Further work is needed to confirm the identification and age of each species. The Service is working with representatives from the Smithsonian Institution and Bishop Museum to properly clean, store, preserve, and identify the bones.

Future work recovering additional avian bones from existing material and material removed from pools restored in the future would continue to build a picture of what the ancient landscape might have looked like thousands of years ago and provide examples of what wildlife lived in the coastal community at that time. Building a more complete picture of these ancient times would aid restoration efforts and help interpret the area to others.

Future collection would be in association with future anchialine pool restoration using techniques described above and direct archaeological recovery methods by paleoarchaeologists. The Smithsonian Institution is interested in conducting further investigations on the Refuge, examining pool contents and determining ages of fossils.

Negligible short-term effects to the area are expected that might result in disturbance of native plants adjacent to anchialine pools. Endangered and threatened plants would not be disturbed and a survey would be conducted to determine presence or absence in proposed pool restoration/archaeological recovery activities. Long-term benefits derived would include greater information dissemination regarding the area and enhanced understanding of the historic composition and plant/animal associations of the area.

6.4.8 Expanded Visitor Services and Environmental Education Program

Environmental education is an important aspect of visitor services on refuges. When dealing with sensitive areas, opportunities to learn about threatened and endangered species are often limited. They are still important and when supervised and planned appropriately open a new world to youth. The Service anticipates enlisting students from local high schools and units of the University system to participate in gaining firsthand knowledge of science and the scientific method by having them conduct monitoring and restoration projects. These activities would be closely monitored by Refuge and/or Refuge-approved leaders and teachers.

Negligible short term effects are expected because of the small footprint of the participants on any given day and the onsite guidance they will be provided. Long-term beneficial effects would include exposing students to opportunities to experience the outdoors and contribute to the knowledgebase of the Refuge. Through these experiences, participants would gain a greater appreciation for nature, wild places, and environmental processes, and their work could potentially guide them into a science-related career. The Refuge will benefit from the information gained that will contribute to more effective management of the biotic and abiotic components of this rare coastal community.

Despite the anticipated increased level of visitor services, including environmental education, public tours, wildlife viewing opportunities, and wildlife and nature photography, effects are expected to be negligible. When compared to other areas on Oahu available for these activities, the increases in public use opportunities at this Refuge would not be noticeable.

The effects of visitor services programs on natural resources, endangered and nonendangered wildlife and plants, and migratory bird species is expected to be negligible as a result of the timing, seasonal access limitations, and limited access and areas available for public use on the Refuge.

6.4.9 Develop and Install Foot Trail System

A foot trail system is planned for development on the Kalaeloa Unit. The purpose is to protect the ground surface from disturbance, protect native and endangered plants, and provide for public safety. Dimensions of the trail will be minimized to reduce the footprint of the system and occupy as little space as necessary to accomplish visitor services needs. The system is intended only for human foot, not vehicular traffic. The trail will provide specific routes visitors will have to follow and provide opportunities for viewing endangered plants and restored anchialine pools. The trail will be designed and routed to avoid damaging or affecting sensitive natural resources and constructed and maintained using best management practices to further reduce the risk of adversely effecting sensitive natural resources.

Short-term impacts are expected to be negligible and will involve minor increased foot traffic and small equipment during brief construction phases. This will be an ongoing process as time and the availability of volunteers allows. Long-term intermediate positive benefits will include increased environmental education and interpretation opportunities in viewing of a restored Hawaiian coastal plant community, restored functioning anchialine pools, and historic World War II military artifacts–without potential damage to natural resources or decreased safety.

6.4.10 Entrance Sign Installation

Presently the Pearl Harbor NWR Units are identified only by boundary/fence line signs stating the land is a unit of the National Wildlife Refuge System (NWRS). As the Refuge Units become more popular and opportunities to visit them improve, Refuge public use areas should be more adequately identified. The standard method within the NWRS is a standard wooden entry sign. Signs are constructed offsite to NWRS standards, shipped to the Refuge and installed. Installation generally takes up to 2 days and consists of drilling two holes to secure the sign posts in, then attaching the sign to the posts. The posts are secured in the ground with cement prior to attachment of the sign.

Negligible short term affects are anticipated and include use of either a manual or mechanized posthole digger and disturbance to the ground in a small several square foot area. Long term minor positive benefits will be to inform the public the area is a unit of the NWRS.

Installing signs has the potential to adversely affect cultural resources; however, no effects to cultural resources are anticipated from this activity or other management actions. Cultural resources Section 106 compliance was undertaken in 2004 for work on the Kalaeloa Unit. The determination was no historic properties of Hawaiian origin occur; therefore, no effect is expected. In the event a discovery is made, any work in progress would cease and coordination with the proper cultural resource specialists would be initiated. World War II structures within the Kalaeloa Unit are outside the sign installation area.

The Waiawa and Honouliuli Units are highly disturbed and modified wetlands. Earth disturbance is shallow and limited and thus it is unlikely that any cultural resources remain on these units.

Prior to implementing all ground disturbing projects, the applicable cultural resource compliance investigation would be undertaken. If cultural resources are found, appropriate procedures and protocols would be followed to protect the cultural resources. Whenever possible, resources would be avoided or mitigated. Mitigation options, in addition to site avoidance by relocating or redesigning facilities, would include data recovery, using either collection techniques, or *in-situ* site stabilization protection.

6.4.11 Construction of Overlook(s) and Maintenance Shed

Overlooks are a way to allow the public to view the Refuge and learn about its resources without actually entering the wetland. Construction of the Betty Bliss Memorial Overlook is being undertaken outside the scope of this CCP. There is a potential for developing a similar type overlook at the Waiawa Unit. No planning for this overlook has been undertaken. If deemed desirable and feasible, the overlook would be placed along the fenceline of the Unit. The overlook would tie into the existing paved path paralleling the unit. Coordination with stakeholders, including the U.S. Navy, City and County of Honolulu, and nearby neighbors would be undertaken before any overlook construction.

If it is determined an overlook will be built, construction would be timed to minimize effects to natural resources of the Refuge, including daylight work only, seasonal construction restrictions based on nesting endangered species, and minimizing disturbance to neighbors. Details of constructing and maintaining a facility such as this would be subject to a separate environmental compliance process.

A small maintenance shed is needed on the Pearl Harbor NWR for short-term storage of equipment (tractors, mowers, etc.) and supplies. A Refuge Unit and a site has not yet been selected for this shed. An appropriate site will be selected that minimizes potential impacts to habitat or management activities. Due to the planned small size of the building (storage for one or two pieces of equipment), ground disturbance due to construction activities will be minimal. Measures to reduce disturbance to wildlife from construction activities will also include seasonal restrictions and designated routes of entry and exit. A major consideration and challenge will be to construct a building in one of these isolated locations that is resistant to break-ins and theft. Benefits to the Refuge will include improved efficiency due to onsite storage (less travel to/from maintenance base at James Campbell NWR), protection of equipment from harsh weather conditions, and improved protection from vandalism and theft.

6.4.12 Economic Impacts

Implementation of either alternative would be expected to result in negligible changes in expenditures in the local economy because staff levels and visitor programs would remain similar to current conditions.

6.4.13 Environmental Justice

The concept of environmental justice has been around since the early 1990s and arose from a need to ensure that negative environmental activities from industry or government projects would not endanger local communities. The U.S. Environmental Protection Agency oversees environmental justice compliance and defines environmental justice as: "the fair treatment and meaningful involvement of all people regardless of race, color, national origin, or income with respect to the development, implementation, and enforcement of environmental laws, regulations, and policies" (USEPA 2010).

Since CCP implementation of any of the alternatives is expected to result in generally positive effects on the human environment, there would be little risk of disproportionate negative effects to low income or minority groups. Therefore, negligible effects related to environmental justice are anticipated under all CCP alternatives.

6.5 Cumulative Effects Assessment

Cumulative effects can result from the incremental effects of a project when added to other past, present, and reasonably foreseeable future projects in the area. Cumulative impacts can result from individually minor but cumulatively significant actions over a period of time. This analysis is intended to consider the interaction of activities at the Pearl Harbor NWR with other actions occurring over a larger spatial and temporal frame of reference.

The Council on Environmental Quality regulations, which implement the provisions of NEPA, define several different types of effects that should be evaluated in an EA, including direct, indirect, and cumulative effects. Direct and indirect effects are addressed above in the resource-specific sections of this Draft CCP/EA. This section addresses cumulative effects.

It should be noted that the cumulative effects analysis has essentially been completed by virtue of the comprehensive nature by which direct and indirect effects associated with implementing the various alternatives was presented in the analysis above. The analysis in this section primarily focuses on effects associated with reasonably foreseeable future events and/or actions regardless of what entity undertakes that action.

6.5.1 Global Climate Changes and Projections

Global climate change is supported by a continuously growing body of unequivocal scientific evidence. During the 20th century, the global environment experienced variations in average worldwide temperatures, sea levels, and chemical concentrations. The Intergovernmental Panel on Climate Change (IPCC) is a scientific intergovernmental body organized by the World

Meteorological Organization and the United Nations Environment Programme in order to assess the causes, impacts, and response strategies to changes in climatic conditions. According to the Fourth Assessment Report by the IPCC, global temperatures on the Earth's surface have increased by 1.33°F over the last 100 years. This warming trend has accelerated within the last 50 years, increasing by 0.23°F each decade (Solomon et al. 2007). Global ocean temperatures to a depth of almost 2,300' have also increased, rising by 0.18°F between 1961 and 2003. During the same time period, mean global sea levels have risen approximately 0.0709" per year (Solomon et al. 2007).

While the concept of global warming is widely accepted, the extent and impact of future changes as well as the exact source (natural or human induced) remains a debate (OPIC 2000). Emerging consensus contends that increasing quantities of greenhouse gases (GHGs) in the atmosphere, especially carbon dioxide (CO_2), are beginning to impact climate and may be the dominant force driving recent warming trends. Glacial and interglacial periods in the Earth's history, as measured from deep Antarctic ice cores, reveal cyclical fluctuations in the concentration of global CO_2. However, recent increases fall outside the range of peak prehistoric CO_2 levels. The atmospheric concentrations of CO_2 and methane in 2005 were 379 ppm^3 and 1774 ppb, respectively. These amounts greatly exceed concentrations recorded in the global environment over the last 650,000 years (Solomon et al. 2007, Buddemeier et al. 2004, Vitousek 1994). The GHGs and other emissions from human activity have enhanced the heat trapping capability of the Earth's atmosphere, causing warmer temperatures. The increase in CO_2 is primarily attributed to fossil fuel use; however, land use changes have also increased the amount of cleared land surfaces, thereby reflecting more solar radiation (IPCC 2007, Solomon et al. 2007).

Global forecasting models offer a variety of predictions based on different emission scenarios. The U.S. government agency Overseas Private Investment Corporation (OPIC) suggests that a further increase in GHG emissions could double atmospheric concentrations of CO_2 by 2060 and subsequently increase temperatures by as much as 2-6.5°F over the next century. Recent model experiments by the IPCC show that if GHGs and other emissions remain at 2000 levels, a further global average temperature warming of about 0.18°F per decade is expected (Solomon et al. 2007). Sea level rise is expected to accelerate by two to five times the current rates due to both ocean thermal expansion and the melting of glaciers and polar ice caps. Recent modeling projects sea level to rise 0.59-1.93' by the end of the 21st century (IPCC 2007). These changes may lead to more severe weather, shifts in ocean circulation (currents, upwelling), as well as adverse impacts to economies and human health (OPIC 2000, IPCC 2001, Buddemeier et al. 2004). The extent and ultimate impact these changes will have on Earth's environment remains under considerable debate.

6.5.2 Climate Change in Hawai'i

Small island groups are particularly vulnerable to climate change. The following characteristics contribute to this vulnerability: small emergent land area compared to the large expanses of surrounding ocean; limited natural resources; high susceptibility to natural disasters; and inadequate funds to mitigate impacts (IPCC 2001). Thus, Hawai'i is considered to have a limited capacity to adapt to future climate changes. The Pacific Islands Regional Integrated Science and Assessment is working to develop programs dealing with climate risk management in the Pacific region. Furthermore, that Hawai'i Climate Change Action Plan (1998) offered initial recommendations to reduce GHGs and the Hawai'i Conservation Alliance is developing a strategy to deal with climate change throughout the State.

Similar to the rest of the world, temperatures in Hawai'i are rising. The U.S. EPA (1998) has estimated that the average surface temperature in Honolulu, Hawai'i has increased by 4.4°F over the last century. In particular, nighttime temperatures are notably warmer, increasing by about 0.5°F per decade over the past 30 years. Recent studies have shown that this rising average night temperature is greater at high elevation sites than lower areas. Sea surface temperature near the islands has been increasing recently, showing a 0.72°F rise 1957-1987. Sea level around the Hawaiian Islands is rising by 6-14 in per century. Over the last 90 years, precipitation has also decreased approximately 20 percent (EPA 1998, Arakawa 2008, Giambelluca 2008).

As a result of these shifts, Hawai'i is developing means to reduce its greenhouse gas emissions. In 1990, it is estimated that 15,985,225 tons of CO_2 were emitted in Hawai'i. Other major green houses gases released that year include 75,736 tons of methane (CH_4) and 690 tons of nitrous oxide (N_2O). These estimates do not include fuels that were exported, used on international aircraft or ship operations, or used by the military in the State. International, military, and overseas CO_2 emissions were estimated to be 7,363,261 tons in 1990 (DBEDT and DOH 1999). In 2007, the State of Hawai'i enacted Act 234, which sets the goal to reduce greenhouse gas emissions to 1990 levels by 2020.

Global and regional predictive climate simulations may not capture unique and important features of the Hawaiian climate. Existing large-scale models show large variability and uncertainty for the Hawaiian Islands; thus, applying these models to predict local conditions must be done with caution until more fine scaled models are developed (Timm 2008). Models from the IPCC and United Kingdom Hadley Centre's climate model suggested that by 2100 annual temperatures in Hawai'i could increase by 3°F, with a slightly higher increase in fall. Other estimates predict a 5-9°F rise by the end of the 21st century (TenBruggencate 2007). Future changes in precipitation are uncertain, dependent largely on shifts in El Niño/La Niña events. Some predictions forecast an additional rise of 17-25 in in by 2100 (USEPA 1998), while others suggested decreased precipitation.

Projected impacts that may have a significant effect on the coastal National Wildlife Refuges on O'ahu are discussed below.

6.5.3 Sea Level Rise

According to the IPCC, the oceans are now absorbing more than 80% percentof the heat added to the Earth's climate system. Since 1961, this absorption has caused average global ocean temperatures to increase and seawater to expand (GAO 2007). Thermal expansion of the sea is the primary cause of global sea level changes. Melting ice-sheets, ice caps, and alpine glaciers also influence ocean levels. Worldwide, sea level changes have historically occurred on a small scale; however, scientific evidence suggests that the current, accelerated rate of global change began between the mid-1800s and 1900s. Similarly, sea levels in the Pacific have regularly changed over the centuries due to variations in solar radiation. Since A.D. 1800, sea levels in the Pacific region have been rising. During the last century, these levels have risen about 6 in and this is likely to rapidly increase in the next century (Noye and Grzechnik 2001).

Due to localized geographic and oceanographic variations, it is not possible to discuss sea level rise (SLR) on a global scale (Michener et al. 1997). Near Pacific Island ecosystems, SLR is influenced by the rate and extent of global sea level rise, as well as changes in episodic events, such as the El Niño Southern Oscillation and storm-related conditions. Topography and exposure to normal and storm swell produce localized differences. Furthermore, it is important to note that shoreline sea levels are historically and currently influenced by isostatic tectonic changes as the islands move with the Pacific Plate, which are not due to global changes in sea level. Thus, sea level change in the Pacific is highly variable due to geologic uplift (Carter et al 2001).

Hawai'i's sea level appears to be rising at a slower rate than the global seas. Based on tide gauge records at the Honolulu Harbor, the sea level surrounding O'ahu has risen at a rate of 0.0551 in per year. Geological uplift contributes about 0.0016 in per year (Caccamise et al. 2005). The University of Hawai'i Sea Level Center has estimated that 1905-2006 mean sea level rose about 0.0417 in per year . A similar estimate was derived from shallow core measurements of a fringing reef crest at Hanauma Bay, which concluded that the island is subsiding at a rate of 0.0394-0.0787 in per year (Nakiboglu et al. 1983). Although most of this rise is due to isostatic sinking of the tectonic plate, global warming induced sea level increases have the potential to intensify this rise.

Tidal marshes are among the most susceptible ecosystems to climate change, especially accelerated SLR. Rising sea levels may result in tidal marsh submergence (Moorhead and Brinson 1995) and habitat migration as salt marshes transgress landward and replace tidal freshwater and brackish marsh. The Sea Level Affecting Marshes Model (SLAMM 6) accounts for the dominant processes involved in wetland conversion and shoreline modifications during long-term SLR (Park et al. 1991).

In an effort to address the potential effects of sea level changes on national wildlife refuges, the Service contracted the application of the SLAMM 6 model for most Pacific Region refuges. This analysis is designed to assist in development of long-term management plans. The SLAMM model predictions for Pearl Harbor NWR suggest that irregularly flooded marshes in the Waiawa unit will start to degrade in scenarios of over 2.2638 ft eustatic SLR and be nearly completely eliminated in scenarios of over 3.2808 ft of eustatic SLR. Predictions for the Honouliuli unit suggest that inland fresh marsh will be subject to saline inundation and conversion to mangrove swamp under SLR scenarios of 3.2808 ft eustatic SLR or greater. Although the Kalaeloa Unit is more resilient to SLR effects than the rest of the Refuge complex, in scenarios exceeding 4.9213 ft of eustatic SLR, considerable stretches of low-lying coastal rocky shelf are predicted to erode. All of these predictions are estimated 50-100 years in the future, well beyond the scope of this CCP.

There is always uncertainty about how regularly flooded marsh will respond to the signal of increased SLR. The most important effects of SLR at the Pearl Harbor NWR are the gradual inundation and flooding of the wetlands and dryland areas, as well as increases in the salinity of wetlands. Salinity alterations have the potential to shift aquatic plants and animal communities that do not tolerate high salinity. Higher sea levels may inundate these low-lying land areas, decreasing habitat for both marine and terrestrial species. For example, waterbird habitat and nesting sites could be reduced as a result of coastal inundation. Flooding at the coastal or estuarine wetlands will facilitate more fish introductions from the ocean, thereby shifting invertebrate communities that provide forage for other organisms. The University of Hawai'i has developed maps of possible changes in O'ahu shoreline depending on various sea level scenarios (Figure 6.1).

6.5.4 Climate Change Effects on Water Resources

The impact of climate change on water resources is dependent on shifts in precipitation amounts, evaporation rates, storms, and events such as the El Niño Southern Oscillation (ENSO). ENSO is an ocean-atmosphere phenomenon in which the normal oceanic and atmospheric circulation patterns of

Figure 6.1 Effect of sea level rise of selected elevations on the Island of Oʻahu.

Source: Hawaiʻi Mapping Research Group, University of Hawaiʻi

the Pacific Ocean temporarily collapse. During normal years, strong trade winds move counterclockwise in the southern hemisphere and clockwise in the northern hemisphere, causing surface water to move westward. These winds also produce upwelling that brings high nutrient waters to the surface. During ENSO, trade winds in the western Pacific stop and the warm mass of water in the west moves eastward, causing shifts in the location of evaporation. As a result, heavy rains occur in normally dry areas such as the central Pacific islands. In addition to more precipitation, these winds upwell warm water, which is devoid of nutrients. This causes productive communities to collapse and subsequent death of fish and birds.

While ENSO events have increased in intensity and frequency over the past decades, some longer-term records have not found a direct link to global warming (Cobb et al. 2003) and do not predict significant changes in ENSO; however, a majority of climate forecasts do suggest an evolution toward more "El Niño-like" patterns (Buddemeier et al. 2004). Most climate projections reveal that this trend is likely to increase rapidly in the next 50 years (Walther et al. 2002). However, other models predict more "La Niña-like" conditions in the Hawaiian Islands (Timm 2008).

A trend toward ENSO patterns will impact sea levels, sea temperatures, rainfall amounts, evaporation rates, and the occurrence of hurricanes; however, the exact impact of climate change on water resources is difficult to predict due to spatial variability. On a global scale, mean precipitation is anticipated to increase. Current climate models project that tropical Pacific and high latitude areas will experience increasing precipitation amounts, while precipitation is likely to decrease in most subtropical regions (Solomon et al. 2007, Parry et al. 2007). A current trend toward this increase is supported by lowered salinity levels in both the mid- and high-latitude oceanic waters (Solomon et al. 2007). If the opposite effect takes place, decreasing precipitation or increasing evaporation will further stress meager surface and groundwater resources. Lack of rain could lower the amount of freshwater lens recharge and decrease available water supplies. Reduced rainfall or increased evaporation will cause a corresponding increase in the demand for residential, commercial, or agricultural water (Giambelluca et al. 1996).

Most climate projections suggest that more intense wind speeds and precipitation amounts will accompany more frequent tropical typhoons/cyclones and increased tropical sea surface temperatures in the next 50 years (Walther et al. 2002, Solomon et al. 2007). The Third Assessment of the IPCC (2001) has concluded with "moderate confidence" that the intensity of tropical cyclones is likely to increase by 10-20 percent in the Pacific region when atmospheric levels of CO_2 reach double pre-industrial levels (McCarthy et al. 2001). One model projects a doubling of the frequency of 4 in per day rainfall events and a 15-18% percent increase in rainfall intensity over large areas of the Pacific (IPCC 2001). Solomon et al. (2007) states that it is "more likely than not" that the rise in intense tropical cyclones is due to anthropogenic activity.

An increase in heavy storms and surf will result in increased flood risks, sedimentation, and impeded drainage in Hawai'i (DBEDT and DOH 1999). In particular, the low-elevation refuge units will be vulnerable to changes in storm frequency, intensity, and directionality. These events have the potential to denude vegetation or affect the biogeochemistry of the wetlands.

6.5.5 Ecological Responses to Climate Change

Evidence suggests that recent climatic changes have affected a broad range of individual species and populations in both the marine and terrestrial environment. Organisms have responded by changes in (1) phenology (timing of seasonal activities) and physiology; (2) range and distribution; (3) community composition and interaction; and (4) ecosystem structure and dynamics (Walther et al. 2002). The reproductive physiology and population dynamics of amphibians and reptiles are highly influenced by environmental conditions such as temperature and humidity. For example, sea turtle sex is determined by the temperature of the nest environment; thus, higher temperatures could result in a higher female to male ratio (Baker et al. 2006). In addition, increases in atmospheric temperatures during seabird nesting seasons will also have an effect on seabirds and water birds (Duffy 1993).

Changes in ocean temperature, circulation, and storm surge due to climate change will impact seabird breeding and foraging. ENSO has been shown to cause seabirds to abandon habitats, nest sites, and foraging areas for colder/warmer waters (Duffy 1993). Studies have found that nesting success is reduced for some species during this climatic event. Oceanographic changes associated with ENSO may also increase or decrease food supply for seabirds and subsequently impact populations that forage offshore. Shifts in marine temperature, salinity, turbidity, currents, depth, and nutrients will have an impact on seabird and water bird prey composition and availability. Although these potential changes may impact seabirds throughout the Hawaiian Island, contrary evidence suggests that seabirds may have coped with and evolved around climatic changes in the past (Duffy 1993). Warming has also caused species to shift toward the poles or higher altitudes and changes in climatic conditions can alter community composition. For example, increases in nitrogen availability can favor those plant species that respond to nitrogen rises (Vitousek 1994). Similarly, increases in CO_2 levels can impact plant photosynthetic rates, decrease nutrient levels, and lower herbivore weights (Ehleringer et al. 2002). Although there is uncertainty regarding these trajectories, it is probable that there will be ecological consequences (Walther et al. 2002).

Climate change has the potential to influence two important ecological issues in the State of Hawai'i: endangered species and invasive species. An overwhelming majority of U.S. endangered species are found in the State of Hawai'i. Species declines have resulted from habitat loss, introduced diseases, and impacts from invasive species. Changes in climate will add an additional threat to the survival of these species (DBEDT and DOH 1998). For example, warmer night temperatures can increase the rate of respiration for native vegetation, resulting in greater competition from nonnative plants (Giambelluca 2008). Furthermore, climate change may enhance existing invasive species issues because alterations in the environment may increase the dispersal ability of flora or fauna. Species response to climate change will depend on the life-history, distribution, dispersal ability, and reproduction requirements of the species (Middleton 2006).

The Service is supporting the development of regional Landscape Conservation Cooperatives that will integrate local climate models with models of climate-change responses by species, habitats, and ecosystems. Cooperatives will collectively plan and design appropriate conservation actions at a landscape scale, monitor responses to climate change, and assess the effectiveness of management strategies. The regional version of these Landscape Conservation Cooperatives is the Pacific Islands Climate Change Cooperative, headquartered in Honolulu, Hawai'i, but working across the Pacific.

Appendices

Appendix A: Species Lists

Common Name	Scientific name	Hawaiian Name
Mammals		
Dog	*Canis familiaris*	ʻīlio
Cat	*Felis catus*	pōpoki
Indian mongoose	*Herpestes auropunctatus*	manakuke
House mouse	*Mus musculus*	ʻiole
Polynesian rat	*Rattus exulans*	ʻiole
Norway rat	*Rattus norvegicus*	ʻiole
Black rat	*Rattus rattus*	ʻiole
Fish		
Milkfish	*Chanos chanos*	awa
Cuban molly	*Limia vittata*	
Engel's mullet	*Moolgarda engeli*	
Mullet	*Mugil cephalus*	ʻamaʻama
Acute-jawed mullet	*Neomyxus leuciscus*	
Sailfin molly	*Poecilia latipinna*	
Shortfin molly	*Poecilia mexicana*	
Gracile lizardfish	*Saurida gracilis*	
Black chin tilapia	*Sarotherodon melanotheron*	
Invertebrates, marine		
Asian clam	*Corbicula fluminea*	
Anchialine snapping shrimp	*Metabetaeus lohena*	
Hawaiian red shrimp	*Halocaradiana rubra*	ʻōpae-ʻula
Feeble shrimp	*Palaemon debilis*	ʻōpae huna
Limpet	*Pyrgophorus coronatus*	ʻopihi
Mud crab	*Scylla serreta*	
Crenate swimming crab	*Thalamita crenata*	
	Thalamita edwardsi	
Invertebrates, terrestrial		
Waterstrider	*Halobates hawaiiensis*	
Cane spider	*Heteropoda venatoria*	
Rambur's forktail damselfly	*Ischnura ramburii*	
Orange-black Hawaiian damselfly	*Megalagrion xanthomelas*	pinapinao
Lesser brown scorpion	*Isometrus maculatus*	kopiana
Centipede	*Scolopendra subspinipes*	kanapī
Reptiles and Amphibians		
Cane toad	*Bufo marinua*	poloka
Common house gecko	*Hemidactylus frenatus*	moʻo ʻalā
Red-eared slider	*Trachemys scripta elegans*	

Common Name	Scientific Name	Hawaiian Name
Migratory Shorebirds		
Plovers & Dotterels		
Black-bellied Plover	*Pluvialis squatarola*	
Pacific Golden-Plover	*Pluvialis fulva*	kōlea
Semipalmated Plover	*Charadrius semipalmatus*	
Killdeer	*Charadrius vociferus*	
Avocets & Stilts		
Hawaiian Stilt	*Himantopus mexicanus knudseni*	aeʻo
Sandpipers & Phalaropes		
Greater Yellowlegs	*Tringa melanoleuca*	
Lesser Yellowlegs	*Tringa flavipes*	
Wandering Tattler	*Heteorscelus incanus*	ʻūlilī
Spotted Sandpiper	*Actitis maclaria*	
Black-tailed Godwit	*Limosa limosa*	
Bar-tailed Godwit	*Limosa lapponica*	
Ruddy Turnstone	*Arenaria interpres*	ʻakekeke
Red Knot	*Calidris canutus*	
Sanderling	*Calidris alba*	hunakai
Semipalmated Sandpiper	*Calidris pusilla*	
Western Sandpiper	*Calidris mauri*	
Least Sandpiper	*Calidris minutilla*	
Pectoral Sandpiper	*Calidris melanotos*	
Sharp-tailed Sandpiper	*Calidris acuminata*	
Solitary Sandpiper	*Tringa solitaria*	
Marsh Sandpiper	*Tringa stagnatilis*	
Dunlin	*Calidris alpina*	
Stilt Sandpiper	*Calidris himantopus*	
Ruff	*Philomachus pugnax*	
Short-billed Dowitcher	*Limnodromus griseus*	
Long-billed Dowitcher	*Limnodromus scolopaceus*	
Common Snipe	*Gallinago gallinago*	
Wilson's Phalarope	*Phalaropus tricolor*	
Seabirds & Gulls		
Great frigatebird	*Fregata minor*	ʻiwa
Laughing gull	*Leucophaeus atricilla*	
Bonaparte's gull	*Chroicocephalus philadelphia*	
Ring-billed gull	*Larus delawarensis*	
Herring gull	*Larus argentatus*	

Common Name	Scientific Name	Hawaiian Name
Herons & Ibises		
Great blue heron	*Ardea herodias*	
Snowy egret	*Egretta thula*	
Cattle egret	*Bubulcus ibis*	
Black-crowned night-heron	*Nycticorax nycticorax*	'auku'u
White-faced ibis	*Plegadis chihi*	
Geese & Ducks		
Greater white-fronted goose	*Anser albifrons*	
Black brant	*Branta bernicla*	
Cackling goose	*Branta hutchinsii*	
Canada goose	*Branta canadensis*	
Gadwall	*Anas strepera*	
Eurasian widgeon	*Anas penelope*	
American widgeon	*Anas americana*	
Mallard	*Anas platyrhynchos*	
Hawaiian duck	*Anas wyvilliana*	Koloa maoli
Blue-winged teal	*Anas discors*	
Northern shoveler	*Anas clypeata*	Koloa mohā
Northern pintail	*Anas acuta*	Koloa māpu
Garganey	*Anas querquedula*	
Green-winged teal	*Anas carolinensis*	
Canvasback	*Aythya valisineria*	
Ring-necked duck	*Aythya collaris*	
Tufted duck	*Aythya fuligula*	
Greater scaup	*Aythya marila*	
Lesser scaup	*Aythya affinis*	
Bufflehead	*Bucephala albeola*	
Diurnal Raptors		
Osprey	*Pandion haliaetus*	
Northern harrier	*Circus cyaneus*	
Peregrine falcon	*Falco peregrinus*	
Upland Game Birds		
Gray francolin	*Francolinus pondicerianus*	
Erckel's francolin	*Francolinus erckelii*	
Ring-necked pheasant	*Phasianus colchicus*	
Gallinules & Coots		
Hawaiian moorhen	*Gallinula chloropus sandvicensis*	'alae 'ula
Hawaiian coot	*Fulica alai*	'alae ke'oke'o
Pigeons & Doves		
Rock pigeon	*Columba livia*	
Spotted dove	*Streptopelia chinensis*	
Zebra dove	*Geopelia striata*	
Mourning dove	*Zenaida macroura*	

Common Name	Scientific Name	Hawaiian Name
Parrots		
Red-crowned Amazon	*Amazona viridigenalis*	
Yellow-headed parrot	*Amazona oratrix*	
Sulphur-crested cockatiel	*Cacatua galerita*	
Owls		
Barn owl	*Tyto alba*	
Hawaiian Short-eared Owl	*Asio flammeus sandwichensis*	pueo
Bulbuls		
Red-vented bulbul	*Pycnonotus cafer*	
Bush-Warblers		
Japanese bush-warbler	*Cettia diphone*	
White-rumped shama	*Copsychus malabaricus*	
Mynas		
Common myna	*Acridotheres tristis*	
White-Eyes		
Japanese white-eye	*Zosterops japonicus*	
Cardinals		
Northern cardinal	*Cardinalis cardinalis*	
Red-crested cardinal	*Paroaria coronata*	
Finches		
Saffron finch	*Sicalis flaveola*	
House finch	*Carpodacus mexicanus*	
Sparrows		
House sparrow	*Passer domesticus*	
Java sparrow	*Padda oryzivora*	
Waxbills & Mannikins		
Common waxbill	*Estrilda astrild*	
Red avadavat	*Amandava amandava*	
Nutmeg mannikin	*Lonchura punctulata*	
Chestnut munia	*Lonchura atricapilla*	

Native Plant Species			
Scientific Name	**Common Name**	**Origin**	**Hawaiian Name**
Aizoaceae			
Sesuvium portulacastrum	sea purslane	Ind.	'ākulikuli
Amaranthaceae			
Achyranthes splendens var. *splendens*	round-leafed chaff-flower	End.	'Ewa hinahina
Boraginaceae			
Heliotropium anomalum var. *argenterum*	hinahina	Ind.	hinahina
Heliotropium curassavicum	seaside heliotrope	Ind.	
Chenopodiaceae			
Chenopodium oahuense	'āheahea	End.	'āheahea
Capparaceae			
Capparis sandwichiana	pilo	End.	maiapilo
Convolvulaceae			
Ipomoea imperati	beach morning glory	Ind.	hunakai
Ipomoea indica	koali'awa	Ind.	koali'awa
Ipomoea pes-carprae	beach morning glory	Ind.	pōhuehue
Jaquemontia ovalifolia	oval-leafed clustervine	Ind.	pā'ūohi'iaka
Cucurbitaceae			
Sicyos sp.	'ānunu	End.	'ānunu
Cuscutaceae			
Cuscuta sandwichiana	kauna'oa	End.	kauna'oa
Cyperaceae			
Bolboschoenus maritimus	kaluhā	Ind.	kaluhā
Mariscus javanicus	marsh cyprus	Ind.	'ahu'awa
Euphorbiaceae			
Chamaesyce skottsbergii var. *skottsbergii*	'Ewa plains 'akoko	End.	'akoko
Fabaceae			
Erythrina sandwicensis	Hawaiian coral tree	End.	wiliwili
Malvaceae			
Abutilon menziesii	red' ilima	End.	ko'oloa'ula
Gossypium tomentosum	Hawaiian cotton	End.	mao
Sida fallax	yellow 'ilima	Ind.	'ilima
Thespesia populnea	Milo	Ind.	milo
Menispermaceae			
Cocculus trilobus	huehue	Ind.	huehue
Myoporaceae			
Myoporum sandwicense	bastard sandalwood	Ind.	naio
Nyctaginaceae			
Boerhavia repens	alena	Ind.	alena
Plumbaginaceae			
Plumbago zeylandica	'ilie'e	Ind.	'ilie'e
Poaceae			
Sporobolus virginicus	beach dropseed	Ind.	'aki'aki
Morinda trimera	noni kuahiwi	End.	noni kuahiwi
Santalaceae			

Scientific Name	Common Name	Origin	Hawaiian Name
Santalum ellipticum	coastal sandalwood	End.	ʻiliahialoʻe
Scrophulariaceae			
Bacopa monnieri	water hyssop	Ind.	ʻaeʻae
Solanaceae			
Lycium sandwicense	Hawaiian desert-thorn	Ind.	ʻohelo kai
Solanum americanum	popolo	Ind.	popolo
Sterculiaceae			
Waltheria indica	ʻuhaloa	Ind.	ʻuhaloa
Verbanaceae			
Vitex rotundifolia	beach vitex	Ind.	pōhinahina
Scaevola taccada	beach naupaka	Ind.	naupaka kahakai

* The taxonomy and nomenclature of the plants are in accordance with Wagner et al. (1999).

Nonnative plants		
Scientific Name	**Common Name**	**Hawaiian Name**
Alternanthera pungens	khaki weed	none
Amaranthus spinosus	spiny amaranth	pakai kukū
Asystasia gangetica	Chinese violet	none
Atriplex semibacatta	Australian saltbush	none
Batis maritima	saltwort, pickleweed	ʻākulikuli kai
Blutaparon vermiculare	silverhead	none
Brachiaria mutica	California grass	none
Cenchrus ciliaris	buffelgrass	none
Cordia subcordata	none	kou
Casuarina equisetifolia	ironwood	none
Cordyline fruticosa	ti	kī
Cynodon spp.	Bermuda grass	none
Cyperus sp.	sedge	none
Cyperus javanicus	Javanese flatsedge	ʻahuʻawa
Cyperus laevigatus	none	makaloa
Cyperus polystayscos	flatsedge	none
Echinochloa sp.	wild millet, millet	none
Eleocharis geniculata	spikerush, bent spikerush	none
Eragrostis sp.	lovegrass	varies by species
Fimbristylis cymosa	button sedge	mauʻu ʻakiʻaki
Fimbristylis milliacea	grass-like fimbry	none
Fimbristylis ferruginea	West Indian fimbry	none
Fimbristylis dichotoma	forked fimbry	none
Leptochloa sp.	sprangletop	none
Leucana leucocephala	none	koa haole
Panicum maximum	Guinea grass	none
Paspalum disticum	knot-grass	none
Pluchea x *fosbergii*	marsh fleabane	none
Pluchea indica	marsh fleabane	none
Pluchea carolinensis	marsh fleabane	none
Pritchardia remota*	none	loulu

Scientific Name	Common Name	Hawaiian Name
Prosopis pallida	mesquite	kiawe
Schinus terebinthifolius	Christmas berry	none
Scirpus californicus	California bulrush	none
*Sesbania tomentosa**	none	'ohai
Tournefortia argentea	tree heliotrope	none
Typha sp.	cattail	none

*Although these are native Hawaiian species (as well as endangered), they were introduced on the Refuge and are not naturally occurring species.

Appendix B. Compatibility and Appropriate Use Determinations

B.1 Introduction

The compatibility determinations (CDs) developed during the CCP planning process evaluate uses projected to occur under Alternative B, the Preferred Alternative in the Draft EA for the Pearl Harbor National Wildlife Refuge CCP/EA. The evaluation of funds needed for management and implementation of each use also assumes implementation as described under Alternative B, the Preferred Alternative. Chapter 6 of the Draft CCP/EA also contains analysis of the impacts of public uses to wildlife and habitats. That portion of the document is incorporated through reference into this set of CDs.

B.1.1 Uses Evaluated At This Time

The following section includes full CDs for all Refuge uses that are required to be evaluated at this time. According to Service policy, compatibility determinations will be completed for all uses proposed under a CCP that have been determined to be appropriate. Existing wildlife-dependent recreational uses must also be reevaluated and new CDs prepared during development of a CCP. According to the Service's compatibility policy, uses other than wildlife-dependent recreational uses are not explicitly required to be reevaluated in concert with preparation of a CCP, unless conditions of the use have changed or unless significant new information relative to the use and its effects have become available or the existing CDs are more than 10 years old. However, the Service planning policy recommends preparing CDs for all individual uses, specific use programs, or groups of related uses associated with the proposed action. Accordingly, the following CDs are included in this document for public review.

Table B-1. Summary of Compatible Use Determinations.

Refuge Use	Page	CD#	Compatible?	Year Due for Reevaluation
Wildlife Observation, Photography, Interpretation	B-5	1	yes	2025
Environmental Education	B-11	2	yes	2025
Research	B-16	3	yes	2020

B.1.2 Compatibility – Legal and Historical Context

Compatibility is a tool refuge managers use to ensure that recreational and other uses do not interfere with wildlife conservation, the primary focus of refuges. Compatibility is not new to the Refuge System and dates back to 1918, as a concept. As policy, it has been used since 1962. The Refuge Recreation Act of 1962 directed the Secretary of the Interior to allow only those public uses of Refuge lands that were "compatible with the primary purposes for which the area was established."

Legally, Refuges are closed to all public uses until officially opened through a compatibility determination. Regulations require that adequate funds be available for administration and protection of refuges before opening them to any public uses. However, wildlife-dependent recreational uses (hunting, fishing, wildlife observation and photography, environmental education, and interpretation) are to receive enhanced consideration and cannot be rejected simply for lack of funding resources unless the refuge has made a concerted effort to seek out funds from all potential partners. Once found compatible, wildlife-dependent recreational uses are deemed the priority public uses at the refuge. If a proposed use is found not compatible, the refuge manager is legally precluded from approving it. Economic uses that are conducted by or authorized by the refuge also require compatibility determinations.

Under compatibility policy, uses are defined as recreational, economic/commercial, or management use of a refuge by the public or a non-Refuge System entity. Uses generally providing an economic return (even if conducted for the purposes of habitat management) are also subject to compatibility determinations. The Service does not prepare compatibility determinations for uses when the Service does not have jurisdiction. For example, the Service may have limited jurisdiction over Refuge areas where property rights are vested by others; where legally binding agreements exist; or where there are treaty rights held by tribes. In addition, aircraft overflights, emergency actions, some activities on navigable waters, and activities by other Federal agencies on "overlay Refuges" are exempt from the compatibility review process.

New compatibility regulations, required by the National Wildlife Refuge System Improvement Act of 1997 (Improvement Act), were adopted by the Service in October 2000. The regulations require that a use must be compatible with both the mission of the System and the purposes of the individual Refuge. This standard helps to ensure consistency in application across the Refuge System. The Improvement Act also requires that compatibility determinations be in writing and that the public have an opportunity to comment on most use evaluations.

The Refuge System mission emphasizes that the needs of fish, wildlife, and plants must be of primary consideration. The Improvement Act defined a compatible use as one that ". . . in the sound professional judgment of the Director, will not materially interfere with or detract from the fulfillment of the mission of the System or the purposes of the Refuge." Sound professional judgment is defined under the Improvement Act as ". . . a finding, determination, or decision, that is consistent with principles of sound fish and wildlife management and administration, available science and resources . . ." Compatibility for priority wildlife-dependent uses may depend on the level or extent of a use.

Court interpretations of the compatibility standard have found that compatibility is a biological standard and cannot be used to balance or weigh economic, political, or recreational interests against the primary purpose of the refuge (Defenders of Wildlife v. Andrus [Ruby Lake Refuge]).

The Service recognizes that compatibility determinations are complex. For this reason, refuge managers are required to consider "principles of sound fish and wildlife management" and "best available science" in making these determinations (House of Representatives Report 105-106). Evaluations of the existing uses on the Pearl Harbor National Wildlife Refuge are based on the professional judgment of Refuge and planning personnel including observations of Refuge uses and reviews of appropriate scientific literature.

B.1.3 Appropriate Use Determinations

The Appropriate Refuge Uses Policy outlines the process that the Service uses to determine when general public uses on refuges may be considered. Priority public uses previously defined as wildlife-dependent uses (hunting, fishing, wildlife observation and photography and environmental education and interpretation) under the National Wildlife Refuge System Improvement Act of 1997 are generally exempt from appropriate use review. Other exempt uses include situations where the Service does not have adequate jurisdiction to control the activity and refuge management activities. In essence, the appropriate use policy, 603 FW 1 (2006), provides refuge managers with a consistent procedure to first screen and then document decisions concerning a public use. When a use is determined to be appropriate, a refuge manager must then decide if the use is compatible before allowing it on a refuge. The policy also requires review of existing public uses. During the CCP process, the Refuge Manager evaluated all existing and proposed Refuge uses at Pearl Harbor NWR using the following guidelines and criteria as outlined in the appropriate use policy:

- Do we have jurisdiction over the use?
- Does the use comply with applicable laws and regulations (Federal, State, tribal and local)?
- Is the use consistent with applicable Executive orders and Department and Service policies?
- Is the use consistent with public safety?
- Is the use consistent with goals and objectives in an approved management plan or other document?
- Has an earlier documented analysis not denied the use or is this the first the use has been proposed?
- Is the use manageable within available budget and staff?
- Will this be manageable in the future within existing resources?
- Does the use contribute to the public's understanding and appreciation of the refuge's natural or cultural resources, or is the use beneficial to the refuge's natural or cultural resources?
- Can the use be accommodated without impairing existing wildlife-dependent recreational uses or reducing the potential to provide quality, compatible, wildlife dependent recreation into the future?

Using this process and these criteria, and as documented on the following pages, the Refuge Manager determined the following additional use is appropriate, and directed that a compatibility determinations be completed for this use: research, scientific collecting, and surveys (B-23, Attachment 1).

B.1.4 References

Defenders of Wildlife v. Andrus (Ruby Lake Refuge I). 11 Envtl. Rptr. Case 2098 (D.D.C. 1978), p. 873.

House of Representatives Report 105-106 (on NWRSIA) - http://refuges.fws.gov/policyMakers/mandates/HR1420/part1.html

Compatibility regulations, adopted by the Service in October 2000: http://Refuges.fws.gov/policymakers/nwrpolicies.html

---

B.2 Compatibility Determination for Wildlife Observation, Photography, and Interpretation

Refuge Name(s):   Pearl Harbor National Wildlife Refuge
(includes Waiawa, Honouliuli, and Kalaeloa Units)

County and State: Honolulu County, Hawai'i

Establishing and Acquisition Authority(ies):

Pearl Harbor NWR was established in 1972 under the authority of the:
- Fish and Wildlife Coordination Act of 1956, as amended (16 U.S.C. 742a – 742j)
- Endangered Species Act of 1973, as amended (16 U.S.C. 1531-1544)
- Additionally for the Kalaeloa Unit (2001): Defense Base Realignment and Closure Act of 1990, as amended (Pub. Law 101-501)

Refuge Purpose(s):

"...to Conserve (A) fish or wildlife which are listed as endangered species or threatened species ... or (B) plants..." 16 U.S.C. 1534 (Endangered Species Act of 1973, as amended)

National Wildlife Refuge System Mission:

"The mission of the National Wildlife Refuge System is to administer a national network of lands and waters for the conservation, management, and where appropriate, restoration of the fish, wildlife, and plant resources and their habitats within the United States for the benefit of present and future generations of Americans" (National Wildlife Refuge System Administration Act of 1966, as amended (16 U.S.C. 668dd-668ee).

Description of Use(s):

Wildlife observation, photography, and interpretation are considered together in this Compatibility Determination (CD) because all are considered to be wildlife-dependent, nonconsumptive uses and many elements of these programs are similar. Currently, all three units of the Pearl Harbor National Wildlife Refuge are closed to the public and entry is only by Special Use Permit for environmental education programs or volunteer projects, including invasive species control, native plant restoration, and wildlife surveys. The closures are due to a combination of reasons including the overriding need to protect sensitive resources (i.e., endangered species) on these very small units, safety considerations, lack of suitable legal public access, and lack of adequate Refuge resources (staff and funding) to administer the uses. The Refuge occasionally receives requests for access to the Waiawa or Honouliuli Units for photography purposes; however, due to the extremely small size of these units which increases the likelihood of disturbance to endangered water birds and other wildlife, these requests are not granted. New, but still limited, wildlife photography opportunities will be provided by the Betty Bliss Memorial Overlook at Honouliuli (see below). Also, in the future, additional viewing and photography opportunities will be offered at the James Campbell NWR where the larger size of the Refuge will allow more options for the development of safe, accessible

---

facilities, while also reducing the levels of disturbance to important concentrations of endangered water birds and other migratory birds.

A new Refuge overlook, called the Betty Bliss Memorial Overlook, will be constructed on the Honouliuli Unit. This overlook will be constructed as a spur off of the adjacent Pearl Harbor Historic Recreation Trail (bikes and pedestrians) and will provide important new first-time, but still limited, public opportunities for wildlife observation, photography, and interpretation on the Refuge. The overlook will be constructed on the northwest corner of the unit, just outside of the existing chain link fence that surrounds the wetland impoundment. In conjunction with bike-trail, the overlook will be open year-round during daylight hours only. Access to the overlook will be open to bike-trail users. No additional access (parking or roads) to serve the overlook is being proposed by the Service.

The Service will evaluate the potential for construction of an additional overlook on the Waiawa Unit.

On the Kalaeloa Unit, existing interpretive panels that describe the natural and cultural history, as well as current management issues and programs, will continue to enhance the Refuge experience for volunteers, students, and the visiting public on guided tours. Under a recently funded environmental education program, local college students under the guidance of Service staff will develop an interpretive trail and materials for the unit. The trail and materials will be used by students for environmental education purposes and by the public on small limited guided tours of the Refuge. Incidental opportunities for wildlife observation and photography will increase proportionally to the increase in environmental education programs and limited guided public tours on that unit.

The limited guided use of the Kalaeloa foot trail will have negligible negative impacts on the Refuge due to the relatively small number of visitors and foot travel, which will be restricted to a designated trail system. The Unit does not have sensitive wildlife species, such as native birds, that would be disturbed by this limited use. This trail system will protect endangered and native plants from trampling and the anchialine pools from surface and soil disturbance in the immediate vicinity of the pools.

Availability of Resources:

Category and Itemization	One-time ($000)	Annual ($000/yr)
Administration and management:	$20,000	$12,000
Maintenance:	$10,000	$3,000
Monitoring costs:	$0	$500
Special equipment, facilities, or improvements:	$45,000*	$0
Offsetting revenues:	$0	$0

*Service/Refuge cost

The Betty Bliss Memorial Overlook is being designed and constructed in partnership with the Hawai'i Department of Transportation (HDOT). Under a Memorandum of Agreement with HDOT the overlook will be constructed in conjunction with improvements being made to Pearl Harbor Historic Trail (Leeward Bike Path) by HDOT. Under the Federal Highway Administration's former

Transportation Enhancement Program, $330,000 has previously been secured that will be used for construction of this overlook.

If the proposed use is a wildlife-dependent public use, what efforts have been made to secure adequate resources to support it?

Once constructed, the new overlook(s) will be entered into the Service Asset Maintenance Management System database to request funding for reoccurring cyclic maintenance needs.

Anticipated Impacts of the Use(s):

Slight short-term impacts would result from the construction of the Betty Bliss Memorial Overlook structure, including removal of adjacent nonnative mangrove. During construction, temporary disturbance to wildlife would occur in the immediate vicinity of the project from noise and movement related to construction activities, operation of equipment, use of tools, etc. A slight, localized impact to water quality (primarily turbidity) would result from removal of +/- 1 acre of the mangrove from disturbance of sediments. Currently, the proposed 0.25-acre site of the overlook is dominated by nonnative invasive vegetation including mangrove, kiawe, and pickleweed. Subsequent management of the site will include restoration by outplanting native vegetation.

Due to a number of design and site considerations, the overlook will be located at the extreme northwest corner of the Honouliuli Unit. While this location will provide new opportunities for these activities, it is located at a sufficient distance to minimize significant disturbance to wetland birds and other wildlife. In particular, the site is located adjacent to a portion of the unit that is rarely used by the highly sensitive ae'o for nesting. Due to the small size and location at one corner of the Refuge, the overlook is not expected to contribute to any adverse long term cumulative impacts to the Refuge. As a feature along the bike trail, the overlook is expected to enhance the trail-user experience in the vicinity of the Refuge and West Loch of Pearl Harbor.

Public Review and Comment:

The period of public review began _____ and ended _____.

The following methods were used to solicit public review and comment:

Public review and comments were solicited in conjunction with release of the draft Pearl Harbor National Wildlife Refuge CCP/ EA (2010) in order to comply with the National Environmental Policy Act and Service policy.

Why was this level of public review and comment selected?

CD was released as integral part of the CCP and received the same level of public review and comments as the CCP, in accordance with Service planning policy.

Summarize comments received and any actions taken or not taken because of comments received.

Determination: (check one below)

___ **Use is Not Compatible**

_X_ **Use is Compatible With Following Stipulations**

Stipulations Necessary to Ensure Compatibility:

Public use of the Betty Bliss Memorial Overlook at the Honouliuli Unit and a Waiawa Overlook, if constructed, will be restricted to daylight hours only, which will be in accordance with the daytime only use of the adjacent bike path. The Refuge is closed at night. This regulation will improve visitor safety and eliminate potential wildlife disturbance at night.

Design of the overlook will incorporate features and materials that provide partial screening of visitors to reduce/minimize visual disturbance of wildlife.

Adequate law enforcement will be provided to enforce Refuge regulations, reduce threat of vandalism, and ensure visitor safety.

Construction crew will erect a visual screen on fence during construction to reduce visual disturbance to wildlife.

Major construction activities will be scheduled outside of peak ae'o nesting season (April – July) to reduce disturbance. Note: Very little nesting habitat and nesting activity occur in close proximity to either the planned Honouliuli Unit or potential Waiawa Unit overlook sites.

On the Kalaeloa Unit, all scheduled public tours will be:
- led by Refuge staff or trained docents to ensure safety of visitors and protection of sensitive resources (endangered plants and anchialine pools).
- limited in number of participants to <20/ tour due to severely limited access, parking, and to enhance the quality of the visitor experience.

Justification:

These wildlife-dependent uses are compatible priority public uses of the National Wildlife Refuge System. Although very limited in scope by necessity due to the size and nature of the Refuge, providing new opportunities for wildlife observation, photography, and interpretation as described in this CD would contribute toward fulfilling provisions of the National Wildlife Refuge System Administration Act, as amended, and one of the goals of the Pearl Harbor National Wildlife Refuge. Even limited opportunities for wildlife observation, photography, and interpretation, as occur on Pearl Harbor National Wildlife Refuge, are important to increasing public understanding and support of the Refuge, the Refuge System and natural resource issues. Therefore, the benefits provided by these opportunities would outweigh anticipated impacts associated with implementation of this small-scale program. The stipulations outlined above will minimize potential impacts relative to wildlife /human interactions.

If the proposed use is an economic use of Refuge natural resources (50 CFR 29.1), how would it contribute to the purposes of the Refuge or the mission of the National Wildlife Refuge System? No economic uses considered or allowed under this CD.

Mandatory Reevaluation Date: (provide month and year for "allowed" uses only)

_____X_____ Mandatory 15-year reevaluation date (for wildlife-dependent public uses)

_____ Mandatory 10-year reevaluation date (for all uses other than wildlife-dependent public uses)

NEPA Compliance for Refuge Use Decision: (check one below)

____ Categorical Exclusion without Environmental Action Statement

____ Categorical Exclusion and Environmental Action Statement

_X_ Environmental Assessment and Finding of No Significant Impact

____ Environmental Impact Statement and Record of Decision

Refuge Determination:

Project Leader,
Pearl Harbor National Wildlife Refuge

_____   _____
(Signature)   (Date)

Project Leader,
Hawaiian and Pacific Islands NWRC

_____   _____
(Signature)   (Date)

Concurrence:

Refuge Supervisor
Pacific Region, National Wildlife Refuge System

_____   _____
(Signature)   (Date)

Regional Chief,
National Wildlife Refuge System:

_____   _____
(Signature)   (Date)

B.3   Compatibility Determination for Environmental Education

Refuge Name(s):   **Pearl Harbor National Wildlife Refuge**
(includes Waiawa, Honouliuli, and Kalaeloa Units)

County and State: Honolulu County, Hawai'i

Establishing and Acquisition Authority(ies):

Legal authorities used for establishment of the Refuge (all units) include:

Pearl Harbor NWR was established in 1972 under the authority of the:
- Fish and Wildlife Coordination Act of 1956, as amended (16 U.S.C. 742a – 742j)
- Endangered Species Act of 1973, as amended (16 U.S.C. 1531-1544)
- Additionally for the Kalaeloa Unit (2001); Defense Base Realignment and Closure Act of 1990, as amended (Pub. Law 101-501)

Refuge Purpose(s):

"...to Conserve (A) fish or wildlife which are listed as endangered species or threatened species ... or (B) plants..." 16 U.S.C. 1534 (Endangered Species Act of 1973)

National Wildlife Refuge System Mission:

"The mission of the National Wildlife Refuge System is to administer a national network of lands and waters for the conservation, management, and where appropriate, restoration of the fish, wildlife, and plant resources and their habitats within the United States for the benefit of present and future generations of Americans" (National Wildlife Refuge System Administration Act of 1966, as amended [16 U.S.C. 668dd-668ee]).

Description of Use(s):

Environmental education (EE) is defined as a wildlife-dependent recreational use under the Refuge Improvement Act. Environmental education consists of educational activities conducted by Refuge staff, volunteers, partners and teachers. Currently, the environmental education program on the Refuge serves a range of 1,500 – 3,700 students annually on the Honouliuli and Kalaeloa Units combined. The Waiawa Unit remains closed to environmental education programs due primarily to lack of a safe, legal access.

1) On the Honouliuli Unit, a Special Use Permit (SUP) has been issued by the Refuge annually to the Hawaii Nature Center (HNC) since 1992. The HNC is a private, nonprofit organization that provides a variety of nature oriented programs to school groups of different ages throughout the year. The Honouliuli Unit is utilized under an SUP as an outdoor field classroom for third grade students as an important part of their wetland curriculum. Programs are conducted September through December and led entirely by HNC staff and teachers. Individual groups are limited in size to no more than 60 students. Based on varying levels of

school participation in the program each year, the annual total number of students may range from 1,500 – 3,500.

2) On the Kalaeloa Unit, current environmental education programs are conducted in conjunction with volunteer work, which is targeted at control of invasive weeds and restoration of native and endangered plants. From 150–200 people may participate in this program annually, which is conducted by volunteers authorized under a Special Use Permit. This is an ongoing year-round program.

3) Also on the Kalaeloa Unit, beginning in the summer of 2010, biologists from the USFWS Pacific Islands Fish and Wildlife Office working in partnership with the Refuge staff received start-up funding to develop and implement a new environmental education program entitled the "Kalaeloa Living Classroom Project". The project will recruit college level interns who under FWS guidance will in turn work with other college and high school students to develop volunteer projects. Projects will include invasive plant removal, native plant restoration, anchialine pool monitoring and development/implementation of a guided environmental education and interpretive trail. When fully developed the program is anticipated to provide environmental education based opportunities for 10-16 student interns and volunteers annually. The guided trail will provide environmental education opportunities to as many as 1,000 area high school students and 500 members of the public each year.

Availability of Resources:

Category and Itemization	One-time ($000)	Annual ($000/yr)
Administration and management:	$	$800
Maintenance:	$	$500
Monitoring costs:	$	$600
Special equipment, facilities, or improvements:	$	$
Offsetting revenues:	$	$

If the proposed use is a wildlife-dependent public use, what efforts have been made to secure adequate resources to support it?

Minimal costs of environmental education will be covered by Refuge visitor services funding.

Anticipated Impacts of the Use(s):

Most of the elements of the EE program already exist and have been in place for many years such as the Hawaii Nature Center Student program at the Honouliuli Unit and the volunteer run invasive species and native plant programs at Kalaeloa Unit. These programs have been conducted over the years in a manner to reduce/minimize adverse impacts to natural resources on the Refuge. These programs are designed and conducted at a level that has minimal and acceptable levels of impacts to Refuge resources in exchange for the benefits that are derived from environmental education activities. Even slight increases in these programs within their existing parameters would not result in additional significant or cumulative impacts. The proposed increase in EE activity at the Kalaeloa Unit through implementation of the "Living Classroom" program would have negligible negative impacts. All activities would occur along established trails or in the case of native plant restoration or invasive species removal under the direct supervision of FWS staff or trained volunteers. The

Kalaeloa Unit is a small isolated tract of land currently inaccessible to the public. Increases in the EE program would have substantial benefits in raising the awareness of local students and communities of the important natural resources on the Refuge and of the substantial ongoing effort to restore and manage these rare resources.

Public Review and Comment:

The period of public review began _____ and ended _____.

The following methods were used to solicit public review and comment:

Public review and comments were solicited in conjunction with release of the draft CCP/ EA (USFWS 2010) in order to comply with the National Environmental Policy Act and Service policy. Appendix _ contains a summary of the comments and Service responses.

Determination: (check one below)

___ Use is Not Compatible

_X_ Use is Compatible with Following Stipulations

Stipulations Necessary to Ensure Compatibility:

All access to the Refuge for environmental education activities not directly supervised by Service personnel are regulated by issuance of annual Special Use Permits (SUPs). The use of SUPs allows the Refuge Manager to continually adjust the activity to any significant new or changing conditions on the Refuge, as needed. However, the current programs are well established and such changes have been infrequent.

Honouliuli Unit
All EE activities are restricted to the time period of September 1st to January 31st. This use period eliminates the possibility of disturbance to highly sensitive ae‘o during their critical nesting and fledging season from April thru August.

A limit of up to 66 students per day (two classes) and accompanying adults is allowed. This number can be accommodated within the small area available on the Refuge for EE activities and represents the most practical and cost efficient numbers of students that can be transported to the Refuge (based on max. class size of 33 students).

During the permitted period (September 1 through January 31) use is restricted to the western edge of the Unit to limit disturbance to all wildlife. All EE activities must end by 2:00 p.m. each day (except teacher orientation programs).

To meet U.S. Navy safety requirements in the vicinity of West Loch, no permanent walled or enclosed structures, such as observation blinds, are allowed on portions of the Unit, including areas utilized for the EE program.

Kalaeloa Unit

Due to lack of open public road access, sensitive resource values and safety considerations, all visiting groups (school and public) will be led by a guide (Refuge staff or volunteer docent).

All groups will be restricted to established trails (to be developed) to minimize potential damage to endangered/native plants, reduce ground disturbance in the vicinity of the anchialine pools, and ensure visitor safety.

Justification:

Environmental education is identified as a priority wildlife dependent public use of the National Wildlife Refuge System and is a goal in the Pearl Harbor NWR Comprehensive Conservation Plan; therefore, implementation of an environmental education program fulfills a part of the Refuge System mission and Refuge goals. The program is intended to foster a better understanding of the Refuge and in turn build a public that is more knowledgeable about and supportive of natural resource issues and needs. Minimal impacts are incurred by implementation of existing EE programs or expected by modest increases as proposed in the CCP and as long as the stipulations to ensure compatibility are followed, the benefits received through public education, participation, and involvement outweigh the minimal impacts and the program is deemed compatible.

Mandatory Reevaluation Date: (provide month and year for "allowed" uses only)

_____X_____ Mandatory 15-year reevaluation date (for wildlife-dependent public uses)

_____ Mandatory 10-year reevaluation date (for all uses other than wildlife-dependent public uses)

NEPA Compliance for Refuge Use Decision: (check one below)

___ Categorical Exclusion without Environmental Action Statement

___ Categorical Exclusion and Environmental Action Statement

_X_ Environmental Assessment and Finding of No Significant Impact

___ Environmental Impact Statement and Record of Decision

Refuge Determination:

Project Leader,
Pearl Harbor National Wildlife Refuge

_____   _____
(Signature)   (Date)

Project Leader,
Hawaiian and Pacific Islands NWRC

_____   _____
(Signature)   (Date)

Concurrence:

Refuge Supervisor
Pacific Region, National Wildlife Refuge System

_____   _____
(Signature)   (Date)

Regional Chief,
National Wildlife Refuge System:

_____   _____
(Signature)   (Date)

B.4   Compatibility Determination for Research, Scientific Collecting, and Surveys

CD Terminology:

Research: Planned, organized, and systematic investigation of a scientific nature.
Scientific collecting: Gathering of Refuge natural resources or cultural artifacts for scientific
    purposes.
Surveys: Scientific inventory or monitoring.

Refuge Name(s):   Pearl Harbor National Wildlife Refuge
                        (includes Waiawa, Honouliuli, and Kalaeloa Units)

County and State: Honolulu County, Hawai'i

Establishing and Acquisition Authority(ies):

Pearl Harbor NWR was established in 1972 under the authority of the:
* Fish and Wildlife Coordination Act of 1956, as amended (16 U.S.C. 742a – 742j)
* Endangered Species Act of 1973, as amended (16 U.S.C. 1531-1544)
* Additionally for the Kalaeloa Unit (2001); Defense Base Realignment and Closure Act of 1990, as amended (Pub. Law 101-501)

Refuge Purpose(s):

"...to Conserve (A) fish or wildlife which are listed as endangered species or threatened species ... or (B) plants..." 16 U.S.C. 1534 (Endangered Species Act of 1973, as amended)

National Wildlife Refuge System Mission:

"The mission of the [National Wildlife Refuge] System is to administer a national network of lands and waters for the conservation, management, and where appropriate, restoration of the fish, wildlife, and plant resources and their habitats within the United States for the benefit of present and future generations of Americans." (National Wildlife Refuge System Administration Act of 1966 (16 U.S.C. 668dd-668ee), as amended by the National Wildlife Refuge System Improvement Act of 1997 (Public Law 105-57).

Description of Use(s):

The Refuge staff receives periodic requests from non-Service entities (e.g., universities, state or territorial agencies, other Federal agencies, nongovernmental organizations) to conduct research, scientific collecting, and surveys on Refuge lands. These project requests can involve a wide range of natural and cultural resources as well as public-use management issues, including basic absence/ presence surveys, collection of new species for identification, habitat use and life-history requirements for specific species/species groups, practical methods for habitat restoration, extent and severity of environmental contaminants, techniques to control or eradicate pest species, effects of climate change on environmental conditions and associated habitat/wildlife response, identification and analyses of paleontological specimens, wilderness character, modeling of wildlife populations, bioprospecting, and assessing response of habitat/wildlife to disturbance from public uses. Projects may be species-specific, Refuge-specific, or evaluate the relative contribution of the Refuge lands to larger landscapes (e.g., ecoregion, region, flyway, national, international) issues and trends.

The Service's research and management and Appropriate Refuge Uses (603 FW1.10D(4)) policies indicate priority for scientific investigatory studies that contribute to the enhancement, protection, use, preservation, and management of native wildlife populations and their habitat as well as their natural diversity. Projects that contribute to refuge-specific needs for resource and/or wilderness management goals and objectives, where applicable, would be given a higher priority over other requests.

Availability of Resources:

Refuge staff responsibilities for projects by non-Service entities will primarily be limited to the following: review of proposals, prepare SUP(s) and other compliance documents (e.g., Section 7 of the Endangered Species Act of 1973, Section 106 of the National Historic Preservation Act), and monitor project implementation to ensure that impacts and conflicts remain within acceptable levels (compatibility) over time. Additional administrative support, logistical and operational support may also be provided depending on each specific request. Estimated costs for one-time (e.g., prepare SUP) and annually recurring tasks by Refuge staff and other Service employees will be determined for each project. Sufficient funding in the general operating budget of the Refuge must be available to cover expenses for these projects. The terms and conditions for funding and staff support necessary to administer each project on the Refuge will be clearly stated in the SUP(s).

The Refuge has the following staffing and funding to administratively support and monitor research that is currently taking place on Refuge lands (see table below). Any substantial increase in the number of projects would create a need for additional resources to oversee the administration and monitoring of the investigators and their projects. Any substantial additional costs above those itemized below may result in finding a project not compatible unless expenses are offset by the investigator(s), sponsoring agency, or organization.

Category and Itemization	One-time ($)	Annual ($/yr)
Administration and management		$3,200
Maintenance		$0
Monitoring		$2,300
Special equipment, facilities, or improvement		$0
Offsetting revenues		$0

Itemized costs in the table above are current estimates calculated using 5 percent of the base cost for a GS-12 Refuge Biologist/Refuge Manager and a 2 percent cost of a GS-13 Refuge Manager.

Anticipated Impacts of the Use:

Use of the Refuge(s) to conduct research, scientific collecting, and surveys will generally provide information that would benefit fish, wildlife, plants, and their habitats. Scientific findings gained through these projects provide important information regarding life-history needs of species and species groups as well as identify or refine management actions to achieve resource management objectives in Refuge management plans (especially CCPs). Reducing uncertainty regarding wildlife and habitat responses to Refuge management actions in order to achieve desired outcomes reflected in resource management objectives is essential for adaptive management in accordance with 522 DM 1.

If project methods impact or conflict with Refuge-specific resources, priority wildlife-dependent public uses, other high-priority research, wilderness, and Refuge habitat and wildlife management programs, then it must be clearly demonstrated that the scientific findings will contribute to resource management and that the project cannot be conducted off Refuge lands for the project to be compatible. The investigator(s) must identify methods/strategies in advance required to minimize or eliminate the potential impact(s) and conflict(s). If unacceptable impacts cannot be avoided, then the project will not be compatible. Projects that represent public or private economic use of the natural resources of any national wildlife refuge (e.g., bioprospecting), in accordance with 16 U.S.C. 715s, must contribute to the achievement of the national wildlife refuge purposes or the National Wildlife Refuge System mission to be compatible (50 C.F.R. 29.1).

Impacts would be project- and site-specific, where they will vary depending upon nature and scope of the field work. Data collection techniques will generally have minimal animal mortality or disturbance, habitat destruction, no introduction of contaminants, or no introduction of nonindigenous species. In contrast, projects involving the collection of biotic samples (plants or animals) or requiring intensive ground-based data or sample collection will have short-term impacts. To reduce impacts, the minimum number of samples (e.g., water, soils, vegetative litter, plants, macroinvertebrates, vertebrates) will be collected for identification and/or experimentation and statistical analysis. Where possible, researchers would coordinate and share collections to reduce sampling needed for multiple projects. For example, if one investigator collects fish for a diet study and another research examines otoliths, then it may be possible to accomplish sampling for both projects with one collection effort.

Investigator(s) obtaining required State and Federal collecting permits will also ensure minimal impacts to fish, wildlife, plants, and their habitats. If, after incorporating the above strategies, the project results in long-term or cumulative effects, it will not be deemed compatible. A Section 7 consultation under the Endangered Species Act (16 U.S.C. 1531-1544, 87 Stat. 884, as amended Public Law 93-205) will be required for activities that may affect a federally listed species and/or critical habitat. Only projects that have no effect or will result in not likely to adversely affect determinations will be considered compatible.

Spread of invasive plants and/or pathogens is possible from ground disturbance and/or transportation of project equipment and personnel, but it will be minimized or eliminated by requiring proper cleaning of investigator equipment and clothing as well as quarantine methods, where necessary. If after all practical measures are taken, an unacceptable spread of invasive species is anticipated to occur, then the project will be found not compatible without a restoration or mitigation plan.

Localized and temporary effects may occur from vegetation trampling, collecting of soil and plant samples, or trapping and handling of wildlife. Impacts may also occur from infrastructure necessary to support a projects (e.g., permanent transects or plot markers, exclosure devices, monitoring equipment, solar panels to power unattended monitoring equipment). Some level of disturbance is expected with these projects, especially if investigator(s) enter areas closed to the public and collect samples or handle wildlife. However, wildlife disturbance (including altered behavior) will usually be localized and temporary in nature. Where long-term or cumulative unacceptable effects cannot be avoided, the project will not be found compatible. Project proposals will be reviewed by Refuge staff and others, as needed, to assess the potential impacts (short, long-term, and cumulative) relative to benefits of the investigation to Refuge management issues and understanding of natural systems.

At least 6 months before initiation of field work (unless an exception is made by prior approval of the Refuge Manager), project investigator(s) must submit a detailed proposal using the format provided in Attachment 1. Project proposals will be reviewed by Refuge staff and others, as needed, to assess the potential impacts (short, long-term, and cumulative) relative to benefits of the investigation to Refuge management issues and understanding of natural systems. This assessment will form the primary basis for allowing or denying a specific project. Projects that result in unacceptable Refuge impacts will not be found compatible. If allowed and found compatible after approval, all projects also will be assessed during implementation to ensure impacts and conflicts remain within acceptable levels.

If the proposal is approved, then the Refuge Manager will issue a SUP(s) with required stipulations (terms and conditions) of the project to avoid and/or minimize potential impacts to Refuge resources as well as conflicts with other public-use activities and Refuge field management operations. After approval, projects also are monitored during implementation to ensure impacts and conflicts remain within acceptable levels based upon documented stipulations.

The combination of stipulations identified above and conditions included in any SUP(s) will ensure that proposed projects contribute to the enhancement, protection, conservation, and management of native wildlife populations and their habitats on the Refuge. As a result, these projects will help fulfill Refuge purpose(s); contribute to the mission of the Refuge System; and maintain the biological integrity, diversity, and environmental health of the Refuge.

Projects that are not covered by the CCP will require additional NEPA documentation.

Public Review and Comment:

This CD was prepared concurrent with the Pearl Harbor NWR CCP/EA. Public notice was provided, open houses were held, and written comments were solicited from the public during the scoping period for the CCP/EA. Public review and comment were solicited during the draft CCP/EA comment period.

Determination: (check one below)

_____ The use is not compatible.

___X___ The use is compatible with the following stipulations.

Stipulations Necessary to Ensure Compatibility:

Each project will require an SUP. Annual or other short-term SUPs are preferred; however, some permits will be a longer period, if needed, to allow completion of the project. All SUPs will have a definite termination date Renewals will be subject to Refuge Manager review and approval based on timely submission of and content in progress reports, compliance with SUP stipulations, and required permits. Other stipulations and provisions would include the following:

- Projects will adhere to scientifically defensible protocols for data collection, where available and applicable.
- Investigators must possess appropriate and comply with conditions of State and Federal permits for their projects.
- If unacceptable impacts to natural resources or conflicts arise or are documented by the Refuge staff, then the Refuge Manager can suspend, modify conditions of, or terminate an on-going project already permitted by SUP(s) on a Refuge.
- Progress reports are required at least annually for multiple-year projects.
- Final reports are due 1 year after completion of the project unless negotiated otherwise with the Refuge Manager.
- Continuation of existing projects will require approval by the Refuge Manager.
- The Refuge staff will be given the opportunity to review draft manuscript(s) from the project before being submitted to a scientific journal(s) for consideration of publication.
- The Refuge staff will be provided with copies (reprints) of all publications resulting from a Refuge project.
- The Refuge staff will be provided with copies of raw data (preferably electronic database format) at the conclusion of the project.
- Upon completion of the project or annually, all equipment and markers (unless required for long-term projects), must be removed and sites must be restored to the Refuge Manager's satisfaction. Conditions for clean-up and removal of equipment and physical markers will be stipulated in the SUP(s).
- All samples collected on Refuge lands are the property of the Service even while in the possession of the investigator(s). Any future work with previously collected samples not clearly identified in the project proposal will require submission of a subsequent proposal for review and approval. In addition, a new SUP will be required for additional project work. For samples or specimens to be stored at other facilities (e.g., museums), a memorandum of understanding will be necessary.
- Sampling equipment as well as investigator(s) clothing and vehicles (e.g., ATV, boats) will be thoroughly cleaned (free of dirt and plant material) before being allowed for use on Refuge lands to prevent the introduction and/or spread of pests.
- The Service, specific Refuge unit, names of Refuge staff and other Service personnel who supported or contributed to the project will be appropriately cited and acknowledged in all written and oral presentations resulting from projects on Refuge lands.
- At any time, Refuge staff may accompany investigator(s) in the field.
- Investigator(s) and support staff will follow all Refuge-specific regulations that specify access and travel on the Refuge.

Justification:

Research, scientific collecting, and surveys on Refuge lands are inherently valuable to the Service because they will expand scientific information available for resource management decisions. In addition, only projects that directly or indirectly contribute to the enhancement, protection, use, preservation, and management of Refuge wildlife populations and their habitats generally will be authorized on Refuge lands. In many cases, if it were not for the Refuge staff providing access to Refuge lands and waters along with some support, the research project would likely not occur and less scientific information would be available to the Service to aid in managing and conserving the Refuge resources. By allowing the use to occur under the stipulations described above, it is anticipated that wildlife species that could be disturbed during the use would find sufficient food resources and resting places so their abundance and use will not be measurably lessened on the Refuge. Additionally, it is anticipated that monitoring, as needed, will prevent unacceptable or irreversible impacts to fish, wildlife, plants, and their habitats. As a result, these projects will not materially interfere with or detract from fulfilling Refuge purpose(s) (including wilderness); contributing to the mission of the Service; and maintaining the biological integrity, diversity, and environmental health of the Refuge.

Mandatory Re-evaluation Date: (provide month and year for "allowed" uses only)

_____ Mandatory 15-year re-evaluation date (wildlife-dependent public uses)

___X___ Mandatory 10-year re-evaluation date (uses other than wildlife-dependent public uses)

NEPA Compliance for Refuge Use Decision: (check one below)

_____ Categorical Exclusion and Environmental Action Statement

___X___ Environmental Assessment and Finding of No Significant Impact

_____ Environmental Impact Statement and Record of Decision

Refuge Determination:

Project Leader
Pearl Harbor National Wildlife Refuge

_____   _____
(Signature)   (Date)

Project Leader
Hawaiian and Pacific Islands NWRC

_____   _____
(Signature)   (Date)

Concurrence:

Refuge Supervisor
Pacific Region, National Wildlife Refuge System

_____   _____
(Signature)   (Date)

Regional Chief
National Wildlife Refuge System:

_____   _____
(Signature)   (Date)

FINDING OF APPROPRIATENESS OF A REFUGE USE

Refuge Name: Pearl Harbor National Wildlife Refuge

Use: Research, Scientific Collecting, and Surveys

This form is not required for wildlife-dependent recreational uses, take regulated by the State, or uses already described in a refuge CCP or step-down management plan approved after October 9, 1997.

Decision Criteria:	YES	NO
(a) Do we have jurisdiction over the use?	✓	
(b) Does the use comply with applicable laws and regulations (Federal, State, tribal, and local)?	✓	
(c) Is the use consistent with applicable Executive orders and Department and Service policies?	✓	
(d) Is the use consistent with public safety?	✓	
(e) Is the use consistent with goals and objectives in an approved management plan or other document?	✓	
(f) Has an earlier documented analysis not denied the use or is this the first time the use has been proposed?	✓	
(g) Is the use manageable within available budget and staff?	✓	
(h) Will this be manageable in the future within existing resources?	✓	
(i) Does the use contribute to the public's understanding and appreciation of the refuge's natural or cultural resources, or is the use beneficial to the refuge's natural or cultural resources?	✓	
(j) Can the use be accommodated without impairing existing wildlife-dependent recreational uses or reducing the potential to provide quality (see section 1.6D, 603 FW 1, for description), compatible, wildlife-dependent recreation into the future?	✓	

Where we do not have jurisdiction over the use ("no" to (a)), there is no need to evaluate it further as we cannot control the use. Uses that are illegal, inconsistent with existing policy, or unsafe ("no" to (b), (c), or (d)) may not be found appropriate. If the answer is "no" to any of the other questions above, we will **generally** not allow the use.

If indicated, the refuge manager has consulted with State fish and wildlife agencies. Yes ___   No ✓

When the refuge manager finds the use appropriate based on sound professional judgment, the refuge manager must justify the use in writing on an attached sheet and obtain the refuge supervisor's concurrence.

Based on an overall assessment of these factors, my summary conclusion is that the proposed use is:

Not Appropriate_____   Appropriate ✓

Refuge Manager:_____   Date:_____

If found to be **Not Appropriate**, the refuge supervisor does not need to sign concurrence if the use is a new use.

If an existing use is found **Not Appropriate** outside the CCP process, the refuge supervisor must sign concurrence.

If found to be **Appropriate**, the refuge supervisor must sign concurrence.

Refuge Supervisor:_____   Date:_____

A compatibility determination is required before the use may be allowed.   **FWS Form 3-2319**
02/06

Attachment 1: Appropriate Uses Justification

Date:

Refuge: Pearl Harbor National Wildlife Refuge (Refuge)

Project: Research, Scientific Collecting, and Surveys

Summary: The Refuge receives requests to conduct scientific research on Refuge lands and waters. Research applicants must submit a proposal that would outline: (1) objectives of the study; (2) justification for the study; (3) detailed methodology and schedule; (4) potential impacts on Refuge wildlife and/or habitat, including disturbance (short and long term), injury, or mortality; (5) personnel required; (6) costs to Refuge, if any; and (7) end products (i.e., reports, publications). Research proposals would be reviewed by Refuge staff, Regional Office Branch of Refuge Biology, and others as appropriate prior to the Refuge issuing a special use permit (SUP). Projects will not be open-ended, and at a minimum, will be reviewed annually.

For each of the findings listed on FWS Form 3-2319, a justification has been provided below:

a. Do we have jurisdiction over the use?

Some or all of the proposed activities would take place within Refuge boundaries. The Refuge has jurisdiction over those research projects that are sited within Refuge boundaries.

b. Does the use comply with applicable laws and regulations (Federal, State, tribal, and local)?

Any proposed research activities would comply with all applicable laws and regulations. Any restrictions or qualifications that are required to comply with law and regulations would be specified in the SUP.

c. Is the use consistent with applicable Executive orders and Department and Service policies?

Through the review of individual projects, the Refuge would ensure that they are consistent with applicable policies, especially Research on Service Lands Policy (803 FW 1).

d. Is the use consistent with public safety?

Through individual project review, the Refuge will ensure that each project is consistent with public safety. If necessary, stipulations to ensure public safety will be included in the project's SUP.

e. Is the use consistent with goals and objectives in an approved management plan or other document?

Research activities are approved in instances where they can provide meaningful data that may contribute to Refuge management and public appreciation of natural resources.

g. Is the use manageable within available budget and staff?

The Refuge receives <10 requests per year for this activity, and it is manageable with available budget and staff.

h. Will this be manageable in the future within existing resources?

The proposed activity at current levels would be manageable in the future with the existing resources.

i. Does the use contribute to the public's understanding and appreciation of the Refuge's natural or cultural resources, or is the use beneficial to the Refuge's natural or cultural resources?

The proposed use is beneficial to the Refuge's natural and cultural resources because the types of research projects approved are those that have the distinct likelihood to help achieve Refuge purposes by providing information useful for the management of trust resources and may contribute to the public's understanding and appreciation of natural and/or cultural resources.

j. Can the use be accommodated without impairing existing wildlife-dependent recreational uses or reducing the potential to provide quality (see section 1.6D, 603 FW 1, for description), compatible, wildlife-dependent recreation into the future?

The Refuge will ensure that the research activities will not impair existing or future wildlife-dependent recreational use of the Refuge during individual project review, prior to issuing a SUP for the project.

Appendix C. Plan Implementation and Costs

Administration

Pearl Harbor National Wildlife Refuge is administered as part of the O'ahu National Wildlife Refuge Complex. The Complex also includes the James Campbell NWR located on the north shore of O'ahu, near the village of Kahuku, and the O'ahu Forest NWR located in the higher elevations of the Ko'olau Mountains in central Oahu. The Complex headquarters is located in leased office space in the north shore town of Hale'iwa, 25–35 miles from the units of Pearl Harbor NWR, and the maintenance shop and equipment storage buildings are located on James Campbell NWR located 50-60 miles from the Pearl Harbor NWR units. A new O'ahu NWR Complex headquarters/visitor center/environmental education facility is being proposed for construction on James Campbell NWR. This facility and associated staff would also serve the Pearl Harbor NWR.

Staffing

As described above, the O'ahu NWR Complex is comprised of the James Campbell, Pearl Harbor and O'ahu Forest National Wildlife Refuges. Out of necessity, all staff positions currently share responsibilities and duties across all three refuges; i.e., no staff is assigned and performs duties only on specific refuges within the complex. Due to projected complexwide workload, priorities, logistics, and supervisory considerations, this arrangement is expected to continue. However, as more staff is eventually added to the Complex, staff may be assigned more specific duties on individual refuges within the complex.

Necessary staffing with current Complex needs for all of the O'ahu Refuge National Wildlife Refuge Complex, as projected by the Service's National Staffing Model, generated 20.5 staff positions. Of these 2.5 staff positions were moved to other offices due to various considerations and needs. Therefore, with the existing core funded complex staff of 6, 12 additional staff are justified to meet current (existing) Refuge needs for all of the O'ahu NWR Complex, including Pearl Harbor NWR. The increased staffing would provide increased coordination with other Federal, State, local agencies, and the public; additional capacity to conduct biological inventory, monitoring, and research, as well as all aspects of habitat management; additional and improved maintenance capability for all Refuge facilities; law enforcement; and visitor services, including interpretation and environmental education.

Current and Necessary Permanent Full-time Staffing for O'ahu NWR Complex, including Pearl Harbor NWR (highlighted positions indicate current core staff)

Staff Position	Salary Rating
Project Leader	GS-13
Deputy Project Leader	GS-11/12
Supervisory Wildlife Biologist	GS-11/ 12
Supervisory Tractor Operator	WS-4
Administrative Technician	GS-7/9
Supervisory Park Ranger	GS-11

Wildlife Refuge Manager	GS-7/9/11
Wildlife Biologist	GS-5/7/9
Refuge Law Enforcement Officer	GS-5/7/9
Environmental Education Specialist	GS-7/9
Park Ranger	GS-5/7/9
Tractor Operator	WG-6
Tractor Operator	WG-6
Maintenance Worker	WG-8
Maintenance Worker	WG-5/6/7
Maintenance Worker	WG-5/6
Biological Technician	GS-5/7
Biological Technician	GS-5/7

Additional Permanent Full-Time staff under Alternative B

Due to the relatively small scale and scope of actions identified as strategies under Alternative B, no additional staff would be required beyond the necessary staff identified above.

Refuge Funding and Budget Requests

Successful and full implementation of the CCP relies on our ability to secure funding and staffing necessary to achieve the actions and strategies described in the CCP. In addition to annual budget allocations, funding can be received through special funding sources and programs geared toward specific resource issues / needs. Examples include grants or project specific funding for endangered species, wetlands, invasive species control, coastal habitats, seabirds, climate change or sea level rise. Currently, budget requests through the Refuge Operating Needs System (RONS) for Pearl Harbor NWR include four additional staff positions as part of the necessary positions identified above. The RONS system will be updated with new/additional projects that are approved under the Pearl Harbor NWR CCP.

Appendix D: Wilderness Review for Pearl Harbor National Wildlife Refuge

General Information on Wilderness Reviews

Wilderness review is the process used to determine whether or not to recommend lands or waters in the National Wildlife Refuge System (System) to the United States Congress (Congress) for designation as wilderness. Planning policy for the System (602 FW 3) mandates conducting wilderness reviews every 15 years through the Comprehensive Conservation Planning (CCP) process.

The wilderness review process has three phases: inventory, study, and recommendation. After first identifying lands and waters that meet the minimum criteria for wilderness, the resulting wilderness study areas (WSA) are further evaluated to determine if they merit recommendation from the Service to the Secretary of the Interior for inclusion in the National Wilderness Preservation System (NWPS). Areas recommended for designation are managed to maintain wilderness character in accordance with management goals, objectives, and strategies outlined in the final CCP until Congress makes a decision or the CCP is amended to modify or remove the wilderness proposal. A brief discussion of wilderness inventory, study, and recommendation follows.

Wilderness Inventory
The wilderness inventory consists of identifying areas that minimally meet the requirements for wilderness as defined in the Wilderness Act of 1964 (Wilderness Act). Wilderness is defined as an area which:
- Has at least 5,000 acres of land or is of sufficient size as to make practicable its preservation and use in an unimpaired condition, or be capable of restoration to wilderness character through appropriate management at the time of review, or be a roadless island;
- Generally appears to have been affected primarily by the forces of nature, with the imprint of man's work substantially unnoticeable;
- Has outstanding opportunities for solitude or a primitive and unconfined type of recreation; and
- May also contain ecological, geological, or other features of scientific, educational, scenic, or historical value. These features and values, though desirable, are not necessary for an area to qualify as a wilderness.

Wilderness Study
During the study phase, lands and waters qualifying for wilderness as a result of the inventory are studied to analyze values (ecological, recreational, cultural, spiritual), resources (e.g., wildlife, water, vegetation, minerals, soils), and uses (habitat management, public use) within the area. The findings of the study help determine whether to recommend the area for designation as wilderness.

Wilderness Recommendation
Once a wilderness study determines that a WSA meets the requirements for inclusion in the NWPS, a wilderness study report that presents the results of the wilderness review, accompanied by a Legislative Environmental Impact Statement (LEIS), is prepared. The wilderness study report and

LEIS that support wilderness designation are then transmitted through the Secretary of the Interior to the President of United States, and ultimately to the United States Congress for approval.

The following section summarizes the inventory phase of the wilderness review for James Campbell and Pearl Harbor NWRs.

Wilderness Inventory

The wilderness inventory is a broad look at the planning area to identify WSAs. These WSAs are roadless areas within refuge boundaries, including submerged lands and their associated water column, that meet the minimum criteria for wilderness identified in Sect. 2. (c) of the Wilderness Act. A WSA must meet the minimum size criteria (or be a roadless island), appear natural, and provide outstanding opportunities for solitude or primitive recreation. Other supplemental values are evaluated, but not required.

<u>Evaluation of Size Criteria for Roadless Areas, Roadless Islands, and Submergent Lands and Associated Water Column</u>
Identification of roadless areas, roadless islands, and submerged lands and associated water column, required gathering land status maps, land use and road inventory data, satellite imagery, aerial photographs, and personal observations of areas within refuge boundaries. "Roadless" refers to the absence of improved roads suitable and maintained for public travel by means of motorized vehicles primarily intended for highway use.

Inventory units meet the size criteria for a WSA if any one of the following standards applies:
- An area with over 5,000 contiguous acres. State and private lands are not included in making this acreage determination.
- A roadless island of any size. A roadless island is defined as an area surrounded by permanent waters or that is markedly distinguished from the surrounding lands by topographical or ecological features.
- An area of less than 5,000 contiguous Federal acres that is of sufficient size as to make practicable its preservation and use in an unimpaired condition, and of a size suitable for wilderness management.
- An area of less than 5,000 contiguous Federal acres that is contiguous with a designated wilderness, recommended wilderness, or area under wilderness review by another Federal wilderness managing agency such as the Forest Service, National Park Service, or Bureau of Land Management.

The Refuge is composed of three highly modified land management units totaling 99 acres on the island of O'ahu and does not meet the size criteria. It is also bounded and bisected by State-owned and Refuge-owned roadways maintained for travel by passenger vehicles.

<u>Evaluation of the Naturalness Criteria</u>
A WSA must meet the naturalness criteria. Section 2.(c) of the Wilderness Act defines wilderness as an area that "…generally appears to have been affected primarily by the forces of nature with the imprint of man's work substantially unnoticeable." The area must appear natural to the average visitor rather than "pristine." The presence of ecologically accurate, historic landscape conditions is not required. An area may include some manmade features and human impacts provided they are

substantially unnoticeable in the unit as a whole. Human-caused hazards, such as the presence of unexploded ordnance from military activity, and the physical impacts of refuge management facilities and activities are also considered in the evaluation of the naturalness criteria. An area may not be considered unnatural in appearance solely on the basis of "sights and sounds" of human impacts and activities outside the boundary of the unit. The cumulative effects of these factors were considered in the evaluation of naturalness for each wilderness inventory unit.

In the wilderness inventory, specific manmade features and other human impacts need to be identified that affect the overall apparent naturalness of the tract. The following factors were primary considerations in evaluating the naturalness of the Refuge:

- Adjacent and highly visible urban structures and military fleet;
- Well pumps, earthen dikes, water control structures;
- Gates, parking lots, and roadways

The Refuge units are all highly modified land parcels, containing earthen dikes, ditches, a perimeter roadway, water control structures, buildings, and water pumping stations. These units do not meet the naturalness criteria.

Evaluation of Outstanding Opportunities for Solitude or Primitive and Unconfined Recreation
In addition to meeting the size and naturalness criteria, a WSA must provide outstanding opportunities for solitude or primitive recreation. The area does not have to possess outstanding opportunities for both solitude and primitive and unconfined recreation, and does not need to have outstanding opportunities on every acre. Further, an area does not have to be open to public use and access to qualify under these criteria. Congress has designated a number of wilderness areas in the NWPS that are closed to public access to protect ecological resource values.

Opportunities for solitude refers to the ability of a visitor to be alone and secluded from other visitors in the area. Primitive and unconfined recreation means nonmotorized, dispersed outdoor recreation activities that do not require developed facilities or mechanical transport. These primitive recreation activities may provide opportunities to experience challenge and risk, self reliance, and adventure.

These two opportunity "elements" are not well defined by the Wilderness Act but in most cases can be expected to occur together. However, an outstanding opportunity for solitude may be present in an area offering only limited primitive recreation potential. Conversely, an area may be so attractive for recreation use that experiencing solitude is not an option.

These inventory units do not offer opportunities for solitude or primitive and unconfined recreation. Daily management activities occur on these inventory units. These activities include road maintenance, mowing and disking of fields, and manipulation of water control structures. Recreational and educational activities are only conducted in group settings, and only allowed as staff-guided activities.

Evaluation of Supplemental Values
Supplemental values are defined by the Wilderness Act as "ecological, geological, or other features of scientific, educational, scenic, or historic value." Based upon the findings of the required components for WSA designation, supplemental values were not evaluated.

Findings

Pearl Harbor NWR does not meet the minimum criteria for consideration as WSAs (see Table D.1).

Table D.1 Wilderness Inventory Summary

Wilderness Inventory Summary Pearl Harbor NWR (99 acres)	
Required Components	
(1) Has at least 5,000 acres of land or is of sufficient size to make practicable its preservation and use in an unconfined condition, or is a roadless island.	No. Does not contain 5,000 acres, is not a roadless island, and is not practicable to manage as a wilderness.
(2) Generally appears to have been affected primarily by the forces of nature, with the imprint of man's work substantially unnoticeable.	No. Landscape is highly modified and actively managed.
(3a) Has outstanding opportunities for solitude.	No. Unit is actively and regularly managed.
(3b) Has outstanding opportunities for a primitive and unconfined type of recreation.	No. Recreation is highly regulated and requires staff presence.
Other Components	
(4) Contains ecological, geological or other features of scientific, educational, scenic, or historical value.	Not evaluated.
Summary	
Parcel qualifies as a wilderness study area (meets criteria 1, 2 & 3a or 3b).	No.

Appendix E: Integrated Pest Management (IPM) Program

1.0 Background

IPM is an interdisciplinary approach utilizing methods to prevent, eliminate, contain, and/or control pest species in concert with other management activities on Refuge lands and waters to achieve wildlife and habitat management goals and objectives. IPM is also a scientifically based, adaptive management process where available scientific information and best professional judgment of the Refuge staff as well as other resource experts would be used to identify and implement appropriate management strategies that can be modified and/or changed over time to ensure effective, site-specific management of pest species to achieve desired outcomes. In accordance with 43 CFR 46.145, adaptive management would be particularly relevant where long-term impacts may be uncertain and future monitoring would be needed to make adjustments in subsequent implementation decisions. After a tolerable pest population (threshold) is determined considering achievement of Refuge resource objectives and the ecology of pest species, one or more methods, or combinations thereof, are selected that are feasible, efficacious, and most protective of non-target resources, including native species (fish, wildlife, and plants), and Service personnel, Service authorized agents, volunteers, and the public. Staff time and available funding will be considered when determining feasibility/practicality of various treatments.

IPM techniques to address pests are presented as CCP strategies prescriptions (see Section 2.0 of this CCP) in an adaptive management context to achieve Refuge resource objectives. In order to satisfy requirements for IPM planning as identified in the Director's Memo (dated September 9, 2004) entitled *Integrated Pest Management Plans and Pesticide Use Proposals: Updates, Guidance, and an Online Database*, the following elements of an IPM program have been incorporated into this CCP:

- Habitat and/or wildlife objectives that identify pest species and appropriate thresholds to indicate the need for and successful implementation of IPM techniques; and
- Monitoring before and/or after treatment to assess progress toward achieving objectives including pest thresholds.

Where pesticides would be necessary to address pests, this Appendix provides a structured procedure to evaluate potential effects of proposed uses involving ground-based applications to Refuge biological resources and environmental quality in accordance with effects analyses presented in Section 4.0 (Environmental Consequences) of this CCP. Only pesticide uses that likely would cause minor, temporary, or localized effects to Refuge biological resources and environmental quality with appropriate best management practices (BMPs), where necessary, would be allowed for use on the Refuge.

This Appendix does not describe the more detailed process to evaluate potential effects associated with aerial applications of pesticides. Moreover, it does not address effects of mosquito control with pesticides (larvicides, pupacides, or adulticides) based upon identified human health threats and presence of disease-carrying mosquitoes in sufficient numbers from monitoring conducted on a Refuge. However, the basic framework to assess potential effects to Refuge biological resources and environmental quality from aerial application of pesticides or use of insecticides for mosquito management would be similar to the process described in this Appendix for ground-based treatments of other pesticides.

2.0 Pest Management Laws and Policies

In accordance with Service policy 7 RM 14 (Pest Control), wildlife and plant pests on units of the National Wildlife Refuge System can be controlled to assure balanced wildlife and fish populations in support of Refuge-specific wildlife and habitat management objectives. Pest control on federal (Refuge) lands and waters also is authorized under the following legal mandates:

- National Wildlife Refuge System Administration Act of 1966, as amended (16 USC 668dd-668ee);
- Plant Protection Act of 2000 (7 USC 7701 *et seq*.);
- Noxious Weed Control and Eradication Act of 2004 (7 USC 7781-7786, Subtitle E);
- Federal Insecticide, Fungicide, and Rodenticide Act of 1996 (7 USC 136-136y);
- National Invasive Species Act of 1996 (16 USC 4701);
- Nonindigenous Aquatic Nuisance Prevention and Control Act of 1990 (16 USC 4701);
- Food Quality Protection Act of 1996 (7 USC 136);
- Executive Order 13148, Section 601(a);
- Executive Order 13112; and
- Animal Damage Control Act of 1931 (7 USC 426-426c, 46 Stat. 1468).

Pests are defined as "…living organisms that may interfere with the site-specific purposes, operations, or management objectives or that jeopardize human health or safety" from Department policy 517 DM 1 (Integrated Pest Management Policy). Similarly, 7 RM 14 defines pests as "Any terrestrial or aquatic plant or animal which interferes, or threatens to interfere, at an unacceptable level, with the attainment of Refuge objectives or which poses a threat to human health." 517 DM 1 also defines an invasive species as "a species that is non-native to the ecosystem under consideration and whose introduction causes or is likely to cause economic or environmental harm or harm to human health." Throughout the remainder of this CCP, the terms pest and invasive species are used interchangeably because both can prevent/impede achievement of Refuge wildlife and habitat objectives and/or degrade environmental quality.

In general, control of pests (vertebrate or invertebrate) on the Refuge would conserve and protect the nation's fish, wildlife, and plant resources as well as maintain environmental quality. From 7 Refuge Manual (RM) 14, animal or plant species, which are considered pests, may be managed if the following criteria are met:

- Threat to human health and well being or private property, the acceptable level of damage by the pest has been exceeded, or State or local government has designated the pest as noxious;
- Detrimental to resource objectives as specified in a Refuge resource management plan (e.g., comprehensive conservation plan, habitat management plan), if available; and
- Control would not conflict with attainment of resource objectives or the purposes for which the Refuge was established.

From 7 RM 14, the specific justifications for pest management activities on the Refuge are the following:

- Protect human health and well being;
- Prevent substantial damage to important to Refuge resources;

- Protect newly introduced or re-establish native species;
- Control non-native (exotic) species in order to support existence for populations of native species;
- Prevent damage to private property; and
- Provide the public with quality, compatible wildlife-dependent recreational opportunities.

In accordance with Service policy 620 FW 1 (Habitat Management Plans), there are additional management directives regarding invasive species found on the Refuge:

- "We are prohibited by Executive Order, law, and policy from authorizing, funding, or carrying out actions that are likely to cause or promote the introduction or spread of invasive species in the United States or elsewhere."
- "Manage invasive species to improve or stabilize biotic communities to minimize unacceptable change to ecosystem structure and function and prevent new and expanded infestations of invasive species. Conduct Refuge habitat management activities to prevent, control, or eradicate invasive species..."

Animal species damaging/destroying federal property and/or detrimental to the management program of a Refuge may be controlled as described in 50 CFR 31.14 (Official Animal Control Operations). Based upon 7 RM 14.7E, a pest control proposal is required, in some cases, to initiate a control program on Refuge lands. The required elements of a pest control proposal are described in 7 RM 14.7A-E. However, a pest control proposal is not required under the following scenarios:

- Routine protection of Refuge buildings, structures (e.g., dikes, levees, water control structures), and facilities not involving prohibited chemicals.
- Incidental control of exotic animals on Refuge lands that are not protected by either federal or state laws, except where chemicals may he used.
- The use of routine habitat management techniques, selective trapping, on-Refuge transfer, and physical and mechanical protection such as barriers and fences (including electric fences).

Trespass and feral animals also may be controlled on Refuge lands. In accordance with 7 RM 14.9B(1), animals trespassing on Refuge lands may be captured and returned to their owners or transferred to humane societies or local animal shelters, where feasible. Based upon 50 CFR 28.43 (Destruction of Dogs and Cats), dogs and cats running at large on a national wildlife Refuge and observed in the act of killing, injuring, harassing or molesting humans or wildlife may be disposed of in the interest of public safety and protection of the wildlife. In accordance with 7 RM 14.9B(2), feral animals should be disposed by the most humane method(s) available and in accordance with relevant Service directives (including Executive Order 11643).

Disposed wildlife specimens may be donated or loaned to public institutions. Donation or loans of resident wildlife species will only be made after securing State approval (50 CFR 30.11 [Donation and Loan of Wildlife Specimens]). Surplus wildlife specimens may be sold alive or butchered, dressed and processed subject to federal and state laws and regulations (50 CFR 30.12 [Sale of Wildlife Specimens]).

As previously stated for controlling animals damaging/destroying federal property and/or detrimental to the management program of a Refuge, incidentally removing such animals from Refuge lands does not require a pest control proposal.

3.0 Strategies

To fully embrace IPM, the following strategies, where applicable, would be carefully considered on the Refuge for each pest species:

- **Prevention.** This would be the most effective and least expensive long-term management option for pests. It encompasses methods to prevent new introductions or the spread of the established pests to un-infested areas. It requires identifying potential routes of invasion to reduce the likelihood of infestation. Hazard Analysis and Critical Control Points (HACCP) planning can be used determine if current management activities on a Refuge may introduce and/or spread invasive species in order to identify appropriate BMPs for prevention. See http://www.haccp-nrm.org/ for more information about HACCP planning.

  Prevention may include source reduction, using pathogen-free or weed-free seeds or fill; exclusion methods (e.g., barriers) and/or sanitation methods (e.g., wash stations) to prevent re-introductions by various mechanisms including vehicles and personnel. Because invasive species are frequently the first to establish newly disturbed sites, prevention would require a reporting mechanism for early detection of new pest occurrences with quick response to eliminate any new satellite pest populations. Prevention would require consideration of the scale and scope of land management activities that may promote pest establishment within un-infested areas or promote reproduction and spread of existing populations. Along with preventing initial introduction, prevention would involve halting the spread of existing infestations to new sites (Mullin et al. 2000). The primary reason of prevention would be to keep pest-free lands or waters from becoming infested. Executive Order 11312 emphasizes the priority for prevention with respect to managing pests.

  The following would be methods to prevent the introduction and/or spread of pests on Refuge lands:
    - Before beginning ground-disturbing activities (e.g., disking, scraping), inventory and prioritize pest infestations in project operating areas and along access routes. Refuge staff would identify pest species on site or within reasonably expected potential invasion vicinity. Where possible, Refuge staff would begin project activities in un-infested areas before working in pest-infested areas.
    - Refuge staff would locate and use pest-free project staging areas. They would avoid or minimize travel through pest-infested areas, or restrict to those periods when spread of seed or propagules of invasive plants would be least likely.
    - Refuge staff would determine the need for, and when appropriate, identify sanitation sites where equipment can be cleaned of pests. Where possible, Refuge staff would clean equipment before entering lands at on-Refuge approved cleaning site(s). This practice does not pertain to vehicles traveling frequently in and out of the project area that will remain on roadways. Seeds and plant parts of pest plants would need to be collected, where practical. Refuge staff would remove mud, dirt, and plant parts from project equipment before moving it into a project area.
    - Refuge staff would clean all equipment, before leaving the project site, if operating in areas infested with pests. Refuge staff would determine the need for, and when appropriate, identify sanitation sites where equipment can be cleaned.
    - Refuge staffs, their authorized agents, and Refuge volunteers would, where possible, inspect, remove, and properly dispose of seed and parts of invasive plants found on their

clothing and equipment. Proper disposal means bagging the seeds and plant parts and then properly discarding of them (e.g., incinerating).

- Refuge staff would evaluate options, including closure, to restrict the traffic on sites with on-going restoration of desired vegetation. Refuge staff would revegetate disturbed soil (except travel ways on surfaced projects) to optimize plant establishment for each specific site. Revegetation may include topsoil replacement, planting, seeding, fertilization, liming, and weed-free mulching as necessary. Refuge staff would use native material, where appropriate and feasible. Refuge staff would use certified weed-free or weed-seed-free hay or straw where certified materials are are reasonably available.
- Refuge staff would provide information, training and appropriate pest identification materials to Refuge staffs, permit holders, and recreational visitors. Refuge staff would educate them about pest identification, biology, impacts, and effective prevention measures.
- Refuge staff would inspect borrow material for invasive plants prior to use and transport onto and/or within Refuge lands.
- Refuge staff would consider invasive plants in planning for road maintenance activities.
- Refuge staff would restrict off road travel to designated routes.

The following would be methods to prevent the introduction and/or spread of pests into Refuge waters:

- Refuge staff would inspect boats (including air boats), trailers, and other boating equipment and, where possible, Refuge remove any visible plants, animals, or mud before leaving any waters or boat launching facilities. Where possible, staff would drain water from motor, live well, bilge, and transom wells while on land before leaving the site.

If possible, Refuge staff would wash and dry boats, downriggers, anchors, nets, floors of boats, propellers, axles, trailers, and other boating equipment to kill pests not visible at the boat launch. These prevention methods to minimize/eliminate the introduction and/or spread of pests were taken verbatim or slightly modified from Appendix E of US Forest Service (2005).

- **Mechanical/Physical Methods.** These methods would remove and destroy, disrupt the growth of, or interfere with the reproduction of pest species. For plants species, these treatments can be accomplished by hand, hand tool (manual), or power tools (mechanical) and include pulling, grubbing, digging, tilling/disking, cutting, swathing, grinding, sheering, girdling, mowing, and mulching of the pest plants.

For animal species, Service employees or their authorized agents could use mechanical/physical methods (including trapping) to control pests as a Refuge management activity. Based upon 50 CFR 31.2, trapping can be used on a Refuge reduce surplus wildlife populations for a "balanced conservation program" in accordance with federal or state laws and regulations. In some cases, non-lethally trapped animals would be relocated to off-Refuge sites with prior approval from the state. A pest control proposal (see 7 RM 14.7A-D for required elements) is needed before initiation of trapping activities, except those operations identified in 7 RM 14.7E. In addition, a separate pest control proposal is not necessary if the required information can be incorporated into an EA (or other appropriate NEPA document).

Each of these tools would be efficacious to some degree and applicable to specific situations. In general, mechanical controls can effectively control annual and biennial pest plants. However, to control perennial plants, the root system has to be destroyed or it would resprout and continue to grow and develop. Mechanical controls are typically not capable of destroying a perennial plants root system. Although some mechanical tools (e.g., disking, plowing) may damage root systems, they may stimulate regrowth producing a denser plant population that may aid in the spread depending upon the target species. In addition, steep terrain and soil conditions would be major factors that can limit the use of many mechanical control methods.

Some mechanical control methods (e.g., mowing), which would be used in combination with herbicides, can be a very effective technique to control perennial species. For example, mowing perennial plants followed sequentially by treating the plant regrowth with a systemic herbicide often would improve the efficacy of the herbicide compared to herbicide treatment only.

- **Cultural Methods.** These methods would involve manipulating habitat to increase pest mortality by reducing its suitability to the pest. Cultural methods would include water-level manipulation, , prescribed burning (facilitate revegetation, increase herbicide efficacy, and remove litter to assist in emergence of desirable species), planting or seeding desirable species to shade or out-compete invasive plants, applying fertilizer to enhance desirable vegetation, irrigation, and other habitat alterations.

- **Biological Control Agents.** Classical biological control would involve the deliberate introduction and management of natural enemies (parasites, predators, or pathogens) to reduce pest populations. Many of the most ecologically or economically damaging pest species in the United States originated in foreign countries. These newly introduced pests, which are free from natural enemies found in their country or region of origin, may have a competitive advantage over cultivated and native species. This competitive advantage often allows introduced species to flourish, and they may cause widespread economic damage to crops or out compete and displace native vegetation. Once the introduced pest species population reaches a certain level, traditional methods of pest management may be cost prohibitive or impractical. Biological controls typically are used when these pest populations have become so widespread that eradication or effective control would be difficult or no longer practical.

Biological control has advantages as well as disadvantages. Benefits would include reducing pesticide usage, host specificity for target pests, long-term self-perpetuating control, low cost/acre, capacity for searching and locating hosts, synchronizing biological control agents to hosts' life cycles, and the unlikelihood that hosts will develop resistance to agents. Disadvantages would include the following: limited availability of agents from their native lands, the dependence of control on target species density, slow rate at which control occurs, biotype matching, the difficulty and expense of conflicts over control of the target pest, and host specificity when host populations are low.

A reduction in target species populations from biological controls is typically a slow process, and efficacy can be highly variable. It may not work well in a particular area although it does work well in other areas. Biological control agents would require specific environmental conditions to survive over time. Some of these conditions are understood; whereas, others are only partially understood or not at all.

Biological control agents would not eradicate a target pest. When using biological control agents, residual levels of the target pest typically are expected; the agent population level or survival would be dependent upon the density of its host. After the pest population decreases, the population of the biological control agent would decrease correspondingly. This is a natural cycle. Some pest populations (e.g., invasive plants) would tend to persist for several years after a biological control agent becomes established due to seed reserves in the soil, inefficiencies in the agents search behavior, and the natural lag in population buildup of the agent.

The full range of pest groups potentially found on Refuge lands and waters would include diseases, invertebrates (insects, mollusks), vertebrates and invasive plants (most common group). Often it is assumed that biological control would address many if not most of these pest problems. Introduced species without desirable close relatives in the United States would generally be selected as biological controls. Natural enemies that are restricted to one or a few closely related plants in their country of origin are targeted as biological controls (Center et al. 1997, Hasan and Ayres 1990).

The Hawai`i Department of Agriculture (HDOA) has a highly successful biocontrol program for the Erythrina gall wasp which has resulted in the rebounding of the native wiliwili trees. In June of 2010, HDOA began another biological control program that releases a tiny parasitic insect to control the stinging Nettle Caterpillar. The release of Brazilian scale to slow the growth rate and spread of strawberry guava has recently been proposed to give Hawai`i's native plants a chance for survival, protect the ability of the forests to provide water, and provide better protection for agricultural crops from the fruit flies that breed in the overabundance of strawberry guava fruit. Due to the success of Hawai`i's biocontrol programs, the state has become a leader in the world on the use of biological control to fight invasive pests.

Refuge staff would ensure introduced agents are approved by the applicable authorities. Except for a small number of formulated biological control products registered by USEPA under FIFRA, most biological control agents are regulated by the US Department of Agriculture (USDA)-Animal Plant Health Inspection Service, Plant Protection and Quarantine (APHIS-PPQ). State departments of agriculture and, in some cases, county agricultural commissioners or weed districts, have additional approval authority.

Federal permits (USDA-APHIS-PPQ Form 526) are required to import biocontrols agents from another state. Form 526 may be obtained by writing:

 USDA-APHIS-PPQ
 Biological Assessment and Taxonomic Support
 4700 River Road, Unit 113
 Riverdale, MD 20737
or
 through the internet at URL address:
 http://www.aphis.usda.gov/ppq/permits/bioligical/weedbio.html.

The Service strongly supports the development, and legal and responsible use of appropriate, safe, and effective biological control agents for nuisance and non-indigenous or pest species.

State and county agriculture departments may also be sources for biological control agents or they may have information about where biological control agents may be obtained. Commercial sources should have an Application and Permit to Move Live Plant Pests and Noxious Weeds (USDA-PPQ Form 226 USDA-APHIS-PPQ, Biological Assessment and Taxonomic Support, 4700 River Road, Unit 113, Riverdale, MD 20737) to release specific biological control agents in a state and/or county. Furthermore, certification regarding the biological control agent's identity (genus, specific epithet, sub-species and variety) and purity (e.g., parasite free, pathogen free, and biotic and abiotic contaminants) should be specified in purchase orders.

Biological control agents are subject to 7 RM 8 (Exotic Species Introduction and Management). In addition, Refuge staff would follow the International Code of Best Practice for Classical Biological Control of Weeds (http://sric.ucdavis.edu/exotic /exotic.htm) as ratified by delegates to the X International Symposium on Biological Control of Weeds, Bozeman, MT, July 9, 1999. This code identifies the following:

- Release only approved biological control agents,
- Use the most effective agents,
- Document releases, and
- Monitor for impact to the target pest, nontarget species and the environment.

Biological control agents formulated as pesticide products and registered by the USEPA (e.g., *Bti*) are also subject to PUP review and approval (see below).

A record of all releases would be maintained with date(s), location(s), and environmental conditions of the release site(s); the identity, quantity, and condition of the biological control agents released; and other relevant data and comments such as weather conditions. Systematic monitoring to determine the establishment and effectiveness of the release is also recommended.

NEPA documents regarding biological and other environmental effects of biological control agents prepared by another federal agency, where the scope is relevant to evaluation of releases on Refuge lands, would be reviewed. Possible source agencies for such NEPA documents include the Bureau of Land Management, US Forest Service, National Park Service, US Department of Agriculture-Animal and Plant Health Inspection Service, and the military services. It might be appropriate to incorporate by reference parts or all of existing document(s) from the review. Incorporating by reference (43 CFR 46.135) is a technique used to avoid redundancies in analysis. It also can reduce the bulk of a Service NEPA document, which only must identify the documents that are incorporated by reference. In addition, relevant portions must be summarized in the Service NEPA document to the extent necessary to provide the decision maker and public with an understanding of relevance of the referenced material to the current analysis.

- **Pesticides.** The selective use of pesticides would be based upon pest ecology (including mode of reproduction), the size and distribution of its populations, site-specific conditions (e.g., soils, topography), known efficacy under similar site conditions, and the capability to utilize best management practices (BMPs) to reduce/eliminate potential effects to non-target species, sensitive habitats, and potential to contaminate surface and groundwater. All pesticide usage (pesticide, target species, application rate, and method of application) would comply with the applicable federal (FIFRA) and state regulations pertaining to pesticide use, safety, storage, disposal, and reporting. Before pesticides can be used to eradicate, control, or contain pests on Refuge lands and waters, pesticide use proposals (PUPs) would be prepared and approved in accordance with 7 RM 14. PUP records would provide a detailed, time-, site-, and target-specific description of the proposed use of pesticides on Refuge. All PUPs would be created, approved or disapproved, and stored in the Pesticide Use Proposal System (PUPS), which is a centralized database only accessible on the Service's intranet (https://systems.fws.gov/pups). Only Service employees would be authorized to access PUP records for a Refuge in this database.

Application equipment would be selected to provide site-specific delivery to target pests while minimizing/eliminating direct or indirect (e.g., drift) exposure to non-target areas and degradation of surface and groundwater quality. Where possible, target-specific equipment (e.g., backpack sprayer, wiper) would be used to treat target pests. Other target-specific equipment to apply pesticides would include soaked wicks or paint brushes for wiping vegetation and lances, hatchets, or syringes for direct injection into stems. Granular pesticides may be applied using seeders or other specialized dispensers. In contrast, aerial spraying (e.g., fixed wing or helicopter) would only be used where access is difficult (remoteness) and/or the size/distribution of infestations precludes practical use of ground-based methods.

Because repeated use of one pesticide may allow resistant organisms to survive and reproduce, multiple pesticides with variable modes of action would be considered for treatments on Refuge lands and waters. This is especially important if multiple applications within years and/or over a growing season likely would be necessary for habitat maintenance and restoration activities to achieve resource objectives. Integrated chemical and non-chemical controls also are highly effective, where practical, because pesticide resistant organisms can be removed from the site.

Cost may not be the primary factor in selecting a pesticide for use on a Refuge. If the least expensive pesticide would potentially harm natural resources or people, then a different product would be selected, if available. The most efficacious pesticide available with the least potential to degrade environment quality (soils, surface water, and groundwater) as well as least potential effect to native species and communities of fish, wildlife, plants, and their habitats would be acceptable for use on Refuge lands in the context of an IPM approach.

- **Habitat restoration/maintenance.** Restoration and/or proper maintenance of Refuge habitats associated with achieving wildlife and habitat objectives would be essential for long-term prevention, eradication, or control (at or below threshold levels) of pests. Promoting desirable plant communities through the manipulation of species composition, plant density, and growth rate is an essential component of invasive plant management (Masters et al. 1996, Masters and Shelly 2001, Brooks et al. 2004). The following three components of succession could be manipulated through habitat maintenance and restoration: site availability, species availability, and species performance (Cox and Anderson 2004). Although a single method (e.g., herbicide treatment) may eliminate or suppress pest species in the short term, the resulting gaps and bare soil create niches that are conducive to further invasion by the species and/or other invasive plants. On degraded sites where desirable species are absent or in low abundance, revegetation with native/desirable grasses, forbs, and legumes may be necessary to direct and accelerate plant community recovery, and achieve site-specific objectives in a reasonable time frame. The selection of appropriate species for revegetation would be dependent on a number of factors including resource objectives and site-specific, abiotic factors (e.g., soil texture, precipitation/temperature regimes, and shade conditions). Seed availability and cost, ease of establishment, seed production, and competitive ability also would be important considerations.

4.0 Priorities for Treatments

The magnitude (number, distribution, and sizes of infestations) for pest problems is too extensive and beyond the available capital resources to effectively address during any single field season. To manage pests in Refuge, it would be essential to prioritize treatment of infestations. Highest priority treatments would be focused on early detection and rapid response to eliminate infestations of new pests, if possible. This would be especially important for aggressive pests potentially impacting species, species groups, communities, and/or habitats associated Refuge purpose(s), System resources of concern (federally listed species, migratory birds, selected marine mammals, and interjurisdictional fish), and native species for maintaining/restoring biological integrity, diversity, and environmental health.

The next priority would be treating established pests that appear in one or more previously un-infested areas. Moody and Mack (1988) demonstrated through modeling that small, new outbreaks of invasive plants eventually would infest an area larger than the established, source population. They also found that control efforts focusing on the large, main infestation rather than the new, small satellites reduced the chances of overall success. The lowest priority would be treating large infestations (sometimes monotypic stands) of well established pests. In this case, initial efforts would focus upon containment of the perimeter followed by work to control/eradicate the established infested area. If containment and/or control of a large infestation is not effective, then efforts would focus upon halting pest reproduction or managing source populations. Maxwell et al. (2009) found treating fewer populations that are sources represents an effective long-term strategy to reduce of total number of invasive populations and decreasing meta population growth rates.

Although state listed noxious weeds would always of high priority for management, other pest species known to cause substantial ecological impact would also be considered. For example, short-spined kiawe may not be listed by a state as noxious, but it can greatly alter fire regimes in the coastal dryland shrub habitat resulting in large monotypic stands that displace native bunch grasses, forbs, and shrubs. Pest control would likely require a multi-year commitment from Refuge staff. Essential to the long-term success of pest management would be pre- and post-treatment monitoring, assessment of the successes and failures of treatments, and development of new approaches when proposed methods do not achieve desired outcomes.

5.0 Best Management Practices (BMPs)

BMPs can minimize or eliminate possible effects associated with pesticide usage to non-target species and/or sensitive habitats as well as degradation of water quality from drift, surface runoff, or leaching. Based upon the Department of Interior Pesticide Use Policy (517 DM 1) and the Service Pest Management Policy and Responsibilities (30 AM 12), the use of applicable BMPs (where feasible) also would likely ensure that pesticide uses may not adversely affect federally listed species and/or their critical habitats through determinations made using the process described in 50 CFR part 402.

The following are BMPs pertaining to mixing/handling and applying pesticides for all ground-based treatments of pesticides, which would be considered and utilized, where feasible, based upon target- and site-specific factors and time-specific environmental conditions. Although not listed below, the most important BMP to eliminate/reduce potential impacts to non-target resources would be an IPM approach to prevent, control, eradicate, and contain pests.

5.1 Pesticide Handling and Mixing

- As a precaution against spilling, spray tanks would not be left unattended during filling.
- All pesticide containers would be triple rinsed and the rinsate would be used as water in the sprayer tank and applied to treatment areas.
- All pesticide spray equipment would be properly cleaned. Where possible, rinsate would be used as part of the make up water in the sprayer tank and applied to treatment areas.
- Refuge staff would empty, triple rinsed pesticide containers that can be recycled at local herbicide container collections.
- All unused pesticides would be properly discarded at a local "safe send" collection.
- Pesticides and pesticide containers would be lawfully stored, handled, and disposed of in accordance with the label and in a manner safeguarding human health, fish, and wildlife and prevent soil and water contaminant.
- Refuge staff would consider the water quality parameters (e.g., pH, hardness) that are important to ensure greatest efficacy where specified on the pesticide label.
- All pesticide spills would be addressed immediately using procedures identified in Refuge spill respond plan.

5.2 Applying Pesticides

- Pesticide treatments would only be conducted by or under the supervision of Service personnel and non-Service applicators with the appropriate, state or BLM certification to safely and effectively conduct these activities on Refuge lands and waters.
- Refuge staff would comply with all federal, state, and local pesticide use laws and regulations as well as Service pesticide-related policies. For example, Refuge staff would use application equipment and apply rates for the specific pest(s) identified on the pesticide label as required under FIFRA.
- Before each treatment season and prior to mixing or applying any product for the first time each season, all applicators would review the labels, MSDSs, and Pesticide Use Proposal (PUPs) for each pesticide, determining the target pest, appropriate mix rate(s), PPE, and other requirements listed on the pesticide label.
- A 1' no-spray buffer from the water's edge would be used, where applicable, and it does not detrimentally influence effective control of pest species.
- Use low impact herbicide application techniques (e.g., spot treatment, cut stump, oil basal, Thinvert system applications) rather than broadcast foliar applications (e.g., boom sprayer, other larger tank wand applications), where practical.
- Use low volume rather than high volume foliar applications where low impact methods above are not feasible or practical, to maximize herbicide effectiveness and ensure correct and uniform application rates.
- Applicators would use and adjust spray equipment to apply the coarsest droplet size spectrum with optimal coverage of the target species while reducing drift.
- Applicators would use the largest droplet size that results in uniform coverage.
- Applicators would use drift reduction technologies such as low-drift nozzles, where possible.

- Where possible, spraying would occur during low (average<7mph and preferably 3-5 mph) and consistent direction wind conditions with moderate temperatures (typically <85 °F).
- Where possible, applicators would avoid spraying during inversion conditions (often associated with calm and very low wind conditions) that can cause large-scale herbicide drift to non-target areas.
- Equipment would be calibrated regularly to ensure that the proper rate of pesticide is applied to the target area or species.
- Spray applications would be made at the lowest height for uniform coverage of target pests to minimize/eliminate potential drift.
- If windy conditions frequently occur during afternoons, spraying (especially boom treatments) would typically be conducted during early morning hours.
- Spray applications would not be conducted on days with >30% forecast for rain within 6 hours, except for pesticides that are rapidly rain fast (e.g., glyphosate in 1 hour) to minimize/eliminate potential runoff.
- Where possible, applicators would use drift retardant adjuvants during spray applications, especially adjacent to sensitive areas.
- Where possible, applicators would use a non-toxic dye to aid in identifying target area treated as well as potential over spray or drift. A dye can also aid in detecting equipment leaks. If a leak is discovered, the application would be stopped until repairs can be made to the sprayer.
- For pesticide uses associated with facilities management, buffers, as appropriate, would be used to protect sensitive habitats, especially wetlands and other aquatic habitats.
- When drift cannot be sufficiently reduced through altering equipment set up and application techniques, buffer zones may be identified to protect sensitive areas downwind of applications. Refuge staff would only apply adjacent to sensitive areas when the wind is blowing the opposite direction.
- Applicators would utilize scouting for early detection of pests to eliminate unnecessary pesticide applications.
- Refuge staff would consider timing of application so native plants are protected (e.g., senescence) while effectively treating invasive plants.
- Rinsate from cleaning spray equipment after application would be recaptured and reused or applied to an appropriate pest plant infestation.
- Application equipment (e.g., sprayer, ATV, tractor) would be thoroughly cleaned and PPE would be removed/disposed of on-site by applicators after treatments to eliminate the potential spread of pests to un-infested areas.

6.0 Safety

6.1 Personal Protective Equipment

All applicators would wear the specific personal protective equipment (PPE) identified on the pesticide label. The appropriate PPE will be worn at all times during handling, mixing, and applying. PPE can include the following: disposable (e.g., Tyvek) or laundered coveralls; gloves (latex, rubber, or nitrile); rubber boots; and/or an NIOSH-approved respirator. Because exposure to concentrated product is usually greatest during mixing, extra care should be taken while preparing pesticide solutions. Persons mixing these solutions can be best protected if they wear long gloves, an apron, footwear, and a face shield.

Coveralls and other protective clothing used during an application would be laundered separately from other laundry items. Transporting, storing, handling, mixing and disposing of pesticide containers will be consistent with label requirements, USEPA and OSHA requirements, and Service policy.

If a respirator is necessary for a pesticide use, then the following requirements would be met in accordance with Service safety policy: a written Respirator Program, fit testing, physical examination (including pulmonary function and blood work for contaminants), and proper storage of the respirator.

6.2 Notification
The restricted entry interval (REI) is the time period required after the application at which point someone may safely enter a treated area without PPE. Refuge staff, authorized management agents of the Service, volunteers, and members of the public who could be in or near a pesticide treated area within the stated re-entry time period on the label would be notified about treatment areas. Posting would occur at any site where individuals might inadvertently become exposed to a pesticide during other activities on the Refuge. Where required by the label and/or state-specific regulations, sites would also be posted on its perimeter and at other likely locations of entry. Refuge staff would also notify appropriate private property owners of an intended application, including any private individuals have requested notification. Special efforts would be made to contact nearby individuals who are beekeepers or who have expressed chemical sensitivities.

6.3 Medical Surveillance
Medical surveillance may be required for Service personnel and approved volunteers who mix, apply, and/or monitor use of pesticides (see 242 FW 7 [Pesticide Users] and 242 FW 4 [Medical Surveillance]). In accordance with 242 FW 7.12A, Service personnel would be medically monitoring if 1 or more of the following criteria is met: exposed or may be exposed to concentrations at or above the published permissible exposure limits or threshold limit values (see 242 FW 4); use pesticides in a manner considered "frequent pesticide use"; or use pesticides in a manner that requires a respirator (see 242 FW 14 for respirator use requirements). In 242 FW7.7A, **"Frequent Pesticide Use** means when a person applying pesticide handles, mixes, or applies pesticides, with a Health Hazard rating of 3 or higher, for 8 or more hours in any week or 16 or more hours in any 30-day period." Under some circumstances, individuals may be medically monitored who use pesticides infrequently (see section 7.7), experience an acute exposure (sudden, short term), or use pesticides with a health hazard ranking of 1 or 2. This decision would consider the individual's health and fitness level, the pesticide's specific health risks, and the potential risks from other pesticide-related activities. Refuge cooperators and other authorized agents (e.g., state and county employees) would be responsible for their own medical monitoring needs and costs.

Standard examinations (at Refuge expense) of appropriate Refuge staff would be provided by the nearest certified occupational health and safety physician as determined by Federal Occupational Health.

6.4 Certification and Supervision of Pesticide Applicators
Appropriate Refuge staff or approved volunteers handling, mixing, and/or applying or directly supervising others engaged in pesticide use activities would be trained and state or federally licensed to apply pesticides to Refuge lands or waters. In accordance with 242 FW7.18A, certification is required to apply restricted use pesticides based upon USEPA regulations. For safety reasons, all

individuals participating in pest management activities with general use pesticides also are encouraged to attend appropriate training or acquire pesticide applicator certification. The certification requirement would be for a commercial or private applicator depending upon the state. New staff unfamiliar with proper procedures for storing, mixing, handling, applying, and disposing of herbicides and containers would receive orientation and training before handling or using any products. Documentation of training would be kept in the files at the Refuge office.

6.5 Record Keeping

6.5.1 Labels and material safety data sheets

Pesticide labels and material safety data sheets (MSDSs) would be maintained at the Refuge shop and laminated copies in the mixing area. These documents also would be carried by field applicators, where possible. A written reference (e.g., note pad, chalk board, dry erase board) for each tank to be mixed would be kept in the mixing area for quick reference while mixing is in progress. In addition, approved PUPs stored in the PUPS database typically contain website links (URLs) to pesticide labels and MSDSs.

6.5.2 Pesticide use proposals (PUPs)

A PUP would be prepared for each proposed pesticide use associated with annual pest management on Refuge lands and waters. A PUP would include specific information about the proposed pesticide use including the common and chemical names of the pesticide(s), target pest species, size and location of treatment site(s), application rate(s) and method(s), and federally listed species determinations, where applicable.

In accordance with 30 AM 12 and 7 RM 14, PUPs would be required for the following:
- Uses of pesticides on lands and facilities owned or managed by the Service, including properties managed by Service personnel as a result of the Food Security Act of 1985;
- Service projects by non-Service personnel on Service owned or controlled lands and facilities and other pest management activities that would be conducted by Service personnel; and
- Where the Service would be responsible or provides funds for pest management identified in protective covenants, easements, contracts, or agreements off Service lands.

In accordance with Service guidelines (Director's memo [December 12, 2007]), Refuge staff may receive up to 5-year approvals for Washington Office and field reviewed proposed pesticide uses based upon meeting identified criteria including an approved IPM plan, where necessary (see http://www.fws.gov/contaminants/Issues/IPM.cfm). For a refuge, an IPM plan (requirements described herein) can be completed independently or in association with a CCP or HMP if IPM strategies and potential environmental effects are adequately addressed within appropriate NEPA documentation.

PUPs would be created, approved or disapproved, and stored as records in the Pesticide Use Proposal System (PUPS), which is centralized database on the Service's intranet (https://systems.fws.gov/pups). Only Service employees can access PUP records in this database.

6.5.3 Pesticide usage

In accordance with 30 AM 12 and 7 RM 14, the Refuge Project Leader would be required to maintain records of all pesticides annually applied on lands or waters under Refuge jurisdiction. This would encompass pesticides applied by other federal agencies, state and county governments, non-government applicators including cooperators and their pest management service providers with Service permission. For clarification, pesticide means all insecticides, insect and plant growth regulators, dessicants, herbicides, fungicides, rodenticides, acaricides, nematicides, fumigants, avicides, and piscicides.

The following usage information can be reported for approved PUPs in the PUPS database:
- Pesticide trade name(s)
- Active ingredient(s)
- Total acres treated
- Total amount of pesticides used (lbs or gallons)
- Total amount of active ingredient(s) used (lbs)
- Target pest(s)
- Efficacy (% control)

To determine whether treatments are efficacious (eradicating, controlling, or containing the target pest) and achieving resource objectives, habitat and/or wildlife response would be monitored both pre- and post-treatment, where possible. Considering available annual funding and staffing, appropriate monitoring data regarding characteristics (attributes) of pest infestations (e.g., area, perimeter, degree of infestation-density, % cover, density) as well as habitat and/or wildlife response to treatments may be collected and stored in a relational database (e.g., Refuge Habitat Management Database), preferably a geo-referenced data management system (e.g., Refuge Lands GIS [RLGIS]) to facilitate data analyses and subsequent reporting. In accordance with adaptive management, data analysis and interpretation would allow treatments to be modified or changed over time, as necessary, to achieve resource objectives considering site-specific conditions in conjunction with habitat and/or wildlife responses. Monitoring could also identify short- and long-term impacts to natural resources and environmental quality associated with IPM treatments in accordance with adaptive management principles identified in 43 CFR 46.145.

7.0 Evaluating Pesticide Use Proposals

Pesticides would only be used on Refuge lands for habitat management as well as facilities maintenance after approval of a PUP. In general, proposed pesticide uses on Refuge lands would only be approved where there would likely be minor, temporary, or localized effects to fish and wildlife species as well as minimal potential to degrade environmental quality. Potential effects to listed and non-listed species would be evaluated with quantitative ecological risk assessments and other screening measures. Potential effects to environmental quality would be based upon pesticide characteristics of environmental fate (water solubility, soil mobility, soil persistence, and volatilization) and other quantitative screening tools. Ecological risk assessments as well as characteristics of environmental fate and potential to degrade environmental quality for pesticides would be documented in Chemical Profiles (see Section 7.5). These profiles would include threshold values for quantitative measures of ecological risk assessments and screening tools for environmental fate that represent minimal potential effects to species and environmental quality. In general, only pesticide uses with appropriate BMPs (see Section 4.0) for habitat management and facilities maintenance on Refuge lands that would potentially have minor, temporary, or localized effects on Refuge biological and environmental quality (threshold values not exceeded) would be approved.

7.1 Overview of Ecological Risk Assessment

An ecological risk assessment process would be used to evaluate potential adverse effects to biological resources as a result of a pesticide(s) proposed for use on Refuge lands. It is an established quantitative and qualitative methodology for comparing and prioritizing risks of pesticides and conveying an estimate of the potential risk for an adverse effect. This quantitative methodology provides an efficient mechanism to integrate best available scientific information regarding hazard, patterns of use (exposure), and dose-response relationships in a manner that is useful for ecological risk decision-making. It would provide an effective way to evaluate potential effects where there is missing or unavailable scientific information (data gaps) to address reasonable, foreseeable adverse effects in the field as required under 40 CFR Part 1502.22. Protocols for ecological risk assessment of pesticide uses on the Refuge were developed through research and established by the US Environmental Protection Agency (2004). Assumptions for these risk assessments are presented in Section 6.2.3.

The toxicological data used in ecological risk assessments are typically results of standardized laboratory studies provided by pesticide registrants to the US Environmental Protection Agency (USEPA) to meet regulatory requirements under the Federal Insecticide, Fungicide and Rodenticide Act of 1996 (FIFRA). These studies assess the acute (lethality) and chronic (reproductive) effects associated with short- and long-term exposure to pesticides on representative species of birds, mammals, freshwater fish, aquatic invertebrates, and terrestrial and aquatic plants. Other effects data publicly available would also be utilized for risk assessment protocols described herein. Toxicity endpoint and environmental fate data are available from a variety of resources. Some of the more useful resources can be found in
Section 7.5.

Table E-1. Ecotoxicity tests used to evaluate potential effects to birds, fish, and mammals to establish toxicity endpoints for risk quotient calculations.

Species Group	Exposure	Measurement endpoint
Bird	Acute	Median Lethal Concentration (LC_{50})
Bird	Chronic	No Observed Effect Concentration (NOEC) or No Observed Adverse Effect Concentration (NOAEC)[1]
Fish	Acute	Median Lethal Concentration (LC_{50})
Fish	Chronic	No Observed Effect Concentration (NOEC) or No Observed Adverse Effect Concentration (NOAEC)[2]
Mammal	Acute	Oral Lethal Dose (LD_{50})
Mammal	Chronic	No Observed Effect Concentration (NOEC) or No Observed Adverse Effect Concentration (NOAEC)[3]

[1]Measurement endpoints typically include a variety of reproductive parameters (e.g., number of eggs, number of offspring, eggshell thickness, and number of cracked eggs).
[2]Measurement endpoints for early life stage/life cycle typically include embryo hatch rates, time to hatch, growth, and time to swim-up.
[3]Measurement endpoints include maternal toxicity, teratogenic effects or developmental anomalies, evidence of mutagenicity or genotoxicity, and interference with cellular mechanisms such as DNA synthesis and DNA repair.

7.2 Determining Ecological Risk to Fish and Wildlife

The potential for pesticides used on the Refuge to cause direct adverse effects to fish and wildlife would be evaluated using USEPA's Ecological Risk Assessment Process (US Environmental Protection Agency 2004). This deterministic approach, which is based upon a two-phase process involving estimation of environmental concentrations and then characterization of risk, would be used for ecological risk assessments. This method integrates exposure estimates (estimated environmental concentration [EEC] and toxicological endpoints [e.g., LC_{50} and oral LD_{50}]) to evaluate the potential for adverse effects to species groups (birds, mammals, and fish) representative of legal mandates for managing units of the NWRS. This integration is achieved through risk quotients (RQs) calculated by dividing the EEC by acute and chronic toxicity values selected from standardized toxicological endpoints or published effect (Table 1).

$$RQ = EEC/Toxicological\ Endpoint$$

The level of risk associated with direct effects of pesticide use would be characterized by comparing calculated RQs to the appropriate Level of Concern (LOC) established by US Environmental Protection Agency (1998 [Table 2]). The LOC represents a quantitative threshold value for screening potential adverse effects to fish and wildlife resources associated with pesticide use. The following are four exposure-species group scenarios that would be used to characterize ecological risk to fish and wildlife on the Refuge: acute-listed species, acute-nonlisted species, chronic-listed species, and chronic-nonlisted species.

Acute risk would indicate the potential for mortality associated with short-term dietary exposure to pesticides immediately after an application. For characterization of acute risks, median values from LC_{50} and LD_{50} tests would be used as toxicological endpoints for RQ calculations. In contrast, chronic risks would indicate the potential for adverse effects associated with long-term dietary exposure to pesticides from a single application or multiple applications over time (within a season and over years). For characterization of chronic risks, the no observed concentration (NOAEC) or no observed effect concentration (NOEC) for reproduction would be used as toxicological endpoints for RQ calculations. Where available, the NOAEC would be preferred over a NOEC value.

Listed species are those federally designated as threatened, endangered, or proposed in accordance with the Endangered Species Act of 1973 (16 USC 1531-1544, 87 Stat. 884, as amended-Public Law 93-205). For listed species, potential adverse effects would be assessed at the individual level because loss of individuals from a population could detrimentally impact a species. In contrast, risks to nonlisted species would consider effects at the population level. A RQ<LOC would indicate the proposed pesticide use "may affect, not likely to adversely effect" individuals (listed species) and it would not pose an unacceptable risk for adverse effects to populations (non-listed species) for each taxonomic group (Table 2). In contrast, a RQ>LOC would indicate a "may affect, likely to adversely affect" for listed species and it would also pose unacceptable ecological risk for adverse effects to nonlisted species.

Table E-2. Presumption of unacceptable risk for birds, fish, and mammals (US EPA 1998).

Risk Presumption		Level of Concern	
		Listed Species	Non-listed Species
Acute	Birds	0.1	0.5
	Fish	0.05	0.5
	Mammals	0.1	0.5
Chronic	Birds	1.0	1.0
	Fish	1.0	1.0
	Mammals	1.0	1.0

7.2.1 Environmental exposure

Following release into the environment through application, pesticides would experience several different routes of environmental fate. Pesticides which would be sprayed can move through the air (e.g., particle or vapor drift) and may eventually end up in other parts of the environment such as non-target vegetation, soil, or water. Pesticides applied directly to the soil may be washed off the soil into nearby bodies of surface water (e.g., surface runoff) or may percolate through the soil to lower soil layers and groundwater (e.g., leaching) (Baker and Miller 1999, Pope et. al. 1999, Butler et. al. 1998, Ramsay et. al. 1995, EXTOXNET 1993a). Pesticides which would be injected into the soil may also be subject to the latter two fates.

The aforementioned possibilities are by no means complete, but it does indicate movement of pesticides in the environment is very complex with transfers occurring continually among different environmental compartments. In some cases, these exchanges occur not only between areas that are close together, but it also may involve transportation of pesticides over long distances (Barry 2004, Woods 2004).

7.2.1.1 Terrestrial exposure

The estimated environmental concentration (ECC) for exposure to terrestrial wildlife would be quantified using an USEPA screening-level approach (US Environmental Protection Agency 2004). This screening-level approach is not affected by product formulation because it evaluates pesticide active ingredient(s). This approach would vary depending upon the proposed pesticide application method: spray or granular.

7.2.1.1.1 Terrestrial-spray application

For spray applications, exposure would be determined using the Kanaga nomogram method (US Environmental Protection Agency 2005a, US Environmental Protection Agency 2004, Pfleeger et al. 1996) through the USEPA's Terrestrial Residue Exposure model (T-REX) version 1.2.3 (US Environmental Protection Agency 2005b). To estimate the maximum (initial) pesticide residue on short grass (<8"m tall) as a general food item category for terrestrial vertebrate species, T-REX input variables would include the following from the pesticide label: maximum pesticide application rate (pounds active ingredient [acid equivalent]/acre) and pesticide half-life (days) in soil. Although there are other food item categories (tall grasses; broadleaf plants and small insects; and fruits, pods, seeds and large insects), short grass was selected because it would yield maximum EECs (240 ppm per lb ai/acre) for worse-case risk assessments. Short grass is not representative of forage for carnivorous species (e.g., raptors), but it would characterize the maximum potential exposure through the diet of avian and mammalian prey items. Consequently, this approach would provide a conservative screening tool for pesticides that do not biomagnify.

For RQ calculations in T-REX, the model would require the weight of surrogate species and Mineau scaling factors (Mineau et. al. 1996). Body weights of bobwhite quail and mallard are included in T-REX by default, but body weights of other organisms (Table E-3) would be entered manually. The Mineau scaling factor accounts for small-bodied bird species that may be more sensitive to pesticide exposure than would be predicted only by body weight. Mineau scaling factors would be entered manually with values ranging from 1 to 1.55 that are unique to a particular pesticide or group of pesticides. If specific information to select a scaling factor is not available, then a value of 1.15 would be used as a default. Alternatively, zero would be entered if it is known that body weight does not influence toxicity of pesticide(s) being assessed. The upper bound estimate output from the T-REX Kanaga nomogram would be used as an EEC for calculation of RQs. This approach would yield a conservative estimate of ecological risk.

Table E-3. Average body weight of selected terrestrial wildlife species frequently used in research to establish toxicological endpoints (Dunning 1984).

Species	Body Weight (kg)
Mammal (15 g)	0.015
House sparrow	0.0277
Mammal (35 g)	0.035
Starling	0.0823
Red-winged blackbird	0.0526
Common grackle	0.114
Japanese quail	0.178
Bobwhite quail	0.178
Rat	0.200
Rock dove (aka pigeon)	0.542
Mammal (1000 g)	1.000
Mallard	1.082
Ring-necked pheasant	1.135

7.2.1.1.2 Terrestrial – granular application

Granular pesticide formulations and pesticide-treated seed would pose a unique route of exposure for avian and mammalian species. The pesticide is applied in discrete units which birds or mammals might ingest accidentally with food items or intentionally as in the case of some bird species actively seeking and picking up gravel or grit to aid digestion or seed as a food source. Granules may also be consumed by wildlife foraging on earthworms, slugs or other soft-bodied soil organisms to which the granules may adhere.

Terrestrial wildlife RQs for granular formulations or seed treatments would be calculated by dividing the maximum milligrams of active ingredient (ai) exposed (e.g., EEC) on the surface of an area equal to 1 square foot by the appropriate LD_{50} value multiplied by the surrogate's body weight (Table 3). An adjustment to surface area calculations would be made for broadcast, banded, and in-furrow applications. An adjustment also would be made for applications with and without incorporation of the granules. Without incorporation, it would be assumed that 100% of the granules remain on the soil surface available to foraging birds and mammals. Press wheels push granules flat with the soil surface, but they are not incorporated into the soil. If granules are incorporated in the soil during band or T-band applications or after broadcast applications, it would be assumed only 15% of the applied granules remain available to wildlife. It would be assumed that only 1% of the granules are available on the soil surface following in-furrow applications.

EECs for pesticides applied in granular form and as seed treatments would be determined considering potential ingestion rates of avian or mammalian species (e.g., 10-30% body weight/day). This would provide an estimate of maximum exposure that may occur as a result of granule or seed treatment spills such as those that commonly occur at end rows during application and planting. The availability of granules and seed treatments to terrestrial vertebrates would also be considered by calculating the loading per unit area (LD_{50}/ft^2) for comparison to USEPA Level of Concerns (US Environmental Protection Agency 1998). The T-REX version 1.2.3 (US Environmental Protection Agency 2005b) contains a submodel which automates Kanaga exposure calculations for granular pesticides and treated seed.

The following formulas will be used to calculate EECs depending upon the type of granular pesticide application:
- In-furrow applications assume a typical value of 1% granules, bait, or seed remain unincorporated.

$$mg\ a.i./ft.^2 = [(lbs.\ product/acre)(\%\ a.i.)(453,580\ mg/lbs)(1\%\ exposed))] / \{[(43,560\ ft.^2/acre)/(row\ spacing\ (ft.))] / (row\ spacing\ (ft.)\}$$

or

$$mg\ a.i./ft^2 = [(lbs\ product/1000\ ft.\ row)(\%\ a.i.)(1000\ ft\ row)(453,580\ mg/lb.)(1\%\ exposed)$$

$$EEC = [(mg\ a.i./ft.^2)(\%\ of\ pesticide\ biologically\ available)]$$

- Incorporated banded treatments assume that 15% of granules, bait, seeds are unincorporated.

$$mg\ a.i./ft.^2 = [(lbs.\ product/1000\ row\ ft.)(\%\ a.i.)(453,580\ mg/lb.)(1-\%\ incorporated)] / (1,000\ ft.)(band\ width\ (ft.))$$

$$EEC = [(mg\ a.i./ft.^2)(\%\ of\ pesticide\ biologically\ available)]$$

- Broadcast treatment without incorporation assumes 100% of granules, bait, seeds are unincorporated.

$$mg\ a.i./ft.^2 = [(lbs.\ product/acre)(\%\ a.i.)(453,590\ mg/lb.)] / (43,560\ ft.^2/acre)$$

$$EEC = [(mg\ a.i./ft.^2)(\%\ of\ pesticide\ biologically\ available)]$$

Where:

- *% of pesticide biologically available = 100% without species specific ingestion rates*

• Conversion for calculating mg a.i./ft.^{2} using ounces: 453,580 mg/lb. /16 = 28,349 mg/oz.

The following equation would used to calculate a RQ based on the EEC calculated by one of the above equations. The EEC would divided by the surrogate LD$_{50}$ toxicological endpoint multiplied by the body weight (Table 3) of the surrogate.

$$RQ = EEC / [LD_{50} (mg/kg) * body\ weight\ (kg)]$$

As with other risk assessments, a RQ>LOC would be a presumption of unacceptable ecological risk. A RQ<LOC would be a presumption of acceptable risk with only minor, temporary, or localized effects to species.

7.2.1.2 Aquatic exposure

Exposures to aquatic habitats (e.g., wetlands, meadows, ephemeral pools, water delivery ditches) would be evaluated separately for ground-based pesticide treatments of habitats managed for fish and wildlife compared with cropland/facilities maintenance. The primary exposure pathway for aquatic organisms from any ground-based treatments likely would be particle drift during the pesticide application. However, different exposure scenarios would be necessary as a result of contrasting application equipment and techniques as well as pesticides used to control pests on agricultural lands and facilities maintenance (e.g., roadsides, parking lots, trails) compared with other managed habitats on the Refuge. In addition, pesticide applications may be done <25' of the high water mark of aquatic habitats for habitat management treatments; whereas, no-spray buffers (≥25') would be used for facilities maintenance treatments.

7.2.1.2.1 Habitat treatments

For the worst-case exposure scenario to non-target aquatic habitats, EECs (Table 4) would be would be derived from Urban and Cook (1986) that assumes an intentional overspray to an entire, non-target water body (1-foot depth) from a treatment <25' from the high water mark using the max application rate (acid basis [see above]). However, use of BMPs for applying pesticides (see Section 4.2) would likely minimize/eliminate potential drift to non-target aquatic habitats during actual treatments. If there would be unacceptable (acute or chronic) risk to fish and wildlife with the simulated 100% overspray (RQ>LOC), then the proposed pesticide use may be disapproved or the PUP would be approved at a lower application rate to minimize/eliminate unacceptable risk to aquatic organisms (RQ=LOC).

Table E.4. Estimated Environmental Concentrations (ppb) of pesticides in aquatic habitats (1' depth) immediately after direct application (Urban and Cook 1986).

Lbs/acre	EEC (ppb)
0.10	36.7
0.20	73.5
0.25	91.9
0.30	110.2
0.40	147.0
0.50	183.7
0.75	275.6
1.00	367.5
1.25	459.7
1.50	551.6
1.75	643.5
2.00	735.7
2.25	827.6
2.50	919.4
3.00	1103.5
4.00	1471.4
5.00	1839
6.00	2207
7.00	2575
8.00	2943
9.00	3311
10.00	3678

7.2.1.2.2 Facilities maintenance treatments

Field drift studies conducted by the Spray Drift Task Force, which is a joint project of several agricultural chemical businesses, were used to develop a generic spray drift database. From this database, the AgDRIFT computer model was created to satisfy USEPA pesticide registration spray drift data requirements and as a scientific basis to evaluate off-target movement of pesticides from particle drift and assess potential effects of exposure to wildlife. Several versions of the computer model have been developed (i.e., v2.01 through v2.10). The Spray Drift Task Force AgDRIFT® model version 2.01 (SDTF 2003, AgDRIFT 2001) would be used to derive EECs resulting from drift of pesticides to Refuge aquatic resources from ground-based pesticide applications >25' from the high water mark. The Spray Drift Task Force AgDRIFT model is publicly available at http://www.agdrift.com. At this website, click "AgDRIFT 2.0" and then click "Download Now" and follow the instructions to obtain the computer model.

The AgDRIFT model is composed of submodels called tiers. Tier I Ground submodel would be used to assess ground-based applications of pesticides. Tier outputs (EECs) would be calculated with AgDRIFT using the following input variables: max application rate (acid basis [see above]), low boom (20"), fine to medium droplet size, EPA-defined wetland, and a ≥25-foot distance (buffer) from treated area to water.

7.2.2 Use of information on effects of biological control agents, pesticides, degradates, and adjuvants

NEPA documents regarding biological and other environmental effects of biological control agents, pesticides, degradates, and adjuvants prepared by another federal agency, where the scope would be relevant to evaluation of effects from pesticide uses on Refuge lands, would be reviewed. Possible source agencies for such NEPA documents would include the Bureau of Land Management, US Forest Service, National Park Service, US Department of Agriculture-Animal and Plant Health Inspection Service, and the military services. It might be appropriate to incorporate by reference parts or all of existing document(s). Incorporating by reference (40 CFR 1502.21) is a technique used to avoid redundancies in analysis. It also would reduce the bulk of a Service NEPA document, which only would identify the documents that are incorporated by reference. In addition, relevant portions would be summarized in the Service NEPA document to the extent necessary to provide the decision maker and public with an understanding of relevance of the referenced material to the current analysis.

In accordance with the requirements set forth in 43 CFR 46.135, the Service would specifically incorporate through reference ecological risk assessments prepared by the US Forest Service (http://www.fs.fed.us/r6/invasiveplant-eis/Risk-Assessments/Herbicides-Analyzed-InvPlant-EIS.htm) and Bureau of Land Management (http://www.blm.gov/wo/st/en/prog/more/veg_eis.html). These risk assessments and associated documentation also are available in total with the administrative record for the Final Environmental Impact Statement entitled *Pacific Northwest Region Invasive Plant Program – Preventing and Managing Invasive Plants* (US Forest Service 2005) and *Vegetation Treatments Using Herbicides on Bureau of Land Management Lands in 17 Western States Programmatic EIS (PEIS)* (Bureau of Land Management 2007). In accordance with 43 CRF 46.120(d), use of existing NEPA documents by supplementing, tiering to, incorporating by reference, or adopting
previous NEPA environmental analyses would avoid redundancy and unnecessary paperwork.

As a basis for completing "Chemical Profiles" for approving or disapproving Refuge PUPs, ecological risk assessments for the following herbicide and adjuvant uses prepared by the US Forest Service would be incorporated by reference:
• 2,4-D
• Chlorosulfuron
• Clopyralid
• Dicamba
• Glyphosate
• Imazapic
• Imazapyr
• Metsulfuron methyl
• Picloram
• Sethoxydim
• Sulfometuron methyl
• Triclopyr
• Nonylphenol polyethylate (NPE) based surfactants

As a basis for completing "Chemical Profiles" for approving or disapproving Refuge PUPs, ecological risk assessments for the following herbicide uses as well as evaluation of risks associated with pesticide degradates and adjuvants prepared by the Bureau of Land Management would be incorporated by reference:

- Bromacil
- Chlorsulfuron
- Diflufenzopyr
- Diquat
- Diuron
- Fluridone
- Imazapic
- Overdrive (diflufenzopyr and dicamba)
- Sulfometuron methyl
- Tebuthiuron
- Pesticide degradates and adjuvants (*Appendix D – Evaluation of risks from degradates, polyoxyethylene-amine (POEA) and R-11, and endocrine disrupting chemicals*)

7.2.3 Assumptions for ecological risk assessments

There are a number of assumptions involved with the ecological risk assessment process for terrestrial and aquatic organisms associated with utilization of the US Environmental Protection Agency's (2004) process. These assumptions may be risk neutral or may lead to an over- or under-estimation of risk from pesticide exposure depending upon site-specific conditions. The following describes these assumptions, their application to the conditions typically encountered, and whether or not they may lead to recommendations that are risk neutral, underestimate, or overestimate ecological risk from potential pesticide exposure.

- Indirect effects would not be evaluated by ecological risk assessments. These effects include the mechanisms of indirect exposure to pesticides: consuming prey items (fish, birds, or small mammals), reductions in the availability of prey items, and disturbance associated with pesticide application activities.

- Exposure to a pesticide product can be assessed based upon the active ingredient. However, exposure to a chemical mixture (pesticide formulation) may result in effects that are similar or substantially different compared to only the active ingredient. Non-target organisms may be exposed directly to the pesticide formulation or only various constituents of the formulation as they dissipate and partition in the environment. If toxicological information for both the active ingredient and formulated product are available, then data representing the greatest potential toxicity would be selected for use in the risk assessment process (US Environmental Protection Agency 2004). As a result, this conservative approach may lead to an overestimation of risk characterization from pesticide exposure.

- Because toxicity tests with listed or candidate species or closely related species are not available, data for surrogate species would be most often used for risk assessments. Specifically, bobwhite quail and mallard duck are the most frequently used surrogates for evaluating potential toxicity to federally listed avian species. Bluegill sunfish, rainbow trout, and fathead minnow are the most common surrogates for evaluating toxicity for freshwater fishes. However, sheep's head minnow can be an appropriate surrogate marine species for coastal environments. Rats and mice are the most common surrogates for evaluating toxicity for mammals. Interspecies sensitivity is a major source of uncertainty in pesticide assessments. As a result of this uncertainty, data is selected for the most sensitive species tested within a taxonomic group (birds, fish, and mammals) given the quality of the data is acceptable. If additional toxicity data for more species of organisms in a particular group are available, the selected data will not be limited to the species previously listed as common surrogates.

- The Kanaga nomogram outputs maximum EEC values that may be used to calculate an average daily concentration over a specified interval of time, which is referred to as a time-weighted-average (TWA). The maximum EEC would be selected as the exposure input for both acute and chronic risk assessments in the screening-level evaluations. The initial or maximum EEC derived from the Kanaga nomogram represents the maximum expected instantaneous or acute exposure to a pesticide. Acute toxicity endpoints are determined using a single exposure to a known pesticide concentration typically for 48 to 96 hours. This value is assumed to represent ecological risk from acute exposure to a pesticide. On the other hand, chronic risk to pesticide exposure is a function of pesticide concentration and duration of exposure to the pesticide. An organism's response to chronic pesticide exposure may result from either the concentration of the pesticide, length of exposure, or some combination of both factors. Standardized tests for chronic toxicity typically involve exposing an organism to several different pesticide concentrations for a specified length of time (days, weeks, months, years or generations). For example, avian reproduction tests include a 10-week exposure phase. Because a single length of time is used in the test, time response data is usually not available for inclusion into risk assessments. Without time response data it is difficult to determine the concentration which elicited a toxicological response.

- Using maximum EECs for chronic risk estimates may result in an overestimate of risk, particularly for compounds that dissipate rapidly. Conversely, using TWAs for chronic risk estimates may underestimate risk if it is the concentration rather than the duration of exposure that is primarily responsible for the observed adverse effect. The maximum EEC would be used for chronic risk assessments although it may result in an overestimate of risk. TWAs may be used for chronic risk assessments, but they will be applied judiciously considering the potential for an underestimate or overestimate of risk. For example, the number of days exposure exceeds a Level of Concern may influence the suitability of a pesticide use. The greater the number of days the EEC exceeds the Level of Concern translates into greater the ecological risk. This is a qualitative assessment, and is subject to reviewer's expertise in ecological risk assessment and tolerance for risk.

- The length of time used to calculate the TWA can have a substantial effect on the exposure estimates and there is no standard method for determining the appropriate duration for this estimate. The T-REX model assumes a 21-week exposure period, which is equivalent to avian reproductive studies designed to establish a steady-state concentration for bioaccumulative compounds. However, this does not necessarily define the true exposure duration needed to elicit a toxicological response. Pesticides, which do not bioaccumulate, may achieve a steady-state concentration earlier than 21 weeks. The duration of time for calculating TWAs will require justification and it will not exceed the duration of exposure in the chronic toxicity test (approximately 70 days for the standard avian reproduction study). An alternative to using the duration of the chronic toxicity study is to base the TWA on the application interval. In this case, increasing the application interval would suppress both the estimated peak pesticide concentration and the TWA. Another alternative to using TWAs would be to consider the number of days that a chemical is predicted to exceed the LOC.

- Pesticide dissipation is assumed to be first-order in the absence of data suggesting alternative dissipation patterns such as bi-phasic. Field dissipation data would generally be the most pertinent for assessing exposure in terrestrial species that forage on vegetation. However, this data is often not available and it can be misleading particularly if the compound is prone to "wash-off". Soil half-life is the most common degradation data available. Dissipation or degradation data that would reflect the environmental conditions typical of Refuge lands would be utilized, if available.

- For species found in the water column, it would be assumed that the greatest bioavailable fraction of the pesticide active ingredient in surface waters is freely dissolved in the water column.

- Actual habitat requirements of any particular terrestrial species are not considered, and it is assumed that species exclusively and permanently occupy the treated area, or adjacent areas receiving pesticide at rates commensurate with the treatment rate. This assumption would produce a maximum estimate of exposure for risk characterization. This assumption would likely lead to an overestimation of exposure for species that do not permanently and exclusively occupy the treated area (US Environmental Protection Agency 2004).

- Exposure through incidental ingestion of pesticide contaminated soil is not considered in the USEPA risk assessment protocols. Research suggests <15% of the diet can consist of incidentally ingested soil depending upon species and feeding strategy (Beyer et al. 1994). An assessment of pesticide concentrations in soil compared to food item categories in the Kanaga nomogram indicates incidental soil ingestion will not likely increase dietary exposure to pesticides. Inclusion of soil into the diet would effectively reduce the overall dietary concentration compared to the present assumption that the entire diet consists a contaminated food source (Fletcher et al. 1994). An exception to this may be soil-applied pesticides in which exposure from incidental ingestion of soil may increase. Potential for pesticide exposure under this assumption may be underestimated for soil-applied pesticides and overestimated for foliar-applied pesticides. The concentration of a pesticide in soil would likely be less than predicted on food items.

- Exposure through inhalation of pesticides is not considered in the USEPA risk assessment protocols. Such exposure may occur through three potential sources: spray material in droplet form at time of application, vapor phase with the pesticide volatilizing from treated surfaces, and airborne particulates (soil, vegetative matter, and pesticide dusts). The USEPA (1990) reported exposure from inhaling spray droplets at the time of application is not an appreciable route of exposure for birds. According to research on mallards and bobwhite quail, respirable particle size (particles reaching the lung) in birds is limited to maximum diameter of 2 to 5 microns. The spray droplet spectra covering the majority of pesticide application scenarios indicate that less than 1% of the applied material is within the respirable particle size. This route of exposure is further limited because the permissible spray drop size distribution for ground pesticide applications is restricted to ASAE medium or coarser drop size distribution.

- Inhalation of a pesticide in the vapor phase may be another source of exposure for some pesticides under certain conditions. This mechanism of exposure to pesticides occurs post application and it would pertain to those pesticides with a high vapor pressure. The USEPA is currently evaluating protocols for modeling inhalation exposure from pesticides including near-field and near-ground air concentrations based upon equilibrium and kinetics-based models. Risk characterization for exposure with this mechanism is unavailable.

- The effect from exposure to dusts contaminated with the pesticide cannot be assessed generically as partitioning issues related to application site soils and chemical properties of the applied pesticides render the exposure potential from this route highly situation specific.

- Dermal exposure may occur through three potential sources: direct application of spray to terrestrial wildlife in the treated area or within the drift footprint, incidental contact with contaminated vegetation, or contact with contaminated water or soil. Interception of spray and incidental contact with treated substrates may pose risk to avian wildlife (Driver et al. 1991). However, available research related to wildlife dermal contact with pesticides is extremely limited, except dermal toxicity values are common for some mammals used as human surrogates (rats and mice). The USEPA is currently evaluating protocols for modeling dermal exposure. Risk characterization may be underestimated for this route of exposure, particularly with high risk pesticides such as some organophosphates or carbamate insecticides. If protocols are established by the USEPA for assessing dermal exposure to pesticides, they will be considered for incorporation into pesticide assessment protocols.

- Exposure to a pesticide may occur from consuming surface water, dew or other water on treated surfaces. Water soluble pesticides have potential to dissolve in surface runoff and puddles in a treated area may contain pesticide residues. Similarly, pesticides with lower organic carbon partitioning characteristics and higher solubility in water have a greater potential to dissolve in dew and other water associated with plant surfaces. Estimating the extent to which such pesticide loadings to drinking water occurs is complex and would depend upon the partitioning characteristics of the active ingredient, soils types in the treatment area, and the meteorology of the treatment area. In addition, the use of various water sources by wildlife is highly species-specific. Currently, risk characterization for this exposure mechanism is not available. The USEPA is actively developing protocols to quantify drinking water exposures from puddles and dew. If and when protocols are formally established by the USEPA for assessing exposure to pesticides through drinking water, these protocols will be incorporated into pesticide risk assessment protocols.

- Risk assessments are based upon the assumption that the entire treatment area would be subject to pesticide application at the rates specified on the label. In most cases, there is potential for uneven application of pesticides through such plausible incidents such as changes in calibration of application equipment, spillage, and localized releases at specific areas in or near the treated field that are associated with mixing and handling and application equipment as well as applicator skill. Inappropriate use of pesticides and the occurrence of spills represent a potential underestimate of risk. It is likely not an important factor for risk characterization. All pesticide applicators are required to be certified by the state in which they apply pesticides. Certification training includes the safe storage, transport, handling, and mixing of pesticides, equipment calibration and proper application with annual continuing education.

- The USEPA relies on Fletcher (1994) for setting the assumed pesticide residues in wildlife dietary items. The USEPA (2004) "believes that these residue assumptions reflect a realistic upper-bound residue estimate, although the degree to which this assumption reflects a specific percentile estimate is difficult to quantify". Fletcher's (1994) research suggests that the pesticide active ingredient residue assumptions used by the USEPA represent a 95th percentile estimate. However, research conducted by Pfleeger et al. (1996) indicates USEPA residue assumptions for short grass was not exceeded. Baehr and Habig (2000) compared USEPA residue assumptions with distributions of measured pesticide residues for the USEPA's UTAB database. Overall residue selection level will tend to overestimate risk characterization. This is particularly evident when wildlife individuals are likely to have selected a variety of food items acquired from multiple locations. Some food items may be contaminated with pesticide residues whereas others are not contaminated. However, it is important to recognize differences in species feeding behavior. Some species may consume whole above-ground plant material, but others will preferentially select different plant structures. Also, species may preferentially select a food item although multiple food items may be present. Without species specific knowledge regarding foraging behavior characterizing ecological risk other than in general terms is not possible.

- Acute and chronic risk assessments rely on comparisons of wildlife dietary residues with LC_{50} or NOEC values expressed as concentrations of pesticides in laboratory feed. These comparisons assume that ingestion of food items in the field occurs at rates commensurate with those in the laboratory. Although the screening assessment process adjusts dry-weight estimates of food intake to reflect the increased mass in fresh-weight wildlife food intake estimates, it does not allow for gross energy and assimilative efficiency differences between wildlife food items and laboratory feed. Differences in assimilative efficiency between laboratory and wild diets suggest that current screening assessment methods are not accounting for a potentially important aspect of food requirements.

- There are several other assumptions that can affect non-target species not considered in the risk assessment process. These include possible additive or synergistic effects from applying two or more pesticides or additives in a single application, co-location of pesticides in the environment, cumulative effects from pesticides with the same mode of action, effects of multiple stressors (e.g., combination of pesticide exposure, adverse abiotic and biotic factors) and behavioral changes induced by exposure to a pesticide. These factors may exist at some level contributing to adverse affects to non-target species, but they are usually characterized in the published literature in only a general manner limiting their value in the risk assessment process.

- It is assumed that aquatic species exclusively and permanently occupy the water body being assessed. Actual habitat requirements of aquatic species are not considered. With the possible exception of scenarios where pesticides are directly applied to water, it is assumed that no habitat use considerations specific for any species would place the organisms in closer proximity to pesticide use sites. This assumption produces a maximum estimate of exposure or risk characterization. It would likely be realistic for many aquatic species that may be found in aquatic habitats within or in close proximity to treated terrestrial habitats. However, the spatial distribution of wildlife is usually not random because wildlife distributions are often related to habitat requirements of species. Clumped distributions of wildlife may result in an under- or over-estimation of risk depending upon where the initial pesticide concentration occurs relative to the species or species habitat.

- For species found in the water column, it would be assumed that the greatest bioavailable fraction of the pesticide active ingredient in surface waters is freely dissolved in the water column. Additional chemical exposure from materials associated with suspended solids or food items is not considered because partitioning onto sediments likely is minimal. Adsorption and bioconcentration occurs at lower levels for many newer pesticides compared with older more persistent bioaccumulative compounds. Pesticides with RQs close to the listed species level of concern, the potential for additional exposure from these routes may be a limitation of risk assessments, where potential pesticide exposure or risk may be underestimated.

- Mass transport losses of pesticide from a water body (except for losses by volatilization, degradation and sediment partitioning) would not be considered for ecological risk assessment. The water body would be assumed to capture all pesticide active ingredients entering as runoff, drift, and adsorbed to eroded soil particles. It would also be assumed that pesticide active ingredient is not lost from the water body by overtopping or flow-through, nor is concentration reduced by dilution. In total, these assumptions would lead to a near maximum possible water-borne concentration. However, this assumption would not account for potential to concentrate pesticide through the evaporative loss. This limitation may have the greatest impact on water bodies with high surface-to-volume ratios such as ephemeral wetlands, where evaporative losses are accentuated and applied pesticides have low rates of degradation and volatilization.

- For acute risk assessments, there would be no averaging time for exposure. An instantaneous peak concentration would be assumed, where instantaneous exposure is sufficient in duration to elicit acute effects comparable to those observed over more protracted exposure periods (typically 48 to 96 hours) tested in the laboratory. In the absence of data regarding time-to-toxic event, analyses and latent responses to instantaneous exposure, risk would likely be overestimated.

- For chronic exposure risk assessments, the averaging times considered for exposure are commensurate with the duration of invertebrate life-cycle or fish-early life stage tests (e.g., 21-28 days and 56-60 days, respectively). Response profiles (time to effect and latency of effect) to pesticides likely vary widely with mode of action and species and should be evaluated on a case-by-case basis as available data allow. Nevertheless, because the USEPA relies on chronic exposure toxicity endpoints based on a finding of no observed effect, the potential for any latent toxicity effects or averaging time assumptions to alter the results of an acceptable chronic risk assessment prediction is limited. The extent to which duration of exposure from water-borne concentrations overestimate or underestimate actual exposure depends on several factors. These include the following: localized meteorological conditions, runoff characteristics of the watershed (e.g., soils, topography), the hydrological characteristics of receiving waters, environmental fate of the pesticide active ingredient, and the method of pesticide application. It should also be understood that chronic effects studies are performed using a method that holds water concentration in a steady state. This method is not likely to reflect conditions associated with pesticide runoff. Pesticide concentrations in the field increase and decrease in surface water on a cycle influenced by rainfall, pesticide use patterns, and degradation rates. As a result of the dependency of this assumption on several undefined variables, risk associated with chronic exposure may in some situations underestimate risk and overestimate risk in others.

- There are several other factors that can affect non-target species not considered in the risk assessment process. These would include the following: possible additive or synergistic effects from applying two or more pesticides or additives in a single application, co-location of pesticides in the environment, cumulative effects from pesticides with the same mode of action, effects of multiple stressors (e.g., combination of pesticide exposure, adverse abiotic [not pesticides] and biotic factors), and sub-lethal effects such as behavioral changes induced by exposure to a pesticide. These factors may exist at some level contributing to adverse affects to non-target species, but they are not routinely assessed by regulatory agencies. Therefore, information on the factors is not extensive limiting their value for the risk assessment process. As this type of information becomes available, it would be included, either quantitatively or qualitatively, in this risk assessment process.

- USEPA is required by the Food Quality Protection Act to assess the cumulative risks of pesticides that share common mechanisms of toxicity, or act the same within an organism. Currently, USEPA has identified four groups of pesticides that have a common mechanism of toxicity requiring cumulative risk assessments. These four groups are: the organophosphate insecticides, N-methyl carbamate insecticides, triazine herbicides, and chloroacetanilide herbicides.

7.3 Pesticide Mixtures and Degradates
Pesticide products are usually a formulation of several components generally categorized as active ingredients and inert or other ingredients. The term active ingredient is defined by the FIFRA as preventing, destroying, repelling, or mitigating the effects of a pest, or it is a plant regulator, defoliant, desiccant, or nitrogen stabilizer. In accordance with FIFRA, the active ingredient(s) must

be identified by name(s) on the pesticide label along with its relative composition expressed in percentage(s) by weight. In contrast, inert ingredient(s) are not intended to affect a target pest. Their role in the pesticide formulation is to act as a solvent (keep the active ingredient is a liquid phase), an emulsifying or suspending agent (keep the active ingredient from separating out of solution), or a carrier such as clay in which the active ingredient is impregnated on the clay particle in dry formulations. For example, if isopropyl alcohol would be used as a solvent in a pesticide formulation, then it would be considered an inert ingredient. FIFRA only requires that inert ingredients identified as hazardous and associated percent composition, and the total percentage of all inert ingredients must be declared on a product label. Inert ingredients that are not classified as hazardous are not required to be identified.

The USEPA (September 1997) issued Pesticide Regulation Notice 97-6 which encouraged manufacturers, formulators, producers, and registrants of pesticide products to voluntarily substitute the term "other ingredients" for "inert ingredients" in the ingredient statement. This change recognized that all components in a pesticide formulation potentially could elicit or contribute to an adverse effect on non-target organisms and, therefore, are not necessarily inert. Whether referred to as "inerts" or "other ingredients," these constituents within a pesticide product have the potential to affect species or environmental quality. The USEPA categorizes regulated inert ingredients into the following four lists (http://www.epa.gov/opprd001/inerts/index.html):
- List 1 – Inert Ingredients of Toxicological Concern
- List 2 – Potentially Toxic Inert Ingredients
- List 3 – Inerts of Unknown Toxicity
- List 4 – Inerts of Minimal Toxicity

Several of the List 4 compounds are naturally-occurring earthen materials (e.g., clay materials, simple salts) that would not elicit toxicological response at applied concentrations. However, some of the inerts (particularly the List 3 compounds and unlisted compounds) may have moderate to high potential toxicity to aquatic species based on MSDSs or published data.

Comprehensively assessing potential effects to non-target fish, wildlife, plants, and/or their habitats from pesticide use is a complex task. It would be preferable to assess the cumulative effects from exposure to the active ingredient, its degradates, and inert ingredients as well as other active ingredients in the spray mixture. However, it would only be feasible to conduct deterministic risk assessments for each component in the spray mixture singly. Limited scientific information is available regarding ecological effects (additive or synergistic) from chemical mixtures that typically rely upon broadly encompassing assumptions. For example, the US Forest Service (2005) found that mixtures of pesticides used in land (forest) management likely would not cause additive or synergistic effects to non-target species based upon a review of scientific literature regarding toxicological effects and interactions of agricultural chemicals (ATSDR 2004). Moreover, information on inert ingredients, adjuvants, and degradates is often limited by the availability of and access to reliable toxicological data for these constituents.

Toxicological information regarding "other ingredients" may be available from sources such as the following:
- TOMES (a proprietary toxicological database including USEPA's IRIS, the Hazardous Substance Data Bank, the Registry of Toxic Effects of Chemical Substances [RTECS]).
- USEPA's ECOTOX database, which includes AQUIRE (a database containing scientific papers published on the toxic effects of chemicals to aquatic organisms).

- TOXLINE (a literature searching tool).
- Material Safety Data Sheets (MSDSs) from pesticide suppliers.
- Other sources such as the Farm Chemicals Handbook.

Because there is a lack of specific inert toxicological data, inert(s) in a pesticide may cause adverse ecological effects. However, inert ingredients typically represent only a small percentage of the pesticide spray mixture, and it would be assumed that negligible effects would be expected to result from inert ingredient(s).

Although the potential effects of degradates should be considered when selecting a pesticide, it is beyond the scope of this assessment process to consider all possible breakdown chemicals of the various product formulations containing an active ingredient. Degradates may be more or less mobile and more or less hazardous in the environment than their parent pesticides (Battaglin et al. 2003). Differences in environmental behavior (e.g., mobility) and toxicity between parent pesticides and degradates would make assessing potential degradate effects extremely difficult. For example, a less toxic and more mobile, bioaccumulative, or persistent degradate may have potentially greater effects on species and/or degrade environmental quality. The lack of data on the toxicity of degradates for many pesticides would represent a source of uncertainty for assessing risk.

An USEPA-approved label specifies whether a product can be mixed with one or more pesticides. Without product-specific toxicological data, it would not possible to quantify the potential effects of these mixtures. In addition, a quantitative analysis could only be conducted if reliable scientific information allowed a determination of whether the joint action of a mixture would be additive, synergistic, or antagonistic. Such information would not likely exist unless the mode of action would be common among the chemicals and receptors. Moreover, the composition of and exposure to mixtures would be highly site- and/or time-specific and, therefore, it would be nearly impossible to assess potential effects to species and environmental quality.

To minimize or eliminate potential negative effects associated with applying two or more pesticides as a mixture, the use would be conducted in accordance with the labeling requirements. Labels for two or more pesticides applied as a mixture should be completely reviewed, where products with the least potential for negative effects would be selected for use on the Refuge. This is especially relevant when a mixture would be applied in a manner that may already have the potential for an effect(s) associated with an individual pesticide (e.g., runoff to ponds in sandy watersheds). Use of a tank mix under these conditions would increase the level of uncertainty in terms of risk to species or potential to degrade environmental quality.

Adjuvants generally function to enhance or prolong the activity of pesticide. For terrestrial herbicides, adjuvants aid in the absorption into plant tissue. Adjuvant is a broad term that generally applies to surfactants, selected oils, anti-foaming agents, buffering compounds, drift control agents, compatibility agents, stickers, and spreaders. Adjuvants are not under the same registration requirements as pesticides and the USEPA does not register or approve the labeling of spray adjuvants. Individual pesticide labels identify types of adjuvants approved for use with it. In general, adjuvants compose a relatively small portion of the volume of pesticides applied. Selection of adjuvants with limited toxicity and low volumes would be recommended to reduce the potential for the adjuvant to influence the toxicity of the pesticide.

7.4 Determining Effects to Soil and Water Quality

The approval process for pesticide uses would consider potential to degrade water quality on and off Refuge lands. A pesticide can only affect water quality through movement away from the treatment site. After application, pesticide mobilization can be characterized by one or more of the following (Kerle et al. 1996):

- Attach (sorb) to soil, vegetation, or other surfaces and remain at or near the treated area;
- Attach to soil and move off-site through erosion from run-off or wind;
- Dissolve in water that can be subjected to run-off or leaching.

As an initial screening tool, selected chemical characteristics and rating criteria for a pesticide can be evaluated to assess potential to enter ground and/or surface waters. These would include the following: persistence, sorption coefficient (K_{oc}), groundwater ubiquity score (GUS), and solubility.

Persistence, which is expressed as half-life ($t_{1/2}$), represents the length of time required for 50% of the deposited pesticide to degrade (completely or partially). Persistence in the soil can be categorized as the following: non-persistent <30 days, moderately persistent = 30 to 100 days, and persistent >100 days (Kerle et. al. 1996). Half-life data is usually available for aquatic and terrestrial environments.

Another measure of pesticide persistence is dissipation time (DT_{50}). It represents the time required for 50% of the deposited pesticide to degrade and move from a treated site; whereas, half-life describes the rate for degradation only. As for half-life, units of dissipation time are usually expressed in days. Field or foliar dissipation time is the preferred data for use to estimate pesticide concentrations in the environment. However, soil half-life is the most common persistence data cited in published literature. If field or foliar dissipation data is not available, soil half-life data may be used. The average or representative half-life value of most important degradation mechanism will be selected for quantitative analysis for both terrestrial and aquatic environments.

Mobility of a pesticide is a function of how strongly it is adsorbed to soil particles and organic matter, its solubility in water, and its persistence in the environment. Pesticides strongly adsorbed to soil particles, relatively insoluble in water, and not environmentally persistent would be less likely to move across the soil surface into surface waters or to leach through the soil profile and contaminate groundwater. Conversely, pesticides that are not strongly adsorbed to soil particles, are highly water soluble, and are persistent in the environment would have greater potential to move from the application site (off-site movement).

The degree of pesticide adsorption to soil particles and organic matter (Kerle et. al. 1996) is expressed as the soil adsorption coefficient (K_{oc}). The soil adsorption coefficient is measured as micrograms of pesticide per gram of soil ($\mu g/g$) that can range from near zero to the thousands. Pesticides with higher Koc values are strongly sorbed to soil and, therefore, would be less subject to movement.

Water solubility describes the amount of pesticide that will dissolve in a known quantity of water. The water solubility of a pesticide is expressed as milligrams of pesticide dissolved in a liter of water (mg/l or ppm). Pesticide with solubility <0.1 ppm are virtually insoluble in water, 100-1000 ppm are moderately soluble, and >10,000 ppm highly soluble (US Geological Survey 2000). As pesticide solubility increases, there would be greater potential for off-site movement.

The Groundwater Ubiquity Score (GUS) is a quantitative screening tool to estimate a pesticide's potential to move in the environment. It utilizes soil persistence and adsorption coefficients in the following formula.

$$GUS = \log_{10}(t_{1/2}) \times [4 - \log_{10}(K_{oc})]$$

The potential pesticide movement rating would be based upon its GUS value. Pesticides with a GUS <0.1 would considered to have an extremely low potential to move toward groundwater. Values of 1.0-2.0 would be low, 2.0-3.0 would be moderate, 3.0-4.0 would be high, and >4.0 would have a very high potential to move toward groundwater.

Water solubility describes the amount of pesticide dissolving in a specific quantity of water, where it is usually measured as mg/l or parts per million (ppm). Solubility is useful as a comparative measure because pesticides with higher values are more likely to move by run-off or leaching. GUS, water solubility, $t_{1/2}$, and K_{oc} values are available for selected pesticides from the OSU Extension Pesticide Properties Database at http://npic.orst.edu/ppdmove.htm. Many of the values in this database were derived from the SCS/ARS/CES Pesticide Properties Database for Environmental Decision Making (Wauchope et al. 1992).

Soil properties influence the fate of pesticides in the environment. The following six properties are mostly likely to affect pesticide degradation and the potential for pesticides to move off-site by leaching (vertical movement through the soil) or runoff (lateral movement across the soil surface).

- Permeability is the rate of water movement vertically through the soil. It is affected by soil texture and structure. Coarse textured soils (e.g., high sand content) have a larger pore size and they are generally more permeable than fine textured soils (i.e., high clay content). The more permeable soils would have a greater potential for pesticides to move vertically down through the soil profile. Soil permeability rates (inches/hour) are usually available in county soil survey reports.
- Soil texture describes the relative percentage of sand, silt, and clay. In general, greater clay content with smaller the pore size would lower the likelihood and rate water that would move through the soil profile. Clay also serves to adsorb (bind) pesticides to soil particles. Soils with high clay content would adsorb more pesticide than soils with relatively low clay content. In contrast, sandy soils with coarser texture and lower water holding capacity would have a greater potential for water to leach through them.
- Soil structure describes soil aggregation. Soils with a well developed soil structure have looser, more aggregated, structure that would be less likely to be compacted. Both characteristics would allow for less restricted flow of water through the soil profile resulting in greater infiltration.
- Organic matter would be the single most important factor affecting pesticide adsorption in soils. Many pesticides are adsorbed to organic matter which would reduce their rate of downward movement through the soil profile. Also, soils high in organic matter would tend to hold more water, which may make less water available for leaching.
- Soil moisture affects how fast water would move through the soil. If soils are already wet or saturated before rainfall or irrigation, excess moisture would runoff rather than infiltrate into the soil profile. Soil moisture also would influence microbial and chemical activity in soil, which effects pesticide degradation.

- Soil pH would influence chemical reactions that occur in the soil which in turn determines whether or not a pesticide will degrade, rate of degradation, and, in some instances, which degradation products are produced.

Based upon the aforementioned properties, soils most vulnerable to groundwater contamination would be sandy soils with low organic matter. In contrast, the least vulnerable soils would be well-drained clayey soils with high organic matter. Consequently, pesticides with the lowest potential for movement in conjunction with appropriate best management practices (see below) would be used in an IPM framework to treat pests while minimizing effects to non-target biota and protecting environmental quality.

Along with soil properties, the potential for a pesticide to affect water quality through run-off and leaching would consider site-specific environmental and abiotic conditions including rainfall, water table conditions, and topography (Huddleston 1996).
- Water is necessary to separate pesticides from soil. This can occur in two basic ways. Pesticides that are soluble move easily with runoff water. Pesticide-laden soil particles can be dislodged and transported from the application site in runoff. The concentration of pesticides in the surface runoff would be greatest for the first runoff event following treatment. The rainfall intensity and route of water infiltration into soil, to a large extent, determine pesticide concentrations and losses in surface runoff. The timing of the rainfall after application also would have an effect. Rainfall interacts with pesticides at a shallow soil depth (¼ to ½ inch), which is called the mixing zone (Baker and Miller 1999). The pesticide/water mixture in the mixing zone would tend to leach down into the soil or runoff depending upon how quickly the soil surface becomes saturated and how rapidly water can infiltrate into the soil. Leaching would decrease the amount of pesticide available near the soil surface (mixing zone) to runoff during the initial rainfall event following application and subsequent rainfall events.
- Terrain slope would affect the potential for surface runoff and the intensity of runoff. Steeper slopes would have greater potential for runoff following a rainfall event. In contrast, soils that are relatively flat would have little potential for runoff, except during intense rainfall events. In addition, soils in lower areas would be more susceptible to leaching as a result of receiving excessive water from surrounding higher elevations.
- Depth to groundwater would be an important factor affecting the potential for pesticides to leach into groundwater. If the distance from the soil surface to the top of the water table is shallow, pesticides would have less distance to travel to reach groundwater. Shallower water tables that persist for longer periods would be more likely to experience groundwater contamination. Soil survey reports are available for individual counties. These reports provide data in tabular format regarding the water table depths and the months during which it is persists. In some situations, a hard pan exists above the water table that would prevent pesticide contamination from leaching.

7.5 Determining Effects to Air Quality
Pesticides may volatilize from soil and plant surfaces and move from the treated area into the atmosphere. The potential for a pesticide to volatilize is determined by the pesticide's vapor pressure which would be affected by temperature, sorption, soil moisture, and the pesticide's water solubility. Vapor pressure is often expressed in mm Hg. To make these numbers easier to compare, vapor pressure may be expressed in exponent form ($I \times 10^{-7}$), where I represents a vapor pressure index. In general, pesticides with $I<10$ would have a low potential to volatilize; whereas, pesticides with $I>1,000$ would have a high potential to volatilize (Oregon State University 1996). Vapor pressure

values for pesticides are usually available in the pesticide product MSDS or the USDA Agricultural Research Service (ARS) pesticide database.

7.6 Preparing a Chemical Profile

The following instructions would be used by Service personnel to complete Chemical Profiles for pesticides. Specifically, profiles would be prepared for pesticide active ingredients (e.g., glyphosate, imazapic) that would be contained in one or more trade name products that are registered and labeled with USEPA. All information fields under each category (e.g., Toxicological Endpoints, Environmental Fate) would be completed for a Chemical Profile. If no information is available for a specific field, then "No data is available in references" would be recorded in the profile. Available scientific information would be used to complete Chemical Profiles. Each entry of scientific information would be shown with applicable references.

Completed Chemical Profiles would provide a structured decision-making process utilizing quantitative assessment/screening tools with threshold values (where appropriate) that would be used to evaluate potential biological and other environmental effects to Refuge resources. For ecological risk assessments presented in these profiles, the "worst-case scenario" would be evaluated to determine whether a pesticide could be approved for use considering the maximum single application rate specified on pesticide labels for habitat management and croplands/facilities maintenance treatments pertaining to Refuges. Where the "worst-case scenario" likely would only result in minor, temporary, and localized effects to listed and non-listed species with appropriate BMPs (see Section 5.0), the proposed pesticide's use in a PUP would have a scientific basis for approval under any application rate specified on the label that is at or below rates evaluated in a Chemical Profile. In some cases, the Chemical Profile would include a lower application rate than the maximum labeled rate in order to protect Refuge resources. As necessary, Chemical Profiles would be periodically updated with new scientific information or as pesticides with the same active ingredient are proposed for use on the Refuge in PUPs.

Throughout this section, threshold values (to prevent or minimize potential biological and environmental effects) would be clearly identified for specific information presented in a completed Chemical Profile. Comparison with these threshold values provides an explicit scientific basis to approve or disapprove PUPs for habitat management and cropland/facilities maintenance on Refuge lands. In general, PUPs would be approved for pesticides with Chemical Profiles where there would be no exceedances of threshold values. However, BMPs are identified for some screening tools that would minimize/eliminate potential effects (exceedance of the threshold value) as a basis for approving PUPs.

Date: Service personnel would record the date when the Chemical Profile is completed or updated. Chemical Profiles (e.g., currently approved pesticide use patterns) would be periodically reviewed and updated, as necessary. The most recent review date would be recorded on a profile to document when it was last updated.

Trade Name(s): Service personnel would accurately and completely record the trade name(s) from the pesticide label, which includes a suffix that describes the formulation (e.g., WP, DG, EC, L, SP, I, II or 64). The suffix often distinguishes a specific product among several pesticides with the same active ingredient. Service personnel would record a trade name for each pesticide product with the same active ingredient.

Common chemical name(s): Service personnel would record the common name(s) listed on the pesticide label or material safety data sheet (MSDS) for an active ingredient. The common name of a pesticide is listed as the active ingredient on the title page of the product label immediately following the trade name, and the MSDS, Section 2: Composition/ Information on Ingredients. A Chemical Profile is completed for each active ingredient.

Pesticide Type: Service personnel would record the type of pesticide for an active ingredient as one of the following: herbicide, dessicant, fungicide, fumigant, growth regulator, insecticide, pisicide, or rodenticide.

EPA Registration Number(s): This number (EPA Reg. No.) appears on the title page of the label and MSDS, Section 1: Chemical Product and Company Description. It is not the EPA Establishment Number that is usually located near it. Service personnel would record the EPA Reg. No. for each trade name product with an active ingredient based upon PUPs.

Pesticide Class: Service personnel would list the general chemical class for the pesticide (active ingredient). For example, malathion is an organophosphate and carbaryl is a carbamate.

CAS (Chemical Abstract Service) Number: This number is often located in the second section (Composition/Information on Ingredients) of the MSDS. The MSDS table listing components usually contains this number immediately prior to or following the % composition.

Other Ingredients: From the most recent MSDS for the proposed pesticide product(s), Service personnel would include any chemicals in the pesticide formulation not listed as an active ingredient that are described as toxic or hazardous, or regulated under the Superfund Amendments and Reauthorization Act (SARA), Comprehensive Environmental Response, Compensation, and Liability Act (CERCLA), Toxic Substances Control Act (TSCA), Occupational Safety and Health Administration (OSHA), State Right-to-Know, or other listed authorities. These are usually found in MSDS sections titled "Hazardous Identifications", "Exposure Control/Personal Protection", and "Regulatory Information". If concentrations of other ingredients are available for any compounds identified as toxic or hazardous, then Service personnel would record this information in the Chemical Profile by trade name. MSDS(s) may be obtained from the manufacturer, manufacturer's website or from an on-line database maintained by Crop Data Management Systems, Inc. (see list below).

Toxicological Endpoints

Toxicological endpoint data would be collected for acute and chronic tests with mammals, birds, and fish. Data would be recorded for species available in the scientific literature. If no data are found for a particular taxonomic group, then "No data available is references" would be recorded as the data entry. Throughout the Chemical Profile, references (including toxicological endpoint data) would be cited using parentheses (#) following the recorded data.

Mammalian LD$_{50}$: For test species in the scientific literature, Service personnel would record available data for oral lethal dose (LD$_{50}$) in mg/kg-bw (body weight) or ppm-bw. Most common test species in scientific literature are the rat and mouse. The lowest LD$_{50}$ value found for a rat would be used as a toxicological endpoint for dose-based RQ calculations to assess acute risk to mammals (see Table 1 in Section 7.1).

Mammalian LC$_{50}$: For test species in the scientific literature, Service personnel would record available data for dietary lethal concentration (LC$_{50}$) as reported (e.g., mg/kg-diet or ppm-diet). Most common test species in scientific literature are the rat and mouse. The lowest LC$_{50}$ value found for a rat would be used as a toxicological endpoint for diet-based RQ calculations to assess acute risk (see Table 1 in Section 7.1).

Mammalian Reproduction: For test species listed in the scientific literature, Service personnel would record the test results (e.g., Lowest Observed Effect Concentration [LOEC], Lowest Observed Effect Level [LOEL], No Observed Adverse Effect Level [NOAEL], No Observed Adverse Effect Concentration [NOAEC]) in mg/kg-bw or mg/kg-diet for reproductive test procedure(s) (e.g., generational studies [preferred], fertility, new born weight). Most common test species available in scientific literature are rats and mice. The lowest NOEC, NOAEC, NOEL, or NOAEL test results found for a rat would be used as a toxicological endpoint for RQ calculations to assess chronic risk (see Table 1 in Section 7.1).

Avian LD$_{50}$: For test species available in the scientific literature, Service personnel would record values for oral lethal dose (LD$_{50}$) in mg/kg-bw or ppm-bw. Most common test species available in scientific literature are the bobwhite quail and mallard. The lowest LD$_{50}$ value found for an avian species would be used as a toxicological endpoint for dose-based RQ calculations to assess acute risk (see Table 1 in Section 7.1).

Avian LC$_{50}$: For test species available in the scientific literature, Service personnel would record values for dietary lethal concentration (LC$_{50}$) as reported (e.g., mg/kg-diet or ppm-diet). Most common test species available in scientific literature are the bobwhite quail and mallard. The lowest LC$_{50}$ value found for an avian species would be used as a toxicological endpoint for dietary-based RQ calculations to assess acute risk (see Table 1 in Section 7.1).

Avian Reproduction: For test species available in the scientific literature, Service personnel would record test results (e.g., LOEC, LOEL, NOAEC, NOAEL) in mg/kg-bw or mg/kg-diet consumed for reproductive test procedure(s) (e.g., early life cycle, reproductive). Most common test species available in scientific literature are the bobwhite quail and mallard. The lowest NOEC, NOAEC, NOEL, or NOAEL test results found for an avian species would be used as a toxicological endpoint for RQ calculations to assess chronic risk (see Table 1 in Section 7.1).

Fish LC$_{50}$: For test freshwater or marine species listed in the scientific literature, Service personnel would record a LC$_{50}$ in ppm or mg/L. Most common test species available in the scientific literature are the bluegill, rainbow trout, and fathead minnow (marine). Test results for many game species may also be available. The lowest LC$_{50}$ value found for a freshwater fish species would be used as a toxicological endpoint for RQ calculations to assess acute risk (see Table 1 in Section 7.1).

Fish Early Life Stage (ELS)/Life Cycle: For test freshwater or marine species available in the scientific literature, Service personnel would record test results (e.g., LOEC, NOAEL, NOAEC, LOAEC) in ppm for test procedure(s) (e.g., early life cycle, life cycle). Most common test species available in the scientific literature are bluegill, rainbow trout, and fathead minnow. Test results for other game species may also be available. The lowest test value found for a fish species (preferably freshwater) would be used as a toxicological endpoint for RQ calculations to assess chronic risk (see Table 1 in Section 7.1).

Other: For test invertebrate as well as non-vascular and vascular plant species available in the scientific literature, Service personnel would record LC_{50}, LD_{50}, LOEC, LOEL, NOAEC, NOAEL, or EC_{50} (environmental concentration) values in ppm or mg/L. Most common test invertebrate species available in scientific literature are the honey bee and the water flea (*Daphnia magna*). Green algae (*Selenastrum capricornutum*) and pondweed (*Lemna minor*) are frequently available test species for aquatic non-vascular and vascular plants, respectively.

Ecological Incident Reports: After a site has been treated with pesticide(s), wildlife may be exposed to these chemical(s). When exposure is high relative to the toxicity of the pesticides, wildlife may be killed or visibly harmed (incapacitated). Such events are called ecological incidents. The USEPA maintains a database (Ecological Incident Information System) of ecological incidents. This database stores information extracted from incident reports submitted by various federal and state agencies and non-government organizations. Information included in an incident report is date and location of the incident, type and magnitude of affects observed in various species, use(s) of pesticides known or suspected of contributing to the incident, and results of any chemical residue and cholinesterase activity analyses conducted during the investigation.

Incident reports can play an important role in evaluating the effects of pesticides by supplementing quantitative risk assessments. All incident reports for pesticide(s) with the active ingredient and associated information would be recorded.

Environmental Fate

Water Solubility: Service personnel would record values for water solubility (S_w), which describes the amount of pesticide that dissolves in a known quantity of water. S_w is expressed as mg/L (ppm). Pesticide S_w values would be categorized as one of the following: insoluble <0.1 ppm, moderately soluble = 100 to 1000 ppm, highly soluble >10,000 ppm (US Geological Survey 2000). As pesticide S_w increases, there would be greater potential to degrade water quality through run-off and leaching.

Sw would be used to evaluate potential for bioaccumulation in aquatic species [see **Octanol-Water Partition Coefficient (K_{ow})** below].

Soil Mobility: Service personnel would record available values for soil adsorption coefficient (K_{oc} [$\mu g/g$]). It provides a measure of a chemical's mobility and leaching potential in soil. K_{oc} values are directly proportional to organic content, clay content, and surface area of the soil. K_{oc} data for a pesticide may be available for a variety of soil types (e.g., clay, loam, sand).

K_{oc} values would be used in evaluating the potential to degrade groundwater by leaching (see **Potential to Move to Groundwater** below).

Soil Persistence: Service personnel would record values for soil half-life ($t_{1/2}$), which represents the length of time (days) required for 50% of the deposited pesticide to degrade (completely or partially) in the soil. Based upon the $t_{1/2}$ value, soil persistence would be categorized as one of the following: non-persistent <30 days, moderately persistent = 30 to 100 days, and persistent >100 days (Kerle et. al. 1996).

Threshold for Approving PUPs:

If soil $t_{1/2} \leq 100$ days, then a PUP would be approved without additional BMPs to protect water quality.

If soil $t_{1/2} > 100$ days, then a PUP would only be approved with additional BMPs specifically to protect water quality. One or more BMPs such as the following would be included in the **Specific Best Management Practices (BMPs) section** *to minimize potential surface run-off and leaching that can degrade water quality:*

- *Do not exceed one application per site per year.*
- *Do not use on coarse-textured soils where the ground water table is <10' and average annual precipitation >12".*
- *Do not use on steep slopes if substantial rainfall is expected within 24 hours or ground is saturated.*

Along with K_{oc}, soil $t_{1/2}$ values would be used in evaluating the potential to degrade groundwater by leaching (see **Potential to Move to Groundwater** below).

Soil Dissipation: Dissipation time (DT_{50}) represents the time required for 50% of the deposited pesticide to degrade and move from a treated site; whereas, soil $t_{1/2}$ describes the rate for degradation only. As for $t_{1/2}$, units of dissipation time are usually expressed in days. Field dissipation time would be the preferred data for use to estimate pesticide concentrations in the environment because it is based upon field studies compared to soil $t_{1/2}$, which is derived in a laboratory. However, soil $t_{1/2}$ is the most common persistence data available in the published literature. If field dissipation data is not available, soil half-life data would be used in a Chemical Profile. The average or representative half-life value of most important degradation mechanism would be selected for quantitative analysis for both terrestrial and aquatic environments.

Based upon the DT_{50} value, environmental persistence in the soil also would be categorized as one of the following: non-persistent <30 days, moderately persistent = 30-100 days, and persistent >100 days.

Threshold for Approving PUPs:

If soil $DT_{50} \leq 100$ days, then a PUP would be approved without additional BMPs to protect water quality.

If soil $DT_{50} > 100$ days, then a PUP would only be approved with additional BMPs specifically to protect water quality. One or more BMPs such as the following would be included in the Specific Best Management Practices (BMPs) section to minimize potential surface run-off and leaching that can degrade water quality:

- *Do not exceed one application per site per year.*
- *Do not use on coarse-textured soils where the ground water table is <10' and average annual precipitation >12".*
- *Do not use on steep slopes if substantial rainfall is expected within 24 hours or ground is saturated.*

Along with K_{oc}, soil DT_{50} values (preferred over soil $t_{1/2}$) would be used in evaluating the potential to degrade groundwater by leaching (see **Potential to Move to Groundwater** below), if available.

Aquatic Persistence: Service personnel would record values for aquatic $t_{1/2}$, which represents the length of time required for 50% of the deposited pesticide to degrade (completely or partially) in water. Based upon the $t_{1/2}$ value, aquatic persistence would be categorized as one of the following: non-persistent <30 days, moderately persistent = 30 to 100 days, and persistent >100 days (Kerle et. al. 1996).

Threshold for Approving PUPs:

If aquatic $t_{1/2}$ ≤100 days, then a PUP would be approved without additional BMPs to protect water quality.
If aquatic $t_{1/2}$ >100 days, then a PUP would only be approved with additional BMPs specifically to protect water quality. One or more BMPs such as the following would be included in the Specific Best Management Practices (BMPs) section to minimize potential surface run-off and leaching that can degrade water quality:
- *Do not exceed one application per site per year.*
- *Do not use on coarse-textured soils where the ground water table is <10' and average annual precipitation >12".*
- *Do not use on steep slopes if substantial rainfall is expected within 24 hours or ground is saturated.*

Aquatic Dissipation: Dissipation time (DT_{50}) represents the time required for 50% of the deposited pesticide to degrade or move (dissipate); whereas, aquatic $t_{1/2}$ describes the rate for degradation only. As for $t_{1/2}$, units of dissipation time are usually expressed in days. Based upon the DT_{50} value, environmental persistence in aquatic habitats also would be categorized as one of the following: non-persistent <30 days, moderately persistent = 30 to 100 days, and persistent >100 days.

Threshold for Approving PUPs:

If aquatic DT_{50} ≤100 days, then a PUP would be approved without additional BMPs to protect water quality.
If aquatic DT_{50} >100 days, then a PUP would only be approved with additional BMPs specifically to protect water quality. One or more BMPs such as the following would be included in the Specific Best Management Practices (BMPs) section to minimize potential surface run-off and leaching that can degrade water quality:
- *Do not exceed one application per site per year.*
- *Do not use on coarse-textured soils where the ground water table is <10' and average annual precipitation >12".*
- *Do not use on steep slopes if substantial rainfall is expected within 24 hours or ground is saturated.*

Potential to Move to Groundwater: Groundwater Ubiquity Score (GUS) = $\log_{10}(\text{soil } t_{1/2})$ x [4 − $\log_{10}(K_{oc})$]. If a DT_{50} value is available, it would be used rather than a $t_{1/2}$ value to calculate a GUS score. Based upon the GUS value, the potential to move toward groundwater would be recorded as one of the following categories: extremely low potential<1.0, low - 1.0 to 2.0, moderate - 2.0 to 3.0, high - 3.0 to 4.0, or very high>4.0.

Threshold for Approving PUPs:

If GUS ≤4.0, then a PUP would be approved without additional BMPs to protect water quality.
If GUS >4.0, then a PUP would only be approved with additional BMPs specifically to protect water quality. One or more BMPs such as the following would be included in the Specific Best Management Practices (BMPs) section to minimize potential surface run-off and leaching that can degrade water quality:

- *Do not exceed one application per site per year.*
- *Do not use on coarse-textured soils where the ground water table is <10' and average annual precipitation >12".*
- *Do not use on steep slopes if substantial rainfall is expected within 24 hours or ground is saturated.*

Volatilization: Pesticides may volatilize (evaporate) from soil and plant surfaces and move off-target into the atmosphere. The potential for a pesticide to volatilize is a function of its vapor pressure that is affected by temperature, sorption, soil moisture, and the pesticide's water solubility. Vapor pressure is often expressed in mm Hg. To make these values easier to compare, vapor pressure would be recorded by Service personnel in exponential form (1×10^{-7}), where I represents a vapor pressure index. In general, pesticides with I<10 would have low potential to volatilize; whereas, pesticides with I >1,000 would have a high potential to volatilize (Oregon State University 1996). Vapor pressure values for pesticides are usually available in the pesticide product MSDS or the USDA Agricultural Research Service (ARS) pesticide database (see **References**).

Threshold for Approving PUPs:

If I ≤1000, then a PUP would be approved without additional BMPs to minimize drift and protect air quality.
If I >1000, then a PUP would only be approved with additional BMPs specifically to minimize drift and protect air quality. One or more BMPs such as the following would be included in the Specific Best Management Practices (BMPs) section to reduce volatilization and potential to drift and degrade air quality:

- *Do not treat when wind velocities are <2 or >10 mph with existing or potential inversion conditions.*
- *Apply the large-diameter droplets possible for spray treatments.*
- *Avoid spraying when air temperatures >85°F.*
- *Use the lowest spray height possible above target canopy.*
- *Where identified on the pesticide label, soil incorporate pesticide as soon as possible during or after application.*

Octanol-Water Partition Coefficient (K_{ow}): The octanol-water partition coefficient (K_{ow}) is the concentration of a pesticide in octanol and water at equilibrium at a specific temperature. Because octanol is an organic solvent, it is considered a surrogate for natural organic matter. Therefore, K_{ow} would be used to assess potential for a pesticide to bioaccumulate in tissues of aquatic species (e.g., fish). If K_{ow} >1000 or S_w<1 mg/L AND soil $t_{1/2}$>30 days, then there would be high potential for a pesticide to bioaccumulate in aquatic species such as fish (US Geological Survey 2000).

Threshold for Approving PUPs:

If there is not a high potential for a pesticide to bioaccumulate in aquatic species, then the PUP would be approved.
If there is a high potential to bioaccumulate in aquatic species (K_{ow}>1000 or S_w<1 mg/L AND soil $t_{1/2}$>30 days), then the PUP would not approved, except under unusual circumstances where approval would only be granted by the Washington Office.

Bioaccumulation/Bioconcentration: The physiological process where pesticide concentrations in tissue would increase in biota because they are taken and stored at a faster rate than they are metabolized or excreted. The potential for bioaccumulation would be evaluated through bioaccumulation factors (BAFs) or bioconcentration factors (BCFs). Based upon BAF or BCF values, the potential to bioaccumulate would be recorded as one of the following: low – 0 to 300, moderate – 300 to 1000, or high >1000 (Calabrese and Baldwin 1993).

Threshold for Approving PUPs:

If BAF or BCF≤1000, then a PUP would be approved without additional BMPs.
If BAF or BCF>1000, then a PUP would not approved, except under unusual circumstances where approval would only be granted by the Washington Office.

Worst-Case Ecological Risk Assessment

Max Application Rates (acid equivalent): Service personnel would record the highest application rate of an active ingredient (ae basis) for habitat management and cropland/facilities maintenance treatments in this data field of a Chemical Profile. These rates can be found in Table CP.1 under the column heading "Max Product Rate – Single Application (lbs/acre – AI on acid equiv basis)". This table would be prepared for a chemical profile from information specified in labels for trade name products identified in PUPs. If these data are not available in pesticide labels, then write "NS" for "not specified on label" in this table.

EECs: An estimated environmental concentration (ECC) represents potential exposure to fish and wildlife (birds and mammals) from using a pesticide. EECs would be derived by Service personnel using an USEPA screening-level approach (US Environmental Protection Agency 2004). For each max application rate [see description under **Max Application Rates (acid equivalent)**], Service personnel would record 2 EEC values in a Chemical Profile; these would represent the worst-case terrestrial and aquatic exposures for habitat management and croplands/facilities maintenance treatments. For terrestrial and aquatic EEC calculations, see description for data entry under **Presumption of Unacceptable Risk/Risk Quotients**, which is the next field for a Chemical Profile.

Presumption of Unacceptable Risk/Risk Quotients: Service personnel would calculate and record acute and chronic risk quotients (RQs) for birds, mammals, and fish using the provided tabular formats for habitat management and/or cropland/facilities maintenance treatments. RQs recorded in a Chemical Profile would represent the worst-case assessment for ecological risk. See Section 7.2 for discussion regarding the calculations of RQs.

For aquatic assessments associated with habitat management treatments, RQ calculations would be based upon selected acute and chronic toxicological endpoints for fish and the EEC would be derived from Urban and Cook (1986) assuming 100% overspray to an entire 1-foot deep water body using the max application rate (ae basis [see above]).

For aquatic assessments associated with cropland/facilities maintenance treatments, RQ calculations would be done by Service personnel based upon selected acute and chronic toxicological endpoints for fish and an EEC would be derived from the aquatic assessment in AgDRIFT® model version 2.01 under Tier I ground-based application with the following input variables: max application rate (acid basis [see above]), low boom (20"), fine to medium/coarse droplet size, 20 swaths, EPA-defined wetland, and 25-foot distance (buffer) from treated area to water.

See Section 7.2.1.2 for more details regarding the calculation of EECs for aquatic habitats for habitat management and cropland/facilities maintenance treatments.

For terrestrial avian and mammalian assessments, RQ calculations would be done by Service personnel based upon dietary exposure, where the "short grass" food item category would represent the worst-case scenario. For terrestrial spray applications associated with habitat management and cropland/facilities maintenance treatments, exposure (EECs and RQs) would be determined using the Kanaga nomogram method through the USEPA's Terrestrial Residue Exposure model (T-REX) version 1.2.3. T-REX input variables would include the following: max application rate (acid basis [see above]) and pesticide half-life (days) in soil to estimate the initial, maximum pesticide residue concentration on general food items for terrestrial vertebrate species in short (<20 cm tall) grass.

For granular pesticide formulations and pesticide-treated seed with a unique route of exposure for terrestrial avian and mammalian wildlife, see Section 7.2.1.1.2 for the procedure that would be used to calculate RQs.

All calculated RQs in both tables would be compared with Levels of Concern (LOCs) established by USEPA (see Table 2 in Section 7.2). If a calculated RQ exceeds an established LOC value (in brackets inside the table), then there would be a potential for an acute or chronic effect (unacceptable risk) to federally listed (T&E) species and nonlisted species. See Section 7.2 for detailed descriptions of acute and chronic RQ calculations and comparison to LOCs to assess risk.

Threshold for approving PUPs:

If RQs≤LOCs, then a PUP would be approved without additional BMPs.
If RQs>LOCs, then a PUP would only be approved with additional BMPs specifically to minimize exposure (ecological risk) to bird, mammal, and/or fish species. One or more BMPs such as the following would be included in the Specific Best Management Practices (BMPs) section to reduce potential risk to non-listed or listed species:
- *Lower application rate and/or fewer number of applications so RQs≤LOCs*
- *For aquatic assessments (fish) associated with cropland/facilities maintenance, increase the buffer distance beyond 25' so RQs≤LOCs.*

Justification for Use: Service personnel would describe the reason for using the pesticide based control of specific pests or groups of pests. In most cases, the pesticide label will provide the appropriate information regarding control of pests to describe in the section.

Specific Best Management Practices (BMPs): Service personnel would record specific BMPs necessary to minimize or eliminate potential effects to non-target species and/or degradation of environmental quality from drift, surface runoff, or leaching. These BMPs would be based upon scientific information documented in previous data fields of a Chemical Profile. Where necessary and feasible, these specific practices would be included in PUPs as a basis for approval.

If there are no specific BMPs that are appropriate, then Service personnel would describe why the potential effects to Refuge resources and/or degradation of environmental quality is outweighed by the overall resource benefit(s) from the proposed pesticide use in the BMP section of the PUP. See Section 4.0 of this document for a complete list of BMPs associated with mixing and applying pesticides appropriate for all PUPs with ground-based treatments that would be additive to any necessary, chemical-specific BMPs.

References: Service personnel would record scientific resources used to provide data/information for a chemical profile. Use the number sequence to uniquely reference data in a chemical profile.

The following on-line data resources are readily available for toxicological endpoint and environmental fate data for pesticides:

1. California Product/Label Database. Department of Pesticide Regulation, California Environmental Protection Agency. (http://www.cdpr.ca.gov/docs/label/labelque.htm#regprods)

2. ECOTOX database. Office of Pesticide Programs, US Environmental Protection Agency, Washington, DC. (http://cfpub.epa.gov/ecotox/)

3. Extension Toxicology Network (EXTOXNET) Pesticide Information Profiles. Cooperative effort of University of California-Davis, Oregon State University, Michigan State University, Cornell University and University of Idaho through Oregon State University, Corvallis, Oregon. (http://extoxnet.orst.edu/pips/ghindex.html)

4. FAO specifications and evaluations for plant protection products. Pesticide Management Unit, Plant Protection Services, Food and Agriculture Organization, United Nations. (http://www.fao.org/WAICENT/FAOINFO/AGRICULT/AGP/AGPP/Pesticid/)

5. Human health and ecological risk assessments. Pesticide Management and Coordination, Forest Health Protection, US Department of Agriculture, US Forest Service. (http://www.fs.fed.us/foresthealth/pesticide/risk.htm)

6. Pesticide Chemical Fact Sheets. Clemson University Pesticide Information Center. (http://entweb.clemson.edu/pesticid/Document/Labels/factshee.htm)

7. Pesticide Fact Sheets. Published by Information Ventures, Inc. for Bureau of Land Management, Dept. of Interior; Bonneville Power Administration, U.S. Dept. of Energy; and Forest Service, US Department of Agriculture. (http://infoventures.com/e-hlth/pesticide/pest-fac.html)

8. Pesticide Fact Sheets. National Pesticide Information Center. (http://npic.orst.edu/npicfact.htm)

9. Pesticide Fate Database. US Environmental Protection Agency, Washington, DC. (http://cfpub.epa.gov/pfate/home.cfm).

10. Pesticide product labels and material safety data sheets. Crop Data Management Systems, Inc. (CDMS) (http://www.cdms.net/pfa/LUpdateMsg.asp) or multiple websites maintained by agrichemical companies.

11. Registered Pesticide Products (Oregon database). Oregon Department of Agriculture. (http://www.oda.state.or.us/dbs/pest_products/search.lasso)

12. Regulatory notes. Pest Management Regulatory Agency, Health Canada, Ontario, Canada. (http://www.hc-sc.gc.ca/pmra-arla/)

13. Reptile and Amphibian Toxicology Literature. Canadian Wildlife Service, Environment Canada, Ontario, Canada. (http://www.cws-scf.ec.gc.ca/nwrc-cnrf/ratl/index_e.cfm)

14. Specific Chemical Fact Sheet – New Active Ingredients, Biopesticide Fact Sheet and Registration Fact Sheet. U.S Environmental Protection Agency, Washington, DC. (http://www.epa.gov/pestidides/factsheets/chemical_fs.htm)

15. Weed Control Methods Handbook: Tools and Techniques for Use in Natural Areas. The Invasive Species Initiative. The Nature Conservancy. (http://tnsweeds.ucdavis.edu/handbook.html)

16. Wildlife Contaminants Online. US Geological Survey, Department of Interior, Washington, D.C. (http://www.pwrc.usgs.gov/contaminants-online/)

17. One-liner database. 2000. US Environmental Protection Agency, Office of Pesticide Programs, Washington, D.C.

Chemical Profile

Date:			
Trade Name(s):		Common Chemical Name(s):	
Pesticide Type:		EPA Registration Number:	
Pesticide Class:		CAS Number:	
Other Ingredients:			

Toxicological Endpoints

Mammalian LD$_{50}$:	
Mammalian LC$_{50}$:	
Mammalian Reproduction:	
Avian LD$_{50}$:	
Avian LC$_{50}$:	
Avian Reproduction:	
Fish LC$_{50}$:	
Fish ELS/Life Cycle:	
Other:	

Ecological Incident Reports

Environmental Fate

Water solubility (S$_w$):	
Soil Mobility (K$_{oc}$):	
Soil Persistence (t$_{1/2}$):	
Soil Dissipation (DT$_{50}$):	
Aquatic Persistence (t$_{1/2}$):	
Aquatic Dissipation (DT$_{50}$):	
Potential to Move to Groundwater (GUS score):	
Volatilization (mm Hg):	
Octanol-Water Partition Coefficient (K$_{ow}$):	
Bioaccumulation/Biocentration:	BAF:` BCF:

Worst Case Ecological Risk Assessment

Max Application Rate (ai lbs/acre – ae basis)	Habitat Management: Croplands/Facilities Maintenance:
EECs	Terrestrial (Habitat Management): Terrestrial (Croplands/Facilities Maintenance): Aquatic (Habitat Management): Aquatic (Croplands/Facilities Maintenance):

Habitat Management Treatments:

Presumption of Unacceptable Risk		Risk Quotient (RQ)	
		Listed (T&E) Species	Nonlisted Species
Acute	Birds	[0.1]	[0.5]
	Mammals	[0.1]	[0.5]
	Fish	[0.05]	[0.5]
Chronic	Birds	[1]	[1]
	Mammals	[1]	[1]
	Fish	[1]	[1]

Cropland/Facilities Maintenance Treatments:

Presumption of Unacceptable Risk		Risk Quotient (RQ)	
		Listed (T&E) Species	Nonlisted Species
Acute	Birds	[0.1]	[0.5]
	Mammals	[0.1]	[0.5]
	Fish	[0.05]	[0.5]
Chronic	Birds	[1]	[1]
	Mammals	[1]	[1]
	Fish	[1]	[1]

Justification for Use: Specific Best Management Practices (BMPs): References:	

Table CP.1 Pesticide Name

Trade Name[a]	Treatment Type[b]	Max Product Rate – Single Application (lbs/acre or gal/acre)	Max Product Rate -Single Application (lbs/acre - AI on acid equiv basis)	Max Number of Applications Per Season	Max Product Rate Per Season (lbs/acre/season or gal/acre/season)	Minimum Time Between Applications (Days)

[a]From each label for a pesticide identified in pesticide use proposals (PUPs), Service personnel would record application information associated with possible/known uses on Service lands.
[b]Treatment type: H – habitat management or CF – cropland/facilities maintenance. If a pesticide is labeled for both types of treatments (uses), then record separate data for H and CF applications.

7.0 References

AgDrift 2001. A user's guide for AgDrift 2.04: a tiered approach for the assessment of spray drift of pesticides. Spray Drift Task Force, PO Box 509, Macon, Missouri.

ATSDR (Agency for Toxic Substances and Disease Registry) US Department of Health and Human Services. 2004. Guidance Manual for the Assessment of Joint Toxic Action of Chemical Mixtures. US Department of Health and Human Services, Public Health Service, ATSDR, Division of Toxicology. 62 pages plus Appendices.

Baehr, C.H., and C. Habig. 2000. Statistical evaluation of the UTAB database for use in terrestrial nontarget organism risk assessment. 10th Symposium on Environmental Toxicology and Risk Assessment, American Society of Testing and Materials.

Baker, J. and G. Miller. 1999. Understanding and reducing pesticide losses. Extension Publication PM 1495, Iowa State University Extension, Ames, Iowa. 6 pages.

Barry, T. 2004. Characterization of propanil prune foliage residues as related to propanil use patterns in the Sacramento Valley, CA. Proceedings of the International Conference on Pesticide Application for Drift Management. Waikoloa, Hawaii. 15 pages.

Battaglin, W.A., E.M. Thurman, S.J. Kalkhoff, and S.D. Porter. 2003. Herbicides and Transformation Products in Surface Waters of the Midwestern United States. Journal of the American Water Resources Association (JAWRA) 39(4):743-756.

Beyer, W.N., E.E. Connor, S. Gerould. 1994. Estimates of soil ingestion by wildlife. Journal of Wildlife Management 58:375-382.

Brooks, M.L., D'Antonio, C.M., Richardson, D.M., Grace, J.B., Keeley, J.E. and others. 2004. Effects of invasive alien plants on fire regimes. BioScience 54:77-88.

Bureau of Land Management. 2007. Vegetation treatments using herbicides on Bureau of Land Management Lands in 17 western states Programmatic EIS (PEIS). Washington Office, Bureau of Land Management.

Butler, T., W. Martinkovic, and O.N. Nesheim. 1998. Factors influencing pesticide movement to ground water. Extension Publication PI-2, University of Florida, Cooperative Extension Service, Gainesville, FL. 4 pages.

Calabrese, E.J. and L.A. Baldwin. 1993. Performing Ecological Risk Assessments. Lewis Publishers, Chelsea, MI.

Center, T.D., Frank, J.H., and Dray Jr., F.A. 1997. Biological Control. Strangers in Paradise: Impact and Management of Nonindigenous Species in Florida. P.245-263.

Cox, R.D., and V.J. Anderson. 2004. Increasing native diversity of cheatgrass-dominated rangeland through assisted succession. Journal of Range Management 57:203-210.

Coombs, E.M., J.K Clark, G.L. Piper, and A.F. Cofrancesco Jr. 2004. Biological control of invasive plants in the United States. Oregon State University Press, Corvallis, 467 pages.

Driver, C.J., M.W. Ligotke, P. Van Voris, B.D. McVeety, B.J. Greenspan, and D.B. Brown. 1991. Routes of uptake and their relative contribution to the toxicologic response of northern bobwhite (*Colinus virginianus*) to an organophosphate pesticide. Environmental Toxicology and Chemistry 10:21-33.

Dunning, J.B. 1984. Body weights of 686 species of North American birds. Western Bird Banding Association. Monograph No. 1.

EXTOXNET. 1993a. Movement of pesticides in the environment. Pesticide Information Project of Cooperative Extension Offices of Cornell University, Oregon State University, University of Idaho, University of California – Davis, and the Institute for Environmental Toxicology, Michigan State University. 4 pages.

Fletcher, J.S., J.E. Nellessen, and T.G. Pfleeger. 1994. Literature review and evaluation of the EPA food-chain (Kenaga) nomogram, and instrument for estimating pesticide residue on plants. Environmental Toxicology and Chemistry 13:1381-1391.

Hasan, S. and P.G. Ayres. 1990. The control of weeds through fungi: principles and prospects. Tansley Review 23:201-222.

Huddleston, J.H. 1996. How soil properties affect groundwater vulnerability to pesticide contamination. EM 8559. Oregon State University Extension Service. 4 pages.

Kerle, E.A., J.J. Jenkins, P.A. Vogue. 1996. Understanding pesticide persistence and mobility for groundwater and surface water protection. EM 8561. Oregon State University Extension Service. 8 pages.

Masters, R.A, and R.L. Sheley. 2001. Invited synthesis paper: principles and practices for managing rangeland invasive plants. Journal of Range Manage 54:502-517.

Masters, R.A., S.J. Nissen, R.E. Gaussoin, D.D. Beran, and R.N. Stougaard. 1996. Imidazolinone herbicides improve restoration of Great Plains grasslands. Weed Technology 10:392-403.

Maxwell, B.D., E. Lehnhoff, L.J. Rew. 2009. The rationale for monitoring invasive plant populations as a crucial step for management. Invasive Plant Science and Management 2:1-9.

Mineau, P., B.T. Collins, and A. Baril. 1996. On the use of scaling factors to improve interspecies extrapolation to acute toxicity in birds. Regulatory Toxicology and Pharmacology 24:24-29.

Moody, M.E., and R.N. Mack. 1988. Controlling the spread of plant invasions: the importance of nascent foci. Journal of Applied Ecology 25:1009-1021.

Morse, L.E., J.M. Randall, N. Benton, R. Hiebert, and S. Lu. 2004. An Invasive Species Assessment Protocol: NatureServe.

Mullin, B.H., L.W. Anderson, J.M. DiTomaso, R.E. Eplee, and K.D. Getsinger. 2000. Invasive Plant Species. Issue Paper (13):1-18.

Oregon State University. 1996. EXTOXNET-Extension Toxicology Network, Pesticide Information Profiles. Oregon State University, Corvallis, Oregon.

Pfleeger, T.G., A. Fong, R. Hayes, H. Ratsch, C. Wickliff. 1996. Field evaluation of the EPA (Kanaga) nomogram, a method for estimating wildlife exposure to pesticide residues on plants. Environmental Toxicology and Chemistry 15:535-543.

Pope, R., J. DeWitt, and J. Ellerhoff. 1999. Pesticide movement: what farmers need to know. Extension Publication PAT 36, Iowa State University Extension, Ames, Iowa and Iowa Department of Agriculture and Land Stewardship, Des Moines, Iowa. 6 pages.

Ramsay, C.A., G.C. Craig, and C.B. McConnell. 1995. Clean water for Washington – protecting groundwater from pesticide contamination. Extension Publication EB1644, Washington State University Extension, Pullman, Washington. 12 pages.

SDTF 2003 Spray Drift Task Force. 2003. A summary of chemigation application studies. Spray Drift Task Force, Macon, Missouri.

Teske, M.E., S.L. Bird, D.M. Esterly, S.L. Ray, S.G. and Perry. 1997. A User's Guide for AgDRIFT^{TM} 1.0: A Tiered Approach for the Assessment of Spray Drift of Pesticides, Technical Note No. 95-10, CDI, Princeton, New Jersey.

Teske, M.E., S.L. Bird, D.M. Esterly, T.B. Curbishley, S.L. Ray, and S.G. Perry. 2002. AgDRIFT®: a model for estimating near-field spray drift from aerial applications. Environmental Toxicology and Chemistry 21: 659-671.

Urban, D.J and N.J. Cook. 1986. Ecological risk assessment. EPA 540/9-85-001. US Environmental Protection Agency, Office of Pesticide Programs, Washington D.C.   94 pages.

US Environmental Protection Agency. 1990. Laboratory Test Methods of Exposure to Microbial Pest Control Agents by the Respiratory Route to Nontarget Avian Species. Environmental Research Laboratory, Corvallis, OR. EPA/600/3-90/070.

US Environmental Protection Agency. 1998. A Comparative Analysis of Ecological Risks from Pesticides and Their Uses: Background, Methodology & Case Study. Environmental Fate & Effects Division, Office of Pesticide Programs, U.S. Environmental Protection Agency, Washington, D.C. 105 pages.

US Environmental Protection Agency. 2004. Overview of the ecological risk assessment process in the Office of Pesticide Programs, US Environmental Protection Agency: endangered and threatened species effects determinations. Office of Pesticide Programs, Washington, DC. 101 pages.

US Environmental Protection Agency. 2005*a*. Technical overview of ecological risk assessment risk characterization; Approaches for evaluating exposure; Granular, bait, and treated seed applications. US Environmental Protection Agency, Office of Pesticide Programs, Washington, DC. http://www.epa.gov/oppefed1/ecorisk_ders/toera_analysis_exp.htm.

US Environmental Protection Agency. 2005*b*. User's Guide TREX v1.2.3. US Environmental Protection Agency, Office of Pesticide Programs, Washington, DC. 22 pages. http://www.epa.gov/oppefed1/models/terrestrial/trex_usersguide.htm.

US Geological Survey. 2000. Pesticides in stream sediment and aquatic biota – current understanding of distribution and major influences. USGS Fact Sheet 092-00, US Geological Survey, Sacramento, California. 4 pages.

US Forest Service. 2005. Pacific Northwest Region Invasive Plant Program Preventing and Managing Invasive Plants Final Environmental Impact Statement. 359 pages.

Wauchope, R.D., T.M. Buttler, A.G. Hornsby, P.M. Augustijn-Beckers, and J.P. Burt. 1992. The SCS/ARS/CES pesticide properties database for environmental decision making. Reviews of Environmental Contamination and Toxicology 123:1-155.

Woods, N. 2004. Australian developments in spray drift management. Proceedings of the International Conference on Pesticide Application for Drift Management, Waikoloa, Hawaii. 8 pages.

Appendix F

STATEMENT OF COMPLIANCE
for Implementation of the
Pearl Harbor National Wildlife Refuge, Honolulu County, Hawai'i
Comprehensive Conservation Plan

The following executive orders and legislative acts have been reviewed as they apply to implementation of the Pearl Harbor National Wildlife Refuge Comprehensive Conservation Plan.

- **National Environmental Policy Act (1969).** The planning process has been conducted in accordance with National Environmental Policy Act Implementing Procedures, Department of the Interior and Service procedures, and has been performed in coordination with the affected public. [add whatever might be pertinent to either release of a draft NEPA document or NEPA decision].

   The CCP is programmatic in many respects and specific details of certain projects and actions cannot be determined until a later date depending on funding and implementation schedules. Certain projects or actions may require additional NEPA compliance.

- **National Historic Preservation Act (1966).** The implementation of the CCP should not affect cultural resources. The proposed action does not meet the criteria of an effect or adverse effect as an undertaking defined in 36CFR800.9 and Service Manual 614FW2. The Service will comply with the National Historic Preservation Act if any management actions have the potential to affect any historic properties which may be present.

- **Executive Order 12372. Intergovernmental Review.** Coordination and consultation with affected Tribal, local and State governments, other Federal agencies, and the landowners has been completed through personal contact by Service Planners, Refuge managers and Supervisors.

- **Executive Order 12898. Federal Actions to Address Environmental Justice in Minority and Low-Income Populations.** All Federal actions must address and identify, as appropriate, disproportionally high and adverse human health or environmental effects of its programs, policies, and activities on minority populations, low-income populations, and Indian Tribes in the United States. The CCP was evaluated and no adverse human health or environmental effects were identified for minority or low-income populations, Indian Tribes, or anyone else.

- **Wilderness Preservation Act of 1964.** The Service has evaluated the suitability of the Refuge for wilderness designation and determined it does not qualify.

- **National Wildlife Administration Act of 1966, as amended by The National Wildlife Refuge System Improvement Act of 1997 (16 U.S.C. 668dd-668ee).** Appropriate Use findings and Compatibility Determinations have been prepared for the following uses: Wildlife Observation, Interpretation and Photography; Environmental Education; and Research.

- **Executive Order 13186. Responsibilities of Federal Agencies to Protect Migratory Birds.** The CCP is consistent with Executive Order 13186 because the CCP and NEPA analyses evaluate the effects of agency actions on migratory birds.

- **Endangered Species Act.** The Service will conduct consultations under Section 7 of the Endangered Species Act for any refuge management program actions that have the potential to affect listed species.

- **Coastal Zone Management Act, Section 307.** Section 307(c)(1) of the Coastal Zone Management Act of 1972 as amended, requires each Federal agency conducting or supporting activities directly affecting the coastal zone, to conduct or support those activities in a manner which is, to the maximum extent practicable, consistent with approved state coastal management programs. The CCP is consistent with Coastal Zone Management Act because CCP implementation would protect the coastal zone from adverse impacts as a result of modification or destruction.

- **Executive Order 11990. Protection of Wetlands.** The CCP is consistent with Executive Order 11990 because CCP implementation would protect and enhance existing wetlands.

- **Executive Order 11988. Floodplain Management.** Under this order Federal agencies "shall take action to reduce the risk of flood loss, to minimize the impact of floods on human safety, health and welfare, and to restore and preserve the natural and beneficial values served by flood plains." The CCP is consistent with Executive Order 11988 because CCP implementation would protect floodplains from adverse impacts as a result of modification or destruction.

- **Integrated Pest Management (IPM), 517 DM 1 and 7 RM 14**
  In accordance with 517 DM 1, an integrated pest management (IPM) approach has been adopted to eradicate, control, or contain pest and invasive species on the refuge. In accordance with 517 DM 1, only pesticides registered with the U.S. Environmental Protection Agency (USEPA) in full compliance with the Federal Insecticide, Fungicide, and Rodenticide Act (FIFRA) and as provided in regulations, orders, or permits issued by USEPA may be applied on lands and waters under Refuge jurisdiction.

_____   _____
Chief, Division of Refuge Planning   Date

Appendix G: Literature Cited

Arakawa, L. 2008. Isle temperatures are rising. Honolulu Advertiser. March 28, 2008.

Baker, J.D., C.L. Littnan, and D.W. Johnston. 2006. Potential effects of sea level rise on the terrestrial habitats of endangered and endemic megafauna in the Northwestern Hawaiian Islands. Endangered Species Research 4:1-10.

Bannor, B.K., and E. Kiviat. 2002. Common Moorhen (*Gallinula chloropus*). *In* The Birds of North America, No. 685. (A. Poole and F. Gill, eds.). The Birds of North America, Inc., Philadelphia, PA.

Blossey, B. and R. Notzold. 1995. Evolution of increased competitive ability in invasive non-indigenous plants: a hypothesis. Journal of Ecology 83:887-889.

Brimacombe, K. 2003. Annual Report II: Applied Research on Use of Native Plants for Coastal Wetland Restoration on Oʻahu, May 2002-May 2003. Department of Botany, University of Hawaii, Manoa.

Brisbin, I.L., Jr., H.D. Pratt, and T.B. Mowbray. 2002. American Coot (*Fulica Americana*) and Hawaiian Coot (*Fulica alai*). *In* The Birds of North America, No. 697. (A. Poole and F. Gill, eds.). Philadelphia, PA.

Buddemeier, R.W., J.A. Kleypas, and R.B. Aronson. 2004. Coral Reefs and Global Climate Change: Potential Contributions of Climate Change to Stresses on Coral Reef Ecosystems. Pew Centre for Global Climate Change: Arlington, VA.

Caccamise, D. J., II, M. A. Merrifield, M. Bevis, J. Foster, Y. L. Firing, M. S. Schenewerk, F. W. Taylor, and D. A. Thomas. 2005. Sea level rise at Honolulu and Hilo, Hawaii: GPS estimates of differential land motion, Geophys. Res. Lett. 32, L03607.

Carter, L.M., E.Shea, M.Hamnett, C.Anderson, G. Dolcemascolo, C.Guard, M. Taylor,T. Barnston,Y. He, M. Larsen, L. Loope, L. Malone, G. Meehl. 2001. Potential Consequences of Climate Variability and Change for the U.S.-Affiliated Islands of the Pacific and Caribbean. pp. 315-349. In Climate Change Impacts on the United States: The Potential Consequences of Climate Variability and Change. National Assessment Synthesis Team, US Global Change Research Program. Cambridge University Press: Cambridge, UK.

Chai, D.K., L.W. Cuddihy, and C.P. Stone. 1989. An Inventory and Assessment of Anchialine the Pools in Hawaii Volcanoes National Park from Waiaʻuia to Kaʻahu, Puna, and Kaʻu, Hawaiʻi. University of Hawaii Cooperative National Park Resources Studies Unit Technical Report 69.

Char, W.P. and N. Balakrishnan. 1979. ʻEwa Plains Botanical Survey. Department of Botany, University of Hawaii at Manoa. Honolulu, Hi.

Choy, Duane. 2007. Koʻoloaʻula coming back from the brink. Honolulu Advertiser. August 3, 2007.

Cobb, K.M., C.Charles, H.Cheng, R.Edwards. 2003. El Niño/Southern Oscillation and tropical Pacific climate during the last millennium.Nature. Vol. 424, No. 6946, pp. 271-276 (17 July 2003)

Coles, S.L., DeFelice, R.C., Eldredge, L.G., and J. T. Carlton. 1997. Biodiversity of Marine Communities in Pearl Harbor, O`ahu, Hawaii with Observations on Introduced Exotic Species. Prepared for the U. S. Navy. Hawaii Biological Survey. Bishop Museum Technical Report No. 10. Bishop Museum Press, Honolulu, HI.

Craft, J.D., Santos. 2008. Islands under islands: the phylogeography and evolution of *Halocaridina rubra* Holthuis, 1963 (Crustacean: Decapoda: Atyidae) in the Hawaiian archipelago. Limnology and Oceanography 53(2).

Cuddihy, L.W and C.P. Stone. 1994. Summary of Vegetation Alteration in the Hawaiian Islands. Pp. 467-472. *in* E. Alison Kay (editor). A Natural History of the Hawaiian Islands. University of Hawaii Press: Honolulu. HI.

Davis, W.E., Jr. 1993. Black-crowned Night-heron (Nycticorax nycticorax). *In* The Birds of North America, No. 74. (A. Poole and F. Gill, eds.). The Birds of North America, Inc., Philadelphia, PA.

DBEDT and DOH (State of Hawai`i Department of Business, Economic Development & Tourism and Department of Health). 1998. Hawai`i climate change action plan. Available at: http://hawaii.gov/dbedt/info/energy/publications/ccap.pdf. Accessed January 20, 2008.

Denslow, J.S. 2005. Survey of Invasive Exotic Plant Species in Conservation Areas on Oahu, Hawaii: Project Report. Institute of Pacific Islands Forestry. Hilo, Hawai`i.

Department of the Navy. 1999. Final Environmental Impact Report for the Disposal and Reuse of Naval Air Station Barbers Point, Hawaii.

Department of the Navy, Commander Navy Region Hawaii. 2001. Pearl Harbor Naval Complex Integrated Natural Resources Management Plan. Final Draft.

Department of Planning and Permitting (DPP), City and County of Honolulu. 2002. General Plan.

Duffy, D. C. 1993. Stalking the Southern Oscillation: Environmental uncertainty, climate change, and North Pacific seabirds. Ottawa, Canada.

Earth Tech, Inc. 2000. Engineering evaluation/cost analysis treatment/disposal alternatives for contaminated soil: NCTAMS PAC, former NAS Barbers Point, and Pearl Harbor Naval Complex, Oahu, Hawaii. Prepared for Department of the Navy, Pacific Division, Naval Facilities Engineering Command.

Earth Tech, Inc. 2001a. Draft engineering evaluation/cost analysis for six sites : former NAS Barbers Point, Oahu, Hawaii / prepared for Department of the Navy, Pacific Division, Naval Facilities Engineering Command.

Earth Tech, Inc. 2006. Record of Decision Building 49 Auxiliary Power Plant Naval Magazine Pearl Harbor West Loch Branch, Oahu, Hawaii. Prepared for Department of the Navy, Pacific Division, Naval Facilities Engineering Command, Hawaii.

Ehleringer, J.R., Cerling, T.E., Dearing, M.D., 2002. Atmospheric CO2 as a global driver influencing plant–animal interactions. Integ. Comp. Biol. 42, 424–430.

Elliott, M.E and E.M. Hall.1977 Wetlands and Wetland Vegetation of Hawaii. Prepared for the United States Army of Engineers, Pacific Ocean Division, Fort Shafter.

Engilis, A., Jr., and M. Naughton. 2004. U.S. Pacific Islands Regional Shorebird Conservation Plan. U.S. Shorebird Conservation Plan. U.S. Department of the Interior, Fish and Wildlife Service. Portland, OR.

Engilis, A., Jr., and T.K. Pratt. 1993. Status and population trends of Hawaii's native waterbirds, 1977-1987. Wilson Bulletin 105:142-158.

Englund, R.A., D.J. Preston, R. Wolff, S.L. Coles, L.G. Eldredge, and K. Arakaki. 2000. Biodiversity of Freshwater and Estuarine Communities in Low Pearl Harbor Oʻahu, Hawaii With Observations on Introduced Species. Prepared for the U.S. Navy. Hawaii Biological Survey, Bishop Museum. Technical Report No. 16.

EPA (U.S. Environmental Protection Agency). 1998. Climate Change and Hawaii. Report no. EPA 236-F-98-007e. Environmental Protection Agency, Office of Policy, Planning and Evaluation. Washington, D.C.

EPA. 2008. Region 9: Superfund website, Pearl Harbor Naval Complex. Available at: http://yosemite.epa.gov/r9/sfund/r9sfdocw.nsf/ViewByEPAID/hi4170090076?OpenDocument#progress. Accessed March 16, 2008.

EPA. 2010. Environmental justice. Available at: http://www.epa.gov/compliance/environmentaljustice/index.html. Accessed July 2010.

Erickson, T.A and C.F. Puttock. 2006. Hawaiʻi Wetland Field Guide: An ecological and identification guide to wetlands and wetland plants of the Hawaiian Islands. U.S. Environmental Protection Agency.

Fletcher III, C. H., E.E. Grossman, B.M. Richmond, and A.E. Gibbs. 2002. Atlas of Natural Hazards in the Hawaiian Coastal Zone. U.S. Geological Survey. U.S. Government Printing Office: Denver, CO.

Foote, D.E., E.L. Hill, S. Nakamura, and F. Stephens. 1972. Soil Survey of the Islands of Kauai, Oʻahu, Maui, Molokai, and Lanai, State of Hawaii. U. S. Department of Agriculture, Soil Conservation Service.

GAO. 2007. Climate Change: Agencies Should Develop Guidance for Addressing the Effects on Federal Land and Water Resources. Report to Congressional Requesters.

Giambelluca, Tom. Recent Historical Temperature and Trade-Wind Inversion Variations in Hawaii. Presented at the Forum on Climate Change in Hawaii, March 2008, in Honolulu, Hawaii.

Giambelluca, T., M. Ridgley, and M. Nullet. 1996. Water balance, climate change and land-use planning in the Pearl Harbor Basin, Hawaii. Water Resources Development 12(4):515-530.

Halliday, W.R. 1998. Current status of the Ewa karst, Honolulu county, Hawaii. Cave Conservationist 16(5):3-8.

Harrison, C.S., M.B. Naughton, and S.I. Fefer. 1984. The status and conservation of seabirds in the Hawaiian Archipelago and Johnston Atoll. Pp. 513-526 in Croxall, J. P., P. G. H. Evans and R. W. Schreiber (eds.). Status and conservation of the World's seabirds. International Council for Bird Preservation Technical Publication No. 2. Cambridge, UK.

Haselwood E.L. and R.T. Hirano. 1983. Handbook of Hawaiian weeds. University of Hawaii Press. Honolulu, Hawaii.

Hawaii Audubon Society. 2005. Hawaii's Birds: 6th Edition. Island Heritage: Waipahu: Hawaii.

Hawaii Climate Change Action Plan. Available at http://hawaii.gov/dbedt/info/energy/publications/ccap.pdf. Accessed January 20, 2008.

Hawaii Community Development Authority (HCDA). 2006. Kalaeloa Master Plan. Prepared by Prepared by Belt Collins, EDAW, SMS, BAE, and Ebisu.

Hawai'i Department of Business, Economic Development and Tourism (DBEDT). 2009. State of Hawai'i Data Book; a statistical abstract. Honolulu, HI.

Hawai'i Department of Land and Natural Resources. 2008. Hawai'i State Comprehensive Outdoor Recreation Plan 2008 Update. Honolulu, HI.

Hawai'i Travel Guide. Available at http://www.hawaiianstyletravel.com/. Accessed June 1, 2010.

Hawaiian Electric Company, Inc. (HECO). 2004. Wind Speed of O'ahu at 50 Meters

Hays, W.S.T. and S. Conant. 2007. Biology and impacts of Pacific Island invasive species. 1. A worldwide review of effects of the small Indian mongoose, Herpestes javanicus (Carnivora : Herpestidae). Pacific Science 61(1):3-16.

Ikuma, E.K., D. Sugano, and J.K. Mardfin. 2002. Filling the gaps in the fight against invasive species. Honolulu, HI: Legislative Reference Bureau.

IPCC. 2007. Climate Change 2007: Synthesis Report. Contribution of Working Groups I, II and III to the Fourth Assessment Report of the Intergovernmental Panel on Climate Change [Core Writing Team, Pachauri, R.K and Reisinger, A. (eds.)].

Juvik, S. P. and J. O. Juvik (eds.) 1998. Atlas of Hawai'i. Third edition. University of Hawai'i Press. Honolulu.

Kakesako, G.K. 2005. Past rounds of closures claimed Barbers Point. Honolulu Star-Bulletin. Friday, May 13, 2005.

Kimura, B.Y. and K.M. Nagata. 1980. Hawaii's Vanishing Flora. The Oriental Publishing Co.: Honolulu, Hi.

Kushlan, J.A., M.J. Steinkamp, K.C. Parsons, J. Capp, M.A. Cruz, M. Coulter, I. Davidson, L. Dickson, N. Edelson, R. Elliot, R.M. Erwin, S. Hatch, S. Kress, R. Milko, S. Miller, K. Mills, R. Paul, R. Phillips, J. E. Saliva, B. Sydeman, J. Trapp, J. Wheeler, and K. Wohl. 2002. Waterbird Conservation for the Americas: The North American Waterbird Conservation Plan, Version 1. Waterbird Conservation for the Americas, Washington, DC.

Lau, L.S. and J.F. Mink. 2006. Hydrology of the Hawaiian Islands. University of Hawai'i Press, Honolulu.

Liu, C.C.K. 2006. Analytical Groundwater Flow and Transport Modeling for the Estimation of Sustainable Yield of Pearl Harbor Aquifer. Water Resources Research Center. University of Hawaii at Manoa, Honolulu.

Loope, L.L., and D. Mueller-Dombois. 1989. Characteristics of invaded islands, p.257-280. In *Biological Invasions: A Global Perspective*. Edited by J. A. Drake, H. A. Mooney, F. D. Castri, R. H. Grooves, F. J. Kruger, M. Rejmanek, and M. Williamson. Chichester, UK: John Wiley and Sons.

Macdonald, G.A. and A.T. Abbott. 1970. Volcanoes in the Sea. University of Hawai'i Press, Honolulu.

Maciolek, J.A. 1983. Distribution and biology of Indo-pacific insular hypogeal shrimps. Bulletin of Marine Science 33:606- 618.

Maciolek, J.A. and R.E. Brock. 1974. Aquatic Survey of the Kona Coast Ponds, Hawaii Island. Sea Grant Advisory Report. UNIHI-SEAGRANT-AR-74-04.

McCarthy, J.J, F. Osvaldo, F. Canziani, N.A. Leary, D.J. Dokken, and K.S. White. 2001. climate change 2001: impacts, adaptation, and vulnerability. Contribution of working group II to the third assessment report of the Intergovernmental Panel on Climate Change. Cambridge University Press, UK.

McKeown, S. 1996. A field guide to reptiles and amphibians in the Hawaiian Islands. Diamond Head Publishing, Inc., Los Osos, CA.

Michener, W.K., E.R. Blood, K.L. Bildstein, M.M. Brinson, and L.R. Gardner. 1997. Climate Change, Hurricanes and Tropical Storms, and Rising Sea Level in Coastal Wetlands. Ecological Applications Vol. 7(3):770-801.

Middleton, B.A. 2006. Invasive Species and Climate Change. U.S. Geological Survey Open-File Report 2006-1153.

Miller, J.A., R.L. Whitehead, D.S. Oki, S.B. Gingerich, and P.G. Olcott. 1999. Ground water atlas of the United States. Segment 13, Alaska, Hawaii, Puerto Rico, and the U.S. Virgin Islands. U.S. Geological Survey.

Mitchell, C., C. Ogura, D.W. Meadows, A. Kane, L. Strommer, S. Fretz, D. Leonard, and A. McClung. 2005. Hawaii's Comprehensive Wildlife Conservation Strategy. Department of Land and Natural Resources. Honolulu, HI.

Mitsch, W.J. and J.G. Gosselink. 1993. Wetlands, Second Edition. New York: Van Nostrand Rinhold

Morden, C.W. and M. Gregoritza. 2005. Population variation and phylogeny in the endangered Chamaesyce skottsbergii (Euphorbiaceae) based on RAPD and ITS analyses. Conservation Genetics 6:969–979.

Motooka, P., L. Castro, D. Nelson, G. Nagai, and L. Ching. 2003. Weeds of Hawai'i's Pastures and Natural Areas; An Identification and Management Guide. College of Tropical Agriculture and Human Resources, University of Hawai'i at Manoa.

Nakiboglu, S.M., K. Lambeck, and P. Aharon. 1983. Post-glacial sealevels in the Pacific: implications with respect to deglaciation regime and local tectonics. Tectonophys. 91: 335-358.

Naval Facilities Engineering Command, Hawaii (NAVFACENGCOM).1998. Draft Environmental Impact Statement for the Disposal and Reuse of Naval Air Station Barbers Point, Hawaii.

NOAA. 1992. Pearl Harbor Naval Complex Waste Site Report. CERCLIS No. HI2170024341.

NOAA. 2002. Climatography of the United States No. 81 Monthly Station Normals of Temperature, Precipitation, and Heating and Cooling Degree Days, 1971 – 2000, 51 Hawaii. National Climatic Data Center Asheville, North Carolina.

Noye, B.J and M.P. Grzechnik. 2001. Sea level changes and their effects. World Scientific Publishing, Singapore.

Oceanit, Townscape, Inc., and Eugene Dashiell. 2007. Central O'ahu Watershed Study. Prepared for the Honolulu Board of Water Supply, U.S. Army Corps of Engineers, and City and County of Honolulu Department of Environmental Services.

Oki, D.S. 2005. Numerical Simulation of the Effects of Low-Permeability Valley-Fill Barriers and the Redistribution of Ground-Water Withdrawals in the Pearl Harbor Area, Oahu, Hawaii. U.S. Geological Survey Scientific Investigations Report 2005-5253
Olson, S.L., and H.F. James. 1982. Prodromus of the fossil avifauna of the Hawaiian Islands. Smithsonian Contributions to Zoology 365:1-59.

Overseas Private Investment Corporation (OPIC). 2000. "Climate Change: Assessing Our Actions."
Washington, D.C.

Park, Gerald. 1999. Final Environmental Assessment, Proposed Transfer of Land to the City and
County of Honolulu for Park and Recreation Purposes, Naval Air Station Barbers Point, Honouliuli,
Ewa District, Oahu, Hawaii. Prepared for Department of Design and Construction, City and County
of Honolulu.

Pattison, R.R., G. Goldstein, and A. Ares. 1998. Growth, biomass allocation and photosynthesis of
invasive and native Hawaiian rainforest species. Oecologia 117(4):449-459.

Parry, M.L., O.F. Canziani, J.P. Palutikof, P.J. van der Linden and C.E. Hanson. 2007. Climate
Change 2007: Impacts, Adaptation and Vulnerability. Contribution of Working Group II to the
Fourth Assessment Report of the Intergovernmental Panel on Climate Change. Cambridge University
Press, Cambridge, UK. 976pp.

PBR Hawaii. 2007. Barbers Point 215' Non-Potable Reservoir NO. 2 Draft Environmental
Assessment. Prepared for Board of Water Supply City and County of Honolulu and The Limtiaco
Consulting Group.

Pearl Harbor Natural Resource Trustees. 1999. Restoration Plan and Environmental Assessment for
the May 14, 1996 Chevron Pipeline Oil Spill into Waiau Stream and Pearl Harbor, O'ahu, Hawaii.
Prepared by U.S. Department of Defense, U.S. Department of the Interior, National Oceanic and
Atmospheric Administration, and State of Hawaii.

Polhemus, D.A. 1996. The Orangeblack Hawaiian Damselfly, *Megalagrion xanthomelas* (Odonata:
Coenagrionidae): Clarifying the Current Range of a Threatened Species. Bishop Museum
Occasional Papers: No. 45, Honolulu, HI.

Polhemus, D.A. 2007. Biology Recapitulates Geology: the Distribution of Megalagrion Damselflies
on the Ko'olau Volcano of O'ahu, Hawai'i. In N.L. Evenhuis & J.M. Fitzsimons (ed.): Bishop
Museum Bulletin in Cultural and Environmental Studies 3:233-246

Rauzon, M.J., D. Drigot, and L. Tanino. 2004. Cattle Egret and Black-crowned Night-heron
observations associated with mangrove removal at Nu'upia Ponds WMA Kane'ohe Bay, Marine
Corps Base Hawai'i in 1996-2000. 'Elepaio 64(41):43-47.

Robinson, J.A., J.M. Reed, J.P. Skorupa, and L.W. Oring. 1999. Black-necked Stilt (*Himantopus
mexicanus*). *In* The Birds of North America, No. 449. (A. Poole and F. Gill, eds.). The Birds of
North America, Inc., Philadelphia, PA.

Sack, L. and K. Frole. 2006. Leaf structural diversity is related to hydraulic capacity in tropical
rainforest trees. Ecology 87:483-491.

Schwartz, C.W., and E.R. Schwartz. 1949. A reconnaissance of the game birds in Hawaii. Board of
Commissioners of Agriculture and Forestry, Division of Fish and Game, Territory of Hawaii, Hilo.

Shaw Environmental, Inc. 2004. Draft Final Baseline Risk Assessment Work Plan. PCP Landfill, Burn Area Site, and Waiawa Unit, Pearl Harbor, O'ahu, Hawaii.

Smith, D.G., J.T. Polhemus, and E.A. VanderWerf. 2002. Comparison of managed and unmanaged Wedge-tailed Shearwater colonies on O'ahu: effects of predation. Pacific Science 56: 451-457.

Smith, N.M. 2002. Weeds of the wet/dry tropics of Australia - a field guide. Environment Centre NT, Inc. 112 pp.

Smucker, T.D., G.D. Lindsey, S.M. Mosher. 2000. Home range and diet of feral cats in Hawaii forests. Pacific Conservation Biology 6: 229-237.

Snetsinger, T.J., S.G. Fancy, J.C. Simon, and J.D. Jacobi. 1994. Diets of owls and feral cats in Hawaii. `Elepaio 54:47-50.

Solomon, S., D. Qin, M. Manning, Z. Chen, M. Marquis, K.B. Averyt, M. Tignor and H.L. Miller. 2007. Climate Change 2007: The Physical Science Basis. Contribution of Working Group I to the Fourth Assessment Report of the Intergovernmental Panel on Climate Change. Cambridge University Press, Cambridge, United Kingdom and New York, NY, USA.

Staples, G.W., and R.H. Cowie (eds.). 2001. Hawai`i's invasive species. Bishop Museum Press: Honolulu, HI.

Stearns, H. T. and K. N. Vacsik. 1931. Geology and ground-water resources of the island of O'ahu, Hawaii. Bulletin No. 7, Hawaii Division of Hydrography, Honolulu.

Stearns, H. T. 1966. Geology of the State of Hawaii. Pacific Books. Palo Alto.

Tabata, R.S. 1980. The Native Coastal Plant of Oahu, Hawaii. pp 321- 346. *In* Smith, C. W. (*Ed.*). June 4-6, 1980. Proceedings of the Third Conference in Natural Sciences, Hawai'i Volcanoes National Park. Cooperative National Park Resources Studies Unit, University of Hawaii at Manoa.

TenBruggencate, J. 2007. Floods, hotter climate in Isles likely by 2090. Honolulu Advertiser. February 25, 2007.

The IT Group. 2000. Final Remediation Verification Report. Removal Action at Pearl City Peninsular Landfill, Pearl Harbor, O'ahu, Hawaii.

Timm, Oliver. Statistical Projection of Global Climate Change Scenarios onto Hawaiian Rainfall. Presented at the Forum on Climate Change in Hawaii, March 26, 2008 in Honolulu, Hawaii.

Tobin, M.E. and R.T. Sugihara. 1992. Abundance and habitat relationships of rats in Hawaiian sugar cane fields. Journal of Wildlife Management 56(4):816-822.

Tomich, P.Q. 1986. Mammals in Hawai`i. Bishop Museum Press: Honolulu, HI.

Tropical Forages. 2005. Online Database. Available at: http://www.tropicalforages.info/key/Forages/Media/Html. Accessed on March 17, 2008.

Tsuru, M.T. and G.D. Cline. 2004. Airfield Pavement Condition Survey Former NAS Barbers Point (Kalaeloa Airport) Oʻahu, Hawaii. Naval Facilities Engineering Command, Pacific Division, Pearl Harbor, Hawaii.

U.S.Department of Agriculture (USDA), ARS, National Genetic Resources Program. *Germplasm Resources Information Network -(GRIN)* [Online Database]. National Germplasm Resources Laboratory, Beltsville, Maryland.

U.S. Department of the Interior, Fish and Wildlife Service, and U.S. Department of Commerce, U.S. Census Bureau. 2006 National Survey of Fishing, Hunting, and Wildlife-Associated Recreation: Hawaiʻi. Washington, D.C.

USFWS (U.S. Fish and Wildlife Service). 1972. First Amendment to the Cooperative agreement for the Conservation and Management of Fish and Wildlife between the U.S. Naval Ammunition Depot, U. S. Bureau of Sport Fisheries and Wildlife, and the Hawaiʻi State Department of Land and Natural Resources.

USFWS (U.S. Fish and Wildlife Service). 1994. Preliminary Project Proposal (PPP) to Establish the Barbers Point Unit of the Pearl Harbor National Wildlife Refuge.

USFWS (U.S. Fish and Wildlife Service). 1996. Pacific Islands Ecoregion Coastal Ecosystem Program Proposal. Pacific Islands Ecoregion. Honolulu, HI.

USFWS (U.S. Fish and Wildlife Service). 1999. Recovery Plan for Multi-Island Plants. U.S. Fish and Wildlife Service, Portland, Oregon.

USFWS (U.S. Fish and Wildlife Service). 1999a. Conceptual Management Plan for the Barbers Point Unit of the Pearl Harbor National Wildlife Refuge, Island of Oʻahu, Hawaii.

USFWS (U.S. Fish and Wildlife Service). 1999b. Level 1 Pre-Acquisition Contaminant Survey for Four Land Parcels on Naval Air Station Barbers Point, Oahu, Hawaii. Pacific Island Field Office.

USFWS (U.S. Fish and Wildlife Service). 2005a. Draft revised recovery plan for Hawaiian waterbirds, second draft of second revision. U.S. Fish and Wildlife Service, Portland, OR.

USFWS (U.S. Fish and Wildlife Service). 2006. Chamaesyce skottsbergii var. kalaeloana (Akoko): 5- Year Review Summary and Evaluation. Pacific Islands Fish and Wildlife Office Honolulu, Hawaii.

USFWS (U.S. Fish and Wildlife Service). 2009. Species Assessment and Listing Priority Assignment Form: *Megalagrion xanthomelas* (Orangeblack Hawaiian damselfly).

USFWS (U.S. Fish and Wildlife Service). 2009. Species Assessment and Listing Priority Assignment Form: Metabetaeus lohena (Anchialine pool shrimp).

University of Hawaiʻi (UH), Sea Grant College Program. 2006. Natural Hazard Considerations for Purchasing Coastal Real Estate in Hawaiʻi: A Practical Guide of Common Questions and Answers.

University of Hawai'I (UH), Sea Grant Extension Service and County of Maui Planning Department. 1997. Beach Management Plan for Maui.

Uyehara, K. J., A. Engilis, Jr., and M. Reynolds. 2007. Hawaiian duck's future threatened by feral Mallards. U.S. Geological Survey Fact Sheet 2007-3047.

Vitousek, Peter M. 1994. Beyond Global Warming: Ecology and Global Change. Ecology 75(7): 1861–1876.

Wagner, W.L., D.R. Herbst, and S.H. Sohmer. 1999. Manual of the flowering plants of Hawai'I, Revised edition. 2 vols, Bishop Museum Special Publication 97. University of Hawaii Press and Bishop Museum Press: Honolulu, HI.

Walther, G-R., Post, E.; Convey, P.; Menzel, A.; Parmesan, C.; Beebee, T.J.C.; Fromentin, J-M.; Hoegh-Guidberg, O.; Bairlein, F. 2002. Ecological responses to recent climate change. Nature. 416: 389-395.

Winter, L. 2003. Popoki and Hawai'i's Native Birds. 'Elepaio 63:43-46.

www.ingramcontent.com/pod-product-compliance
Lightning Source LLC
Chambersburg PA
CBHW081206280526
45787CB00006B/2347